Moral Minefields

Moral Minefields

HOW SOCIOLOGISTS
DEBATE GOOD SCIENCE

Shai M. Dromi and Samuel D. Stabler

THE UNIVERSITY OF CHICAGO PRESS
CHICAGO AND LONDON

The University of Chicago Press, Chicago 60637
The University of Chicago Press, Ltd., London
© 2023 by The University of Chicago
Published 2023
Printed in the United States of America

32 31 30 29 28 27 26 25 24 23   1 2 3 4 5

ISBN-13: 978-0-226-82816-9 (cloth)
ISBN-13: 978-0-226-82818-3 (paper)
ISBN-13: 978-0-226-82817-6 (e-book)
DOI: https://doi.org/10.7208/chicago/9780226828176.001.0001

Library of Congress Cataloging-in-Publication Data

Names: Dromi, Shai M., author. | Stabler, Samuel D., author.
Title: Moral minefields : how sociologists debate good science /
    Shai M. Dromi and Samuel D. Stabler.
Description: Chicago ; London : The University of Chicago Press, 2023. |
    Includes bibliographical references and index.
Identifiers: LCCN 2022056855 | ISBN 9780226828169 (cloth) |
    ISBN 9780226828183 (paperback) | ISBN 9780226828176 (ebook)
Subjects: LCSH: Sociology—Research—Moral and ethical aspects. |
    Social sciences and ethics.
Classification: LCC HM571 .D766 2023 | DDC 301.072—dc23/eng/20221222
LC record available at https://lccn.loc.gov/2022056855

♾ This paper meets the requirements of ANSI/NISO Z39.48-1992
(Permanence of Paper).

Contents

Eternity in Cincinnati

Moments after being crushed to death between a row of shopping carts and a truck, Eleanor Shellstrop wakes up in Heaven. She is immediately reassured that her lifelong quest of exonerating innocent death row inmates as a pro bono defense lawyer has paid off. Her calculated morality score, based on each and every choice she made in life, has placed her at the top percentile of human moral virtuousness. She is one of the select few allowed into the Good Place. Most others—whose lives fell even slightly short of exemplary—are doomed to eternity in the Bad Place.

While outwardly rejoicing, Eleanor is secretly uneasy. As she meets her new neighbors—the world-renowned moral philosopher, the billionaire philanthropist, and the silence-vowed monk—her unease turns to dread. Unbeknownst to her new acquaintances, real-life Eleanor was not an altruistic justice warrior. She was a selfish, frivolous, and occasionally mean-spirited pharmaceutical salesperson who pushed questionable medication on the elderly. She was not *all* bad, but she certainly did not lead a flawless life like her Good Place neighbors. As Eleanor quickly realizes, she has reached the Good Place in error.

But should she be sent to the Bad Place? Eleanor protests:

> "What, one in a million gets to live in paradise and everyone else is tortured for eternity? Come on! I mean, I wasn't freaking Gandhi, but I was okay. I was a *medium person*. I should get to spend eternity in a medium place! Like Cincinnati. Everyone who wasn't perfect but wasn't terrible should get to spend eternity in Cincinnati."

While Eleanor does not make it to Cincinnati, her innate ability to contest the fairness of the different metrics of moral worth that determined her fate takes her on a much longer journey over the course of the television comedy *The Good Place*. Eleanor takes it upon herself to become a better person and to avoid eternal damnation based on her improvement, rather than on her lifelong balance of good and evil deeds. Eleanor's personal transformation shifts her focus from saving herself from the Bad Place to advocating for radical changes in the afterlife's scales of evaluation. Rather than being judged by balancing their lifetime moral checkbook, by the end Eleanor insists that people should be judged by their ability to improve. The show traces the contest between those believing moral standing should be judged by one's *past* and those believing one's *potential* is the true marker. By employing their innate human critical capacities to deliberate between different measures of worth, the characters not only improve their own standing but make the afterlife better for everyone.

Back on Earth, arguments about how to judge goodness also animate countless scholarly conversations among sociologists today. Routine debates about the quality of academic work are punctuated by broader conversations about whether such work should be conducted and about how the *moral worth* of a scholarly contribution should be evaluated. In 2021, Aldon Morris, president of the American Sociological Association (ASA), called on his colleagues to decide if the discipline is "a science of emancipation," or if it will "continue to pretend to be an aloof, detached science."[1] Measuring sociological work based on its contribution to social justice has certainly been *one* way to determine its worth, tracing back to Karl Marx, W. E. B. Du Bois, and Ida Wells-Barnett, to name a few who contended that social scientists work to push against oppressive social structures and who attached their scholarship to activism.[2] However, others have long maintained that worthwhile sociological work *is* scientific, and would see little problem in maintaining detachment (although they might object to the negative connotations Morris assigns them).[3] Others still would insist that good scientific research is neither engaged nor detached; it produces parsimonious and universally valid laws (like "supply and demand") that capture human behavior across contexts.[4] They too have critics: post-positivists, who see the search for such laws as empirically inadequate and as underserving its own research subjects.[5] Instead, these scholars insist, historical and cultural nuance is the mark of good sociology.[6] But don't mention these arguments to Kieran Healy, whose article "Fuck Nuance" rejected sociologists' demands for contextuality as "fundamentally antitheoretical."[7] Academic work is fraught with debates about which research is right and which is wrong and, more importantly, how to evaluate right and wrong to begin with.

It is beyond the scope of this book to retell the long history of moral reasoning in sociological thinking.[8] Instead, we take on a much narrower task: to show that scholars use multiple cultural frameworks delineating how sociological work contributes to the common good to debate what type of work qualifies as "good sociology" and what makes it worthwhile. While scholars constantly disqualify each other's definitions of good sociology (and will voice claims like "what you're doing is not real sociology!"), the book will show that American sociology offers its members *multiple* definitions of sociological worth, based on different conceptions of morality. Sociologists constantly disagree with, but also tolerate, alternate ways of defining good scholarship. In this, they operate in an environment much like that of everyday folk—one where multiple moral registers are available to debate the worth of an object, idea, or situation. In doing so, sociologists constantly debate the moral underpinnings of academic work, regardless of subfield or methodological approach. The book will argue that contention over questions of right and wrong—of *morality*—has contributed to the scientific progress of the discipline by provoking scholars to redesign research programs, to devise innovative solutions to contentious questions, and to discard unethical avenues of research.

To delve into the frameworks sociologists use to evaluate research, we examine historical debates about what justifies certain strands of sociological research and about how sociology should contribute to the social world. We do not hold that questions of methodological rigor are secondary in these debates; rather, we believe that methodological rigor is one of many perspectives sociologists use to evaluate the worthiness of research products. By focusing on the role of these debates in sociological knowledge production, we show how sociologists navigate a field rich with moral diversity, at times rejecting research practices incompatible with the discipline's ethics and at times forming community in the face of multiple competing claims about the social good.

As with all things academic, the complex and difficult terrain this book covers features its own jargon-laden debates. To situate ourselves in these discussions, we draw on resources from pragmatist sociology and cultural sociology to capture how actors use collective cultural understandings of justice to address dilemmas in situ. Whether they rely on market principles, patrimonial logics, or the pull of a charismatic individual, each of those understandings provides a mode that others can agree upon as a proper principle for action. Our approach unpacks the multiple ways scholars define the good and how they work together in the context of deep divisions and contention between them.

Many moral philosophers and social scientists use the concept *moral* to denote an objective universal standard for the good, manifested through avoiding harm to others, adhering to social norms, and exercising fairness.[9] However, throughout the book, we use the term *moral* to define "understandings of good and bad, right and wrong, worthy and unworthy that vary between persons and between social groups"[10]—in other words, as a lived phenomenon, rather than a prescribed set of rules.[11] In this we follow a long lineage of sociologists who have defined the concept as a *formal* rather than substantive concept by referring to historically and culturally variable understandings of good and bad.[12] As the sociologists Steven Hitlin and Stephen Vaisey note, while the opposite of moral in the first sense is *immoral*, the opposite of moral in the second sense—the one we use going forward—is *nonmoral* or *morally irrelevant*.[13] In our definition, morality is rooted in publicly shared conceptions about what serves the common good. Individuals evaluate objects in light of one possible definition of the common good, and may face criticism from those holding other definitions.[14]

Accordingly, we use the term *moral repertoires* throughout the book to denote the collectively held grammars individuals use to define what constitutes the common good.[15] Moral repertoires allow academics to define why a research project is worthy (e.g., its findings help address social inequality, it develops original theory, it connects previously unconnected scholars, etc.). Conversely, moral repertoires allow academics to reject other projects as deplorable (e.g., the project ignores the voices of underrepresented minorities, it wastes resources on redundant data collection, it is plagiarized).[16] While some would see a claim like "sociology should simply follow the rules of the hard sciences and focus on facts" as nonmoral, a long line of critical sociologists and philosophers of science have shown that such claims are no less normative than claims like "sociologists should pursue social justice." Understanding these and other arguments about how sociology should be waged as instances of moral repertoires allows us to trace how conceptions of "good sociology" develop and how debates around this topic unfold. As this book shows, scholarly creativity emerges as researchers employ moral repertoires to navigate such debates.

With an eye toward keeping this book accessible to scholars who are not familiar with the theoretical frameworks we use here (and who, perhaps, would not normally think of their research as having anything to do with morality), we have endeavored to keep the jargon to a minimum. The Afterword provides the technical essentials of our approach, including a summary of the moral repertoires we describe throughout the book, as a reference. Readers with a stronger interest in the underpinnings of our theoretical frameworks will find an in-depth theoretical discussion in the endnotes.

Given the messiness of the deliberations we cover in the coming chapters, we do not offer one single solution to moral contention among academics, and certainly do not hold up individual sociologists as exemplary moral beings. Nor do we claim that working sociologists hold "real" agendas that covertly shape their research through their moral motivations. Rather, we maintain that morality in science means something more than "bias" or "tradition"; that when academics make commitments in the name of justice, their words are not *always* a cover for other interests. Rather, much like the characters in *The Good Place*, scholars justifying their research in moral terms are systematizing the concrete dilemmas of working in an academic community with a plurality of opinions about what constitutes the good. Such plurality certainly breeds contention, and the solutions to such debates are far from perfect. Indeed, as the analyses ahead will demonstrate, resolutions to academic controversies over the moral good are often fragile, leading to additional contention down the road. But through ongoing struggle over what makes sociology good, scholars refine moral repertoires and open new directions for inquiry.[17]

Sociology is hardly the only discipline to grapple with its moral underpinnings. Famously, post–World War II physicists wrestled with the implications for their discipline of the newly invented atomic bomb and its wartime uses.[18] But the social sciences in particular have a long history of debating the positive goods they offer to the world and of denouncing types of research they believe are socially harmful. Sociology, as we will demonstrate, is an excellent case study for such dynamics because of its historic links with social policy circles and the ease with which the public interprets sociological claims as bearing moral value. Nevertheless, sociology also exemplifies processes that other disciplines weather as well. It is our hope that scholarship will continue to explore moral debate across academia, beyond sociology.

Because we examine sociology in the United States as one field of contention, we are admittedly limited to a Western-centric European view. Indeed, scholars like Raewyn Connell and Julian Go have critiqued Western sociology for its parochial view and its exclusion of the voices of subaltern communities and non-Western theorists.[19] Our case selection and our reconstruction of the debates therein are certainly in themselves consequential for disciplinary collective memory, and we are cognizant of the fact that our focus on Northern Hemisphere scholarship may inadvertently exacerbate Eurocentricity in the discipline.[20] However, by analyzing the US as a study case, we hope to stimulate others to examine additional fields of scholarly contention and to identify the predominant moral quandaries there. The dynamics we analyze in what follows are constitutive of social science debates beyond the US context, even if the substantive moral repertoires American sociologists use are historically and culturally specific. While moral repertoires manifest themselves differently in American sociology and in other national contexts, their plurality is shared across national contexts, to varying extents.[21]

We are writing this book at a time when confrontations between sociologists appear to be reaching new lows. The rise of so-called "cancel culture" on social media platforms has only exacerbated the personal strife that academics famously foster.[22] Scholarly interpersonal strife is now part of the public debate on Twitter, and stories of departmental colleagues hurling personal insults behind closed doors occasionally emerge on public message boards. Our core message—that a plurality of moral repertoires animates creative social science—stands in stark contrast to these trends toward strife. While this book should not be read as a conflict management book (and the reader is not urged to think of sociologists as uniquely virtuous creatures!), our analysis provides concrete examples of scholarly communities working through fundamental disagreements. The book demonstrates that the discipline has thrived by acknowledging multiple ways of evaluating the goods that sociology should provide. Vincent Jeffries, the founder of the ASA Altruism, Morality, and Social Solidarity Section, defined "the sociology of the good" as an endeavor focusing upon "the meaningful content of moral ideas that appears most likely to produce and maintain maximum altruism and a universalistic solidarity."[23] Such a morally cognizant sociology may not be in Cincinnati, but we hope this book may provide a step in its direction.

moral repertoires
rise of so-called
"Cancel culture"

Rules of the Road

Social scientific debates over research ethics have reached an unprecedented fervor in recent decades. Clashes between scholars over ethical issues have devolved into personal insults and public shaming on Twitter. Controversies have erupted over issues like using social scientific data to preemptively police individuals statistically seen as more likely to commit violent crime[1] and over whether theoretical frameworks like critical race theory are essential or harmful.[2] Criticisms of the all-white, all-male, all-European canon have split departments in various disciplines over what (if any) curricular revisions are required.[3] Responses to controversial journal articles now include demands to fire authors, to publicly reveal the names of the anonymous reviewers who recommended publication, and to replace the editorial staff.[4] Allegations of an ethnographer's complicity in her subjects' crimes trended on anonymous online forums and the author was "dragged"—publicly shamed on social media—with scholars clashing over her work's ethical standing, sparking a broader debate over the principles of urban ethnographies.[5] Across these cases, vocal and personal disputes erupted over questions of research standards, where participants evaluated the empirical and theoretical claims in question in terms of ethical principles they believe sociologists at large should uphold: for example, commitment to equality, loyalty to research subjects, respect for leading researchers in an academic field, or cooperation with academics from different backgrounds. Conversations across the social sciences, then, have revolved as much around questions of *what values should guide our disciplines* as around questions of empirical findings.

Contention over the right ways to conduct scientific research have been endemic throughout academic history.[6] But the discipline of sociology has stood out as a major site for contention over the place researchers' values should take in conducting research.[7] Over recent decades, disciplinary conversations on the matter have developed two contrasting and outspoken positions. Despite a diversity of opinions on the matter, proponents of both positions have become increasingly emphatic about the values they believe should guide social research.

On the one hand, scholars like Steven Morgan, Jesper Sorensen, Duncan Watts, and Ezra Zuckerman have argued for stricter scientific protocols in the social sciences to reduce the biases that researchers' values may cause, especially in research on controversial topics.[8] Although these sociologists largely acknowledge that some level of value judgment inevitably affects their choice of subject matter and their research conclusions,[9] they have called for enhancing objectivity in the discipline by using randomized control trials, large-N datasets, replication studies, and computational analysis methods.[10] Referencing Max Weber's canonical work on value-freedom in science as a justification,[11] critics have claimed that scholars' moral values—while unavoidable—ultimately distort the true fact-finding mission of the discipline and cause unnecessary strife between researchers. Some have criticized the activist bent of contemporary sociology, claiming that sociologists largely harbor liberal moralistic worldviews that blind them to evidence contrary to their preexisting beliefs.[12] These claims have, at times, echoed popular conservative pundits' critique of liberal biases in academia as distorting the truth.[13]

On the other hand, a prominent contingent of sociologists has been calling for explicit normative commitment to social justice among their peers. Drawing on the philosophy of Thomas Kuhn and Paul Feyerabend, who wrote against classical positivist views of science,[14] and on social theorists like Howard Becker, Alvin Gouldner, and C. Wright Mills, who rejected the possibility and desirability of value-free social sciences,[15] scholars in this camp have asserted that individual academics *never* detach from their social positions, and that sociologists should therefore be explicit about how values guide their research, as this will bolster the broader mission of pursuing equality and justice.[16] In making such claims, scholars like Dorothy Smith and Patricia Hill Collins have critiqued the idea of an "unbiased" or "value-free" sociology as an inherently racialized and gendered concept.[17] As part of this growing criticism, leading sociologists have demanded that the discipline recover an explicitly value-oriented stance in order to confront present sociopolitical ills. Michael Burawoy, as president of the American Sociological Association (ASA), famously pleaded for sociologists to recognize their commitment to the public and to defending civil society. More recently, Mary Romero and others maintained that American sociology has been an activist discipline from the very beginning,[18] pointing to pioneering turn-of-the-twentieth-century social theorists like Jane Addams, W. E. B. Du Bois, and Ida Wells-Barnett. For such scholars, sociological research is intertwined with the active pursuit of social justice, and the persistent demands for increased objectivity in sociology are merely a cover to marginalize non-white, non-male scholars.[19]

While mutually opposed, proponents of both camps would agree on one point: that most sociologists need to change their normative commitments. For advocates of increased neutrality in sociology, academics are currently too caught up in activism and must instead uphold *objectivity* as their guiding value. Committing to producing accurate facts about the social world requires them to put aside their moral orientations. For supporters of enhanced normative engagement in sociology, scholars at large are detached from the real injustices of the world, and must adopt *justice* as their core value (if they have not done so already). But by calling for their colleagues to readjust their moral compasses, both camps endorse several unwarranted assumptions about working sociologists.

First, both sides assume that many of their colleagues lack the critical sense to determine how their moral predispositions shape their research. This view of individuals as generally unable to provide an account of the causes for their thought, speech, and action owes much to the legacy of the sociologist Émile Durkheim, who argued that sociology needs "concepts that adequately express things as they actually are, and not as everyday life finds it useful to conceive them" and that sociology—as a new social science for his time—"has to create new concepts" and to "dismiss all lay notions and the terms expressing them."[20] In studies of academia, the sociologist Pierre Bourdieu popularized a similar approach by arguing that academics produce work reflecting their positions in their academic fields as shaped by their class backgrounds.[21] For Bourdieu, academics are largely unaware of their predispositions and must exercise reflexivity in order to counteract the "unconscious determinations that are inscribed in the scientist's mind,"[22] which are inextricably tied to the field dynamics that compel them toward certain research trajectories.[23] Sociologists of science have produced nuanced work in this vein, and have related the explicit utterances scientists make to their positions in academic fields, with the understanding that these relations may be indirect and historically contingent.[24] However, the assumption that academics at large are generally unaware of the moral stakes of their research ignores the fact that social scientists discuss this exact topic on many occasions. Indeed, even a brief walk through an ASA annual meeting will reveal myriad simultaneous debates about what makes research worthwhile, with participants weighing the moral worth of certain types of research against each other, reflecting on the criteria that guide them in doing so, criticizing others, and (occasionally) changing their positions on the matter. Such debates include questions about how social science can be more objective in its assessments, but also questions about how research contributes to broader movements for social justice.[25]

Second, and relatedly, supporters and detractors of explicit social justice orientation in sociology exempt *themselves* from the obliviousness they ascribe to their colleagues. In this, critics in both camps assume that they themselves can deduce other sociologists' unarticulated (perhaps unconscious) motives and biases.[26] Proponents of increased scientific objectivity argue that their methods help identify and counteract other researchers' preexisting biases.[27] Proponents of social justice–oriented research describe themselves as uniquely qualified to identify the class-, gender-, and race-based patterns that mar their colleagues' work.[28] In this, both sides share an epistemological orientation that the French philosopher Paul Ricœur called *the hermeneutics of suspicion*:[29] the position that seeks to reveal the hidden truths that undergirds actors' words and actions. Those taking this position often depict actors who disagree with them as misrecognizing the realities of social life.[30] This position has thus allowed a conversation about sociologists' true, unseen underlying commitments and the effects of those commitments on their research to burgeon while disregarding what working sociologists might say about their research aims.

Third, many commentators assume that only *some* sociologists "do" morality whereas others do not. Defenders of scientific neutrality in sociology have depicted their own position as nonmoral—in contradistinction to "social justice warriors" whom they depict as moralistic.[31] Conversely, proponents of social justice–oriented sociology, seeing moral stance-taking as an essential component of research, have presented themselves as the ones who best realize the fundamental moral aims of the discipline, in contrast to most others.[32] The latter camp has been joined by a chorus of authors who claim that sociologists at large have lost sight of essential human goodness and needs, and that the discipline needs to recover its moral compass by drawing on neuroscientific discoveries about human capacities or on moral philosophical ideas about thriving personhood.[33] But in making the assumption that only *some* research is infused with moral values, commentators ignore the literature dating back to Max Weber that shows how researchers' notions about the good society affect social research—starting from the selection of problems to research and conceptualization of key terms and continuing through final delivery of findings.[34] In fact, as the myriad critics of the notion of objectivity have argued, statements such as "sociology should be value free" are, in themselves, value judgments.[35]

Thus, disciplinary discussions of the role of morality in the discipline have assumed that sociologists are largely oblivious to the underlying structures that produce their stated positions; that some sociologists have unique insight into their colleagues' underlying motivations; and that some statements about how science ought to be conducted are moralistic whereas others are not. But these assumptions leave us ill equipped to capture the robust and diverse civic world sociologists animate. They fly in the face of existing knowledge about how actors engage with questions of morality and devalue the critical competencies of our own colleagues. If we are to understand the role morality plays in sociological research, we need a more robust theoretical framework that takes actors' capacities seriously.

This book parts ways with this suspicious view of the role of morality in sociological research. It moves away from a view of morality as preexisting norms and values that covertly shape research practices. Instead, it examines morality as a set of shared cultural repertoires. Each repertoire provides actors with a possible definition of the common good by which to justify their research. While some might describe the common good as civic equality, others might identify it as creativity and entrepreneurship, and others still might see it as giving voice to disadvantaged populations. Sociologists—like all actors—commonly draw on such repertoires to promote specific social goods, to respond to criticisms of their work, to rebuke others' research, and to navigate their way through a terrain rife with disputes about what would constitute a good society and what types of research practices would take us there. Adopting this view allows us to take account of the ways sociologists employ moral distinctions in their work: how they articulate morality in their own research, how they criticize research they deem immoral, how they resist or evade moral criticism, and how shared notions of morality come to organize research areas. While we do not deny that sociologists may harbor deep-seated moral values that guide their thinking on research questions, we reject the view that sociologists at large are unqualified to negotiate their moral views with multiple others. In our analysis, we draw on strands of pragmatist and cultural sociology that consider the social analyses individuals produce to be as valuable as those the analysts offer, and that maintain that non-sociologists do not need our help in uncovering hidden truths about their predispositions. Our task in this book is to show how sociologists respond to the diversity of opinions their colleagues hold about what is moral about sociology.

Common intuition would suggest that academic communities require consensus for scholarly production.[36] After all, without agreement over academic standards, basic research assumptions, and empirical relevance to the discipline, how would any article manuscript make it past the editorial gatekeepers of the top journals? But this book argues the opposite: that debate—in particular *moral* debate—between sociologists is a core engine of progress for the discipline. With sociologists advocating a plurality of positions about what qualifies as good sociology, such debates provide opportunities to refine the broader aims of the discipline, to negotiate the boundaries of what qualifies as "sociology," to rethink research trajectories in light of their ethical limitations, and to devise new research trajectories in contentious terrains. While sociologists of science have long recognized that consensus does not characterize sociology, they have lamented this as a failure. Randall Collins has argued that the social sciences, because of their slow-moving empirical discovery front, remain embroiled in arguments about how to interpret existing empirical knowledge.[37] Andrew Abbott has depicted sociology as repeatedly recreating preexisting binary oppositions between theoretical positions, even as it creates new subfields and new research areas.[38] Unlike these scholars, we follow organizational sociologists like David Stark[39] and sociologists of religion like Robert Wuthnow,[40] who have shown that environments where actors grapple with multiple views about the good promote organizational innovation and engaged civic life. The study cases we examine in the following chapters—controversies over core topics in sociology—demonstrate that scientific progress in sociology can be achieved precisely through such disagreements.

WHAT DOES MORALITY HAVE TO DO WITH SOCIOLOGY?

Ideas about the social good are central to the production of social scientific knowledge. Comparative-historical sociologists have shown that academic disciplines such as business, economics, and psychology developed in relation to publicly held notions of the good life, which shaped the questions academics asked and the answers they provided.[41] Scholars have also shown that some nascent academic disciplines failed to gain traction when the core issues they addressed (e.g., men's reproductive health) were deemed immoral.[42] But moral repertoires have not only shaped the historical emergence of disciplines; they also remain relevant to contemporary academia. Indeed, sociologists of knowledge have pointed out that the very definition of a social problem worthy of sociological research requires taking a moral stance on how one ought to assess the key indicators of relevance to study it.[43] Andrew Abbott, for example, has noted that sociologists take the concept of inequality—a foundational one for the discipline—to mean *injus-*

tice, rather than as a neutral descriptor. This conflation causes researchers to operationalize the concept of inequality as a normative-cum-empirical term in their research.[44] Andrew Sayer has similarly noted that sociologists pursue topics "thick" with meaning, wherein "attempting to replace [evaluative terms] with non-evaluative descriptions is likely to result in a loss of descriptive adequacy."[45] Related studies have also shown that scholars' policy ideas carry with them broad ethical theories relating to the common good.[46] The fact that sociologists evaluate the "right" social problems to study through a moral lens means that disciplinary gatekeepers often deem scholarship dealing with morally polluted issues unworthy of publication.[47] Indeed, sociologists have pointed to an implicit "analytic ontology" that shapes the kinds of social processes researchers consider morally worth investigating,[48] and disincentivizes sociologists to pursue topics that are viewed as controversial.[49] Sociologists have also shown how moral deliberation informs routine academic situations, such as evaluating grant applications, discussing standards of excellence, or assessing research ethics.[50]

Morality and sociology dovetail not only in the assumptions undergirding research, but also in the public-facing roles the discipline has adopted. As Bourdieu pointed out, sociologists face difficulties claiming scientific authority and autonomy from political influences because non-sociologists can counter sociologists' pronouncements about society with common sense (with claims like "what is this structural inequality nonsense? Obviously, the richest people are the ones who've worked the hardest!").[51] Because the boundaries of the discipline are porous, with politicians, advocates, legal experts, pundits, and others often participating in sociological conversations, actors from different professional fields may interpret sociological claims as demonstrating a moral-political position. Readers may, for example, interpret statements of empirical findings (e.g., "African Americans' incarceration rates quintuple those of whites") or methodological criticism (e.g., "surveys that allow only two genders exclude a range of additional possible categories") as direct normative statements (e.g., "the prison system contradicts the principle of equality before the law and must be reformed" or "uninformed research practices deny some social groups' right to recognition and must be censured"). The porous boundaries of the discipline and the diversity of its stakeholders has also expanded sociological research interests. As Abbott wrote, "sociology has become a discipline of many topics—always acquiring them, seldom losing them."[52] Given the field's increasing breadth, sociologists are even more likely to become embroiled in a debate about the social good. The "public sociology" movement, which has urged academics to attune themselves to public ethical concerns and social problems, has further bolstered the affinity between sociological and political claims.[53]

But beyond its interface with politics and policy makers, the discipline is also rife with internal conversations about what moral goods it *should* promote. Robert Bellah suggested that sociologists are often aware of and actively pursue moral aims influenced by "socially current notions about what is a good society, a satisfactory marriage, an able person, and so on."[54] And indeed, sociologists raise explicit questions about how to promote the good society on a regular basis. A regional sociological association sought in its annual meeting to "invoke conversations about new visions of human flourishing" involving a "serious reconsideration of the meaning of terms such as responsibility, sustainability, morality, and love (even unlimited love for all others without exception)."[55] Other examples include the model proposed by Erik Olin Wright for a sociological research informed by a commitment to active intervention in social ills in order to promote "real utopias" and the eponymous ASA annual meeting theme,[56] as well as Peter Hall and Michèle Lamont's investigation of the conditions underpinning "successful societies."[57] The new ASA Section on Altruism, Morality, and Social Solidarity has also taken the "sociology of the good" to be one of its core missions—that is, a program geared toward promoting human flourishing.[58]

Yet, if scholars have argued that morality is central to sociology, they have paid little attention to the ways sociologists maintain a vision of *themselves* as worthy moral agents in an academic world characterized by moral contention. Indeed, cultural sociologists and social psychologists have shown that actors constantly grapple with questions about their own moral standing and rely on cultural schemes to construct a sense of themselves as good people.[59] It should come as no great surprise, then, that entire disciplines struggle with whether they are conducting themselves in a decent way: as Abbott points out, social sciences positioned similarly to sociology—notably, law and political science—handle such puzzles of scientific ethics within specialized semi-autonomous subdisciplines—i.e. jurisprudence and political philosophy.[60] In this book, we draw on sociology's already existing history of moral debate to construct such a field of study.

FROM CRITICISM TO CRITICAL CAPACITIES IN THE SOCIOLOGY OF KNOWLEDGE PRODUCTION

To capture how sociologists' moral repertoires affect longue durée research trajectories, we adopt a pragmatist approach to the study of knowledge production. Pragmatist philosophical influences have seen a renaissance in sociology, in ways that highlight community capacities to deliberate on and resolve social problems. Pragmatism in sociology goes back to the earliest days of the discipline in the US,[61] to the work of W. E. B. Du Bois[62] in the sociology of race and to George Herbert Mead's thought on self and society.[63] After several decades of disregard, sociologists recently rediscovered the work of pragmatist philosophers like Charles Peirce, John Dewey, and William James, and applied it to social phenomena ranging from historical bird-watching to responding to microaggressions.[64] As Neil Gross notes, while many of his fellow sociologists have tended to use pragmatist concepts to study micro-level occurrences such as interpersonal interaction or problem solving, pragmatism has much to say about macro-level phenomena as well.[65] Meanwhile, French sociologists like Luc Boltanski, Laurent Thévenot, Ève Chiapello, Ilana Silber, and Cyril Lemieux[66] have recently developed a view of participatory democracy wherein actors employ different "moral theories" to make sense of common situations and to criticize injustice. This "Sociology of Critique" (often called "the New French Pragmatist Sociology"[67]) shares core concerns with US pragmatist sociology.

By adopting a pragmatist approach, we turn attention from questions about what sociologists *ought* to do, to questions about what sociologists *already* do when it comes to the moral underpinnings of their research. Indeed, John Dewey's thinking on public deliberation highlights individuals' capacity to reflect on their own moral stances and societies' ability to deliberate between multiple views of the social good.[68] For Dewey, actors deliberate on potential solutions to social problems by drawing on various notions of morality (what Dewey refers to as *moral theories*) to reach a decision about what action to take next.[69] Dewey envisioned a moral theory as a historically contingent system of addressing social problems (rather than a universally valid one) by providing individuals the conceptual tools to create value judgments in deliberations over the common good.[70] Democratic forms and practices complement moral theories by providing a participatory system where individuals constantly work to define together what qualifies as an ethical community, sharing with each other a "moral and spiritual association."[71] In this deliberative project, science and democracy are mutually supportive enterprises: through academic inquiry, actors debate public problems and devise provisional solutions that support better democracies.

Dewey believed science and democracy are ideally egalitarian and progressive, and rest on habits of open social communication. In practice, both are messy affairs. In order to examine how scholars grapple with often contentious implications of sociological research, we adapt several guiding pragmatist principles for the purpose of this book.

First, we subscribe to Dewey's view that individuals—academics or others—can grasp complex ethical orders and deliberate between moral theories. Boltanski and Thévenot aimed their studies of social critique at describing "the actor's sense of justice—or, more precisely, their sense of injustice" and charting the "models of the competence with which actors have to be endowed in order to face ordinary critical situations."[72] Pragmatist sociology sees individuals as capable of comprehending nuanced logics of worth and applying them to concrete situations in their daily lives.[73] This includes actors who articulate their understanding not as refined philosophical arguments, but as concrete statements about the moral worth of their actions.[74] In the academic context, we identify the frameworks of ethical reasoning that inform sociological debates. To this end, we develop tools to trace nuanced logics of reasoning and to follow sociological debates in action.[75] Even the mundane decisions of academic life require moral evaluations: when comparing the value of research proposals in a grants committee; when addressing controversial research; when cooperating with department members who have diverging research agendas on securing a new hire. Thus, we see engagement with questions of good and bad, of *morality*, as a core aspect of sociological knowledge production and as integral to the lived experience of working sociologists. Our approach is pragmatist in that it focuses on the history and cultural limits of moral debate, "to understand the practice of critique and, thus, understand why it is so difficult to criticize," as Boltanski put it.[76]

Second, in contrast to structural or ideological critiques of academia,[77] we take authors' stated intentions in conducting research at face value, rather than seeking out unseen factors that predetermine their stances or treating their positions as some form of false consciousness.[78] Thus, while we analyze existing research studies in the following chapters, we do not attach unseen reasons to the scholarship we examine. Instead, we base our analyses on the explicit statements those academics make. In no way do we imply that scholars' positionality and institutional belonging do not play important roles in shaping their research agendas. But by highlighting the plurality of available repertoires sociologists use to engage with moral controversy, we include the possibility that actors bring their own positionality into the academic conversation. Our working assumption, drawing on a long pragmatist tradition in sociology, is that actors can *choose* how they engage morality—a central capacity that purely structural accounts underplay.[79]

Relatedly, we maintain that we, as outside observers, cannot use academics' published scholarship to decipher what psychological nuts and bolts moved them to conduct their research. In this, our book does not seek to join the ongoing conversation between social psychologists, cultural sociologists, and cognitive sociologists about whether and how morality affects individual human behavior.[80] Instead, we follow Ann Swidler in asserting that analyses of culture on the individual level and the social-psychological level cannot come at the expense of thinking about how culture is organized to begin with, and how its organization provides actors with opportunities for action.[81] Accordingly, we restrict our discussion to the *public* roles moral repertoires take: how actors use them and what opportunities they afford.

Third, in our view, claims to truth are intertwined with forms of moral reasoning. For this reason, we treat academic conversations as important sites of disagreement about the common good, with sociology being one tradition that addresses these problems explicitly. Readers often interpret sociological findings as bearing political implications and demanding further debate.[82] Thus, a sociological claim—say, that the children of same-sex marriage have different life outcomes than those of opposite-sex marriage—will be perceived as taking a *political* position against same-sex parents' adoption rights.[83] The ensuing public outcry can elicit a scholarly debate over the theoretical framing of the questions researchers pose and the research norms they use.[84] Disagreements over scientific matters in sociology are laden with political meanings and are open to engagement with the wider public. Thus, our claim that scholars engage with moral frameworks in discussing research has no bearing on the empirical validity of their research. We do not suggest that research is empirically inadequate because its authors make moral claims about their findings; and we do not suggest that some research is more legitimate because of the normative discourse its authors use. Our point is merely that sociologists across subfields make moral and empirical questions beholden to one another.[85]

Fourth, while we examine disagreements, we emphasize that actors can and do achieve peaceful coexistence despite abysmal differences between worldviews.[86] Some disagreements culminate with one side prevailing over the other, but many other controversies end with a compromise where the parties agree to disagree. Such compromises emerge as actors devise ways to continue to cooperate without pursuing their disagreement further, out of a pragmatic intention to maintain their interaction. We argue that individuals, even in the face of significant differences, maintain the capacity to cooperate with one another to find common goals that transcend their differences.[87] Indeed, scientists may harbor strong disagreements with each other, but will often cooperate to facilitate increased social awareness, to renew thinking on a pressing public problem, or simply to be able to move forward with their own research. As our examples of routine department life suggest, academics are required not only to understand multiple viewpoints about what constitutes the common good, but also to reach compromises with colleagues despite stark differences in their understanding of the social goods sociology should provide. Focusing on how sociologists criticize but also continue to work in the face of critique will help explain how moral debates within the discipline can generate new types of research.[88]

In short, to study the history of how sociologists criticize one another, we maintain that individuals can grasp complex ethical order, mean what they say when they use such ethical systems to justify their actions, and reach compromises that transcend their differences in moral perspective. Overall, we draw attention to the ways sociology can not only critique existing social arrangements, but also justify changes that promote a more just social world.

MORAL META-COMMUNICATIONS

Within the cases we explore in the following chapters, we focus specifically on what Paul Lichterman and Isaac Reed call *meta-communication*—the "active reflection on foundational assumptions behind the concepts we choose or reflection on entire lines of scholarly inquiry or debate."[89] Meta-communication is commentary about the scholarly conversation academics are having. Taking a step back and noting that a surveying methodology is flawed and calling into question the findings it generated is one example; debating the ethics of ethnographers' engagement with field sites is another. For Lichterman and Reed, meta-communication is essential for the progress of science because it allows members of a community of inquiry to express concerns about theory, method, and research questions.[90] Meta-communicating is an explicitly collective activity, so while an individual may seek to start a conversation on a particular controversial research topic, they must convince others that the chosen topic is worthwhile. For this reason, while numerous sociologists of science have interviewed individual scholars about their own stances on research,[91] we analyze scholars' written meta-communication as they position themselves in relation to their colleagues' research (even if implicitly). Moreover, the following chapters will show that meta-communication can also pertain to the moral standing of a research trajectory: whether it is *good* and—if so—how and for whom. Such meta-communication could be pointing out that an entire research stream is based on racist assumptions and is thus unacceptable; claiming that a sociological study in fact harms the populations it seeks to help; or defending the value of a research program for promoting positive social relations. If sociology is indeed a combative discipline, it is because of this kind of moral meta-communication.

Furthermore, while *some* moral meta-communication is indeed explosive, the chapters ahead also highlight the more implicit forms it can take.[92] As we show, meta-communication need not be confrontational: even if some moral meta-communication may involve explicit statements like "we need to stop using this survey method because it harms certain populations by excluding them," others may involve indirect statements like "survey methodologies such as these fall short of giving all populations proper representation, and thus fail to live up to the discipline's standards."[93] Indeed, research on moral framing has shown that when it comes to signaling the moral standing of an object, implicit cues are as powerful as explicit injunctions in conveying moral judgment.[94]

In each of the following chapters, we focus on historic debates that demonstrate how moral creativity and scholarly ingenuity interlock. Each of these examples is a case where meta-communication about a controversial topic caught the attention of a broad community of scholars and generated a dispute. Rather than focus on the fervor of the debate, we highlight how some scholars in each case strove to avoid a zero-sum war in the name of advancing sociology's shared commitments to diversity of thought and social justice. We follow the historical sociologist William Sewell in seeing our task as tracing relationships between social structures and the agents who reproduce and transform them in action, rather than as identifying universally generalizable cause-and-effect mechanisms. As Sewell had it, scholars should conceptualize societies as "the sites of a multitude of overlapping and interlocking cultural structures,"[95] and see historical events as occurring in the conjunctures (or situations) where actors are forced to coordinate between cultural frameworks and changing social conditions.[96] We similarly view new forms of moral meta-communication as emerging when academics publicly negotiate historically specific conjunctures between dominant academic paradigms, public *zeitgeist*, and their own professional trajectories. In so doing, we follow the spirit of third-wave comparative-historical sociology and emphasize the particularity of historical conjunctures, and the ways actors creatively and collectively make sense of them.[97] Thus, rather than inquire about the psychological or career factors that led certain scholars to make certain claims at certain times, we ask how scholars constructed justifications and criticisms of research trajectories at specific conjunctures in the history of their discipline. In this model, actors' agency is constrained only by their ability to get others to recognize relevant schemata to explain what's happening.[98]

We selected our study cases because they provide particularly clear ways of observing how scholarly moral meta-communication unfolds. Using a purposive method of case selection,[99] we identified a series of cases that demonstrate our theoretical and normative concerns, rather than seeking an average or a truly representative selection of cases. Thus, while certainly not all sociological debates involve competing moral repertoires,[100] the cases we have chosen highlight particular instances where moral debate served as an engine of creativity.[101] It is not our task to decide whether the outcomes of debates are positive or negative, or whether they were ultimately resolved; rather, our aim is to demonstrate that they push scholars to reassess work in their research field and to devise new ways to move forward.

THE ROAD AHEAD

Crucial to our claim that moral debate pushes sociological debates forward is that we envision moral repertoires as emerging from ongoing social interaction. Open debate—often spurred by making public pronouncements about the flawed nature of existing research—makes this interaction tractable. In chapter 1 we unpack the notion of a *moral repertoire* and use the sociology of religion as a jumping-off point to show how clashing moral repertoires can cause serious debate but also generate new avenues for research as scholars devise new ways of addressing and circumventing controversy. The sociology of religion is a convenient starting point for us because sociologists had long held that religious decline is a persistent feature of modernization and had largely seen this as a positive trend. However, as religious revival increasingly gripped politics throughout the turn from the twentieth to the twenty-first century, the secularization thesis faced a slew of empirical and normative critiques. This case is illustrative of the patterned methods of assessing research, each of which relies on a different preconception of the social goods scholarship ought to provide; it is particularly helpful because it resulted in a diverse set of research strains that found ways to coexist with and transcend one another. Thus, the chapter provides tools to study how scholars delimit controversial academic pursuits and how they construct new ways to address or bypass such sensitivities. The case studies examined in the following chapters demon-strate the broad applicability of these tactics across sociology.

Chapter 2 delves deeper into what we mean when we refer to a moral debate in sociology. It examines what we call *no-go zones* in the social sciences—topics that academic communities consider to be morally con-taminated—in order to outline how the situations where sociologists in-voke competing moral repertoires are constructed. Focusing on the once sociologically fashionable, but now widely discredited, ideas of Herbert Spencer, the chapter traces the repeated resurgence of two parallel sites of research: the link between race, genetics, and inequality; and the link between culture and poverty. Emphasizing how scholars debate the nature of the research situation to advance claims in such contested research do-mains, we develop a typology of scholarly engagement with controversy, wherein actors treat academic research as unproblematic, as debatable, as a community-building opportunity, or as radically unacceptable. Rather than simply banning topics outright, we show how scholars of supposedly "forbidden" topics devise ways to frame their research as morally worthy. In fact, despite controversy, contemporary sociologists of health do use new genetic data, claiming that such research helps promote a more just future by emphasizing processes of collective genetic trauma and the heri-tability of many health characteristics.[102] Conversely, we show how those who fail in making a compelling case that their controversial research is morally worthy face community sanctions. While academic controversy may result from forceful provocation, we highlight how sociologists also mark their own moral boundaries through overtly good-faith discussions about whether it is possible to explore polluted research topics.

While chapter 2 shows how moral debate is constructed and negotiated among sociologists, chapters 3 and 4 focus on the different ways scholars navigate such debates. In this, criticized parties may adopt new discur-sive frameworks that allow them to justify their research as worthwhile despite possible limitations, and to thus redeem or transform their topic of inquiry.

One method for handling contentious moral terrain is to seek com-promise. Here, scholars add nuance to their claims by tempering them in recognition of competing moral interpretation. Chapter 3 focuses on this strategy of partially reforming research practices, and examines as a study case the 1990s denunciations of methodological nationalism offered by cosmopolitan theorists, who intertwined theoretical and empirical claims with normative injunctions about world politics. These denunciations be-gan with scholars like Ulrich Beck and John Urry who advocated for a new, cosmopolitan sociology that could address a world increasing permeated by transnational social activity, identities, and thought. As part of this new wave in sociology, scholars working on sites bounded within traditional nation-states found themselves critiqued for implicitly endorsing a pernicious world order of boundaries and nations. The chapter focuses on how sociologists subsequently maneuvered to reframe their research in ways that continued to explore how the category of the nation-state remains salient today, but also evaded criticism of endorsing nation-states as a phenomenon. The chapter highlights the efforts scholars make to reach compromises with their peers rather than spark further controversy among them. The analysis shows how scholars who reframed the role of nationalism as a concrete empirical question also worked to situate their moral concerns in an increasingly globalized world.

While a plurality of moral repertoires can breed contention amongst scholars, it can also serve as the foundation of different research trajectories altogether. Occasionally, scholars launch new research trajectories that acknowledge the gravity of some ongoing debate, but also allow the scholar to reframe their research discursively to transcend the existing argument. Chapter 4 focuses on two such cases at the intersection of gender, family, and inequality. These cases emerged from debates on the utility of stated fertility intentions for demographic analysts and in the study of intensive mothering practices. The chapter shows how sociologists use this maneuver (which we call *reconstitution*) to seek a way out of moral deadlocks. In the first example, demographers widely debated the notion that mothers' stated fertility intentions early in life predict their future number of children, with some scholars accusing others of causing actual harm to the women they were studying. However, a new generation of sociologists working in this area suggested that the gap between intended and achieved fertility could be understood as cultural data that could be used to reshape their subfield. Examining this cultural data through historical and ethnographic methods was thus portrayed as valuable not only empirically, but also morally, to highlight women's agency. In the second example, we investigate the lengthy scholarly controversy over whether public health recommendations for mothers to breastfeed are legitimate or whether they ignore the costs of breastfeeding to mothers, particularly regarding their lifelong wages. We focus on a group of scholars who highlighted how debates about breastfeeding recommendations could be used to re-center women's voices and concerns in society. In this, scholars built upon existing debates about breastfeeding—some of which reached considerable fervor and devolved into ad hominem attacks—to pursue other research trajectories that can transcend the debate through focusing on an alternative moral good. In both cases, scholars turned to alternate notions of how research ought to promote the common good, resisting the impulse to delve directly into existing controversies and attempt to refute or reform existing approaches to the topic. Together, chapters 3 and 4 draw attention to the creative ways scholars respond to moral critique, which ultimately contribute to the empirical vibrancy of the discipline.

Throughout the book, we argue that moral debate within the field is a healthy and to some extent desirable activity amongst sociologists. Of course, our argument is also a moral claim. We do not argue that more controversy automatically results in better science, but we do argue that any "big tent" approach to sociology will recognize that explicit moral debate *can* help advance analysis within specific historical and institutional contexts. We maintain that controversy has multifaceted effects on social scientific research and that (in certain instances) it can drive disciplinary change and spur breakthroughs rather than hinder research. In the conclusion, we argue for value pluralism, which acknowledges that multiple mutually exclusive definitions of the good may coexist productively. Value pluralism, we maintain, will contribute to a forthright discussion of the social contributions social scientists provide through their research, and will increase mutual respect among different factions in the discipline. The Afterword provides a summary guide to our theoretical approach, which will be a useful reference for readers as they navigate the core chapters of the book.

While Bourdieu described sociology as a martial art,[103] we see it as a moral minefield.[104] By naming the book *Moral Minefields*, we agree that sociology is itself a battlefield. But our aim is not to underscore the combativeness of the field; instead we intend to highlight how in moments of heated debate sociology finds ways to navigate critiques and to come out stronger as a discipline.[105] We highlight how sociologists seeking to forward an argument learn to maneuver *through* a space of moral contention rather than engaging in a battle. In this sense, sociology is important not only because it justifies criticism, but also because it provides the intellectual resources to resolve social ruptures and bolster respect for diversity. In a similarly militaristic analogy, C. Wright Mills once explained to a friend that his most aggressive critics also served as the basis for his own scholarly renewal:

> The pragmatic meaning of all this [scholarly criticism] is that you become aware of where the bayonet is thrust from; you know the milieu across which it comes. You try to avoid being struck. But if you don't

in fact know what part of the body to take the bayonet from, then you take it with eyes wide open. You make an *experience* out of it, even if it is your last.[106]

Much like Mills, we argue that as sociologists we take the body blows of moral debate and make something of them. Where possible, we also show how we can avoid the need for body blows, and still make something out of these disputes in the end.

CHAPTER ONE

Navigating in a Minefield

Moral Repertoires and Sociological Research

In the case of sociology . . . we are always walking on hot coals, and the things we discuss are alive, they are not dead and buried.

PIERRE BOURDIEU[1]

While numerous sociologists have been admired for their uncompromising criticisms of existing social arrangements, such figures often made difficult colleagues. In fact, some of the more prominent debates in the discipline involved academics claiming not only that their opponents are empirically wrong, but that they are morally corrupt for harboring certain opinions. C. Wright Mills was a notoriously belligerent academic who infused his scathing criticism of midcentury American society with personal attacks on his colleagues. Mills was scornful of sociology as a discipline for failing to attract the best and brightest, and—the public appeal of his work notwithstanding—made very few allies among his academic peers.[2] Several months after his death, his contemporary Edward Shils wrote, "Now he is dead and his rhetoric is a field of broken stones, his analyses empty, his strenuous pathos limp. He was a victim of his own vanity and of a shriveled Marxism, which will not die."[3] A generation later, Norman K. Denzin called *The Sociological Imagination* "a hypocritical text, with dubious ethics," and highlighted how Mills's bravado alienated not only his peers, but future generations of scholars too.[4] Similarly, W. E. B. Du Bois's growing intellectual disagreement with Booker T. Washington escalated from a professional to a personal feud over the early 1900s. Convinced that Washington was attempting to cut off funds for his own institute at Atlanta University, Du Bois eventually resigned from the university in order to prevent further loss of funds. Historians now believe that the sparring between Du Bois and Washington detracted from the scholarly legacy of both in the long term.[5] Given that taking a position on a sociological question usually means taking a stance on a political issue,[6] scholars' stated positions about the common good (and condemnation of alternate views) have repeatedly sparked ad hominem debates that ended in research topics being quarantined.

Even scholars who avoid ad hominem attacks still criticize fellow sociologists' work based on moral judgments, particularly around the question of what constitutes good sociological research. Sociologists have developed an array of repertoires to criticize the work of their peers based on notions of the social good. Using such repertoires, sociologists have constructed claims about the moral character of their peers and the ethical status of their work, alongside critiques of its methodological adequacy. In sociological controversies, critics formulate denunciations by identifying certain research practices as transgressing against a broad notion of the expected contribution of the discipline to the common good. Given the heightened polarization characterizing US campuses over the last decade, clashes surrounding different views of unacceptable research have become even more prevalent.[7]

In this chapter, we develop the notion of *moral repertoires*: abstract meaning systems that each define one possible conception of worthy scholarly work. Moral repertoires offer scholars the cultural logics to justify their research and evaluate the research of others. Any one discipline can provide speakers with multiple possible repertoires: while one repertoire may focus strictly on the empirical worth of a paper, another may assess the commitment of the researchers to the populations they study, and a third may evaluate a paper based on the types of political claims the findings enable. Such repertoires allow working sociologists to demarcate certain types of research and researcher conduct as unacceptable, regardless of what findings they may yield, but they may also help generate new directions for researchers to follow. Indeed, the plurality of repertoires in the discipline allows scholars to switch between different registers and to justify new research avenues.

Thus, some of the "state of the art" of any discipline includes work that either finds ways to address previously criticized research topics while avoiding censure or builds on existing debates to explore new directions for research and circumvent contentious issues altogether. Scholars taking such avenues are, to use Bourdieu's metaphor, "walking on hot coals,"[8] and to do so successfully they develop ways to acknowledge the gravity of the moral controversy at hand while at the same time continuing to advance social thinking around and engagement with contentious moral propositions.

In what follows, we draw on recent work in the cultural and pragmatist sociology of knowledge production to highlight the agency of social scientists as they negotiate research practices or make decisions on value in research. Scholarship in this area has shown that the micro-level discussions social scientists carry on about worthiness matter greatly for larger shifts in the production of knowledge.[9] Questions about the perceived morality of scholars and their research play key roles in such interactions.[10] This chapter draws insights from the new "sociology of critique" to highlight the patterned logics by which sociologists conceive of ways in which sociology contributes to the common good, and outlines how sociologists negotiate a reality where some of their colleagues harbor very different ideas about what constitutes that good. We do not aim to provide an exhaustive account of *all* the trajectories a scholarly disagreement might take or to provide suggestions for conflict resolution. Instead, we identify a set of common claims that sociologists make about research and demonstrate the paths their debates take and the resolutions they reach. After outlining our approach, we examine the history of one of the most contentious sociological debates in recent decades—the debate over the secularization thesis and its implications—and show how different scholars switched between moral repertoires to continue conducting research in such a contentious field.

SOCIOLOGISTS AS MORAL AGENTS: FROM MANNHEIM TO PRAGMATIST SOCIOLOGY

The frequent "lack of conviction" of the intellectuals is merely the reverse side of the fact that they alone are in a position to have intellectual convictions. . . . Should the capacity to acquire a broader point of view be considered merely as a liability? Does it not rather present a mission?

KARL MANNHEIM[11]

Alongside the aspiration for value-neutrality that the Weberian paradigm imparted to sociology, the discipline has had a long tradition of explicit discussion of what constitutes the good society and how sociologists might help bring it forth. As a founding figure for the sociology of knowledge, Karl Mannheim saw immense promise in sociology as a program that could hold the liberal political order accountable. In Mannheim's view, sociology provided a way beyond Marx's single-minded critique of ideology: rather than simply providing the tools for denouncing existing arrangements, sociology's scientific development hinged on its ability to reveal the diversity of human experience and to reach consensus about the collective implications of those experiences.[12] As a result, sociology can produce the sort of critiques that both revive the scientific quest for truth and also—particularly through the sociology of knowledge—bring those arguments about truth into conversation with utopian visions of the good society.

Cultural[13] and structural[14] analyses within mainstream sociological discourse have incorporated Mannheim's work. However, a heterodox stream of "relatively unattached" professional sociologists—scholars who, according to Mannheim, are "not too firmly situated in the social order"[15] and can therefore take critical distance from existing party, institutional, and class loyalties—have made the largest inroads drawing from Mannheim's ideas. C. W. Mills, for instance, was trained by one of Mannheim's students (Hans Gerth). Mills reformulated Mannheim's ideas through an engagement with American Pragmatism.[16] While his masterpiece on the meanings of sociology as a science, *The Sociological Imagination*, does not address Mannheim outright, his engagement with Mannheim's project clearly influenced his hope to make "the moral problems of social study—the problem of social science as a public issue"[17] the central concern of the discipline. In a very different way, as Patricia Hill Collins developed her renowned treatise on Black feminist thought, she also alluded to Mannheim's ideas about the need to rethink how actors can produce social criticism.[18] Collins has since turned her attention outside of the sociology of science to focus on the significance of these ideas for public life.[19]

Mannheim's work presented a vision of sociology as a discipline that brings into conversation for public reflection diverse social experiences, and as a discipline that recognizes that certain actors' class position may leave them in a "relatively unattached" position where they can make informed moral arguments. At the same time, the ideas Mannheim put forth succeeded primarily when scholars like Mills and Collins utilized them to legitimize heterodox scholarly practices and to criticize the dominant sociology of the day, rather than to assess the more common moral positions sociologists articulate and their relative influence on disciplinary development. While these sociologists grew to notoriety by developing their own unique descriptions of the links between morality and social science, in what follows we elaborate on the ways the common moral positions sociologists take constitute repertoires of logics that shape broad disciplinary outcomes.

REPERTOIRES OF MORALITY IN SOCIOLOGY

To begin exploring the diverse ways of evaluating research sociologists employ, consider the following responses a scholarly presenter might receive after concluding their talk:

1. "Your data does not support your claims. Let me point out some of the most glaring measurement and inference problems in your paper."
2. "I'm surprised you're not in conversation with scholars in a field adjacent to yours. You really should do more interdisciplinary work!"
3. "You've said nothing about your position in the field, in relation to your interviewees. I'm concerned about the power dynamics between you as a privileged interviewer and them."
4. "Bourdieu is the most eminent scholar in this field, and what you are saying contradicts his theories. You clearly haven't read his work on your subject."
5. "I'm concerned about the political implications of your findings. If we think this through, your paper all too easily reinforces existing biases and supports regressive, conservative politics."
6. "There is no theoretical or methodological originality here. You're basically applying other scholars' frameworks as they are, without any creativity on your part."
7. "For a non-specialist in your area, how would you frame the importance of your research? I'm concerned that there is currently very little public interest or funding for your topic. Perhaps consider reframing your findings."

While versions of these responses are common enough across academic settings, their logics are considerably different. The first response posits methodological adequacy as a key measure of worth. Subsequent responses go in different directions: the second places interconnectivity as the central evaluative category of good research; the third refers to maintaining positive, equal relations with research subjects; the fourth sees respect for charismatic leaders in the field as key; the fifth presents the ultimate contribution to civil society and equality as the fundamental measure of worth; the sixth focuses on the originality and innovativeness of the contribution; and the seventh asks about whether the findings will be of wide interest. Each key measure of worth, in turn, is embedded in a broad understanding of how good research ought to be conducted and where its social benefits lie:

- The first cherishes the generation of facts that will shed light on social phenomena—we call it the *Efficiency Repertoire*.
- The second values dialogue and cooperation within the discipline and beyond as the way to advance—we call it the *Network Repertoire*.

- The third sees the mission of sociology as giving voice to underrepresented groups—we call it the *Anchored Repertoire.*
- The fourth views the worthiest work in the discipline as capitalizing on and developing the work of leading intellectual figures—we call it the *Charismatic Repertoire.*
- The fifth depicts sociology as a science devoted to furthering social equality and civic values—we call it the *Civic Repertoire.*
- The sixth focuses on originality and creativity as the marker of good sociology—we call it the *Creativity Repertoire.*
- And the seventh ties the worth of sociological research to its marketability, to its public relevance and its potential to draw attention and funding—we call it the *Marketability Repertoire.*

Each of these different logics of evaluating sociological work provides scholars with a repertoire from which to form moral claims about what research ought to be pursued and what research is abhorrent. While this list is not exhaustive of all types of logics critics in the discipline employ, it demonstrates the *diversity* of repertoires that scholars routinely voice in discussions of academic work.

Moral repertoires resemble what Luc Boltanski and Laurent Thévenot called *cités*,[20] which are systems of moral logic, each of which establishes one way of evaluating worth. Each repertoire specifies relevant categories for evaluation, the adequate methods for establishing worth, and the expected investment for achieving a status of greatness. Each also excludes all other methods of evaluation: an object one repertoire of evaluation deems worthy could be considered ordinary by a different repertoire. However, rather than being confined to one framework of argumentation, actors may use different repertoires in different situations: a university administrator may start their day demanding that faculty teach courses appealing to student demands, around lunchtime criticize a professor for their minimal contribution to campus life, and end the day arguing that a report on campus climate uses questionable methodology. Actors move this way between logics of argumentation regardless of their own background or position because each repertoire formalizes widely available commonsense metrics. The unit of our analysis is not an actor but an *utterance*, such as a comment made at a colloquium, a justification for writing a book in its preface, or a scathing critique of a manuscript in a peer review. Actors may use different repertoires at different times, and may even use several mutually exclusive repertoires to justify the same object (e.g., "not only is this book meticulously researched using cutting-edge methodologies, it also informs policy in ways that can reduce inequality").

Each repertoire not only specifies the center of moral worth, but also provides *tests*—types of proof and measurement relevant to establishing worth—that allow for their consistent emergence, use, and consolidation in everyday practice. For example, consider a university tenure committee. While one university administrator may evaluate professors based on their service to the university, another may see a scholar's research productivity as crucial. While most in academia will agree that both are important metrics, most will also agree that the two measures are on different registers, or in other words represent different moral orientations for the research university: for the first it is a civic institution, for the second it is a knowledge production institution. A third administrator may argue that the university is designed to support an intellectual avant-garde, and that the first two have missed the point entirely—they should be after a measure of uniqueness of contribution. Since such repertoires are diverse, the acceptance of a given moral framework can become grounds for further dispute.[21] Furthermore, even if all three administrators agree to evaluate a professor for tenure based on her research productivity, they may disagree on what indicators to use: quantitative counts of publications and impact factors, or the quality of her recommendation letters? In this instance, both sides of a debate can even use the same repertoire but disagree on the practical implications of the result of a single "test."[22] In short, a repertoire defines a category of evaluation, but also includes a host of definitions, facts, and fact-finding procedures that allow actors to reach conclusions about worth.[23]

Crucially, moral repertoires are historically constituted, shaped by the relevant modes of social experience and criticism available at a particular time, and are a result of efforts to elaborate in situ moral claims into scientific claims about the nature of social reality. For this reason, new moral repertoires often emerge in "unsettled times,"[24] when a new mode of cultural resistance emerges and captures the imagination of societies and sociologists. These periods of renewal often give rise to *épreuves*[25]—moments of trial, when actors debate the worth of an object. In academia these could be award committees, tenure discussions, or curriculum development conversations, among other options.[26] Periods of broad deliberation over research practices and ethics similarly give rise to moral meta-communication—namely, commentary about the assumptions undergirding research, which appear in thought pieces in professional newsletters, lengthy justifications of approaches in research articles, or agenda-setting keynote addresses at conferences. Moral repertoires take shape in these periods, when actors feel obliged to spell out what they see as the moral underpinnings of their stances.

Durable repertoires—those with a wide breadth of cultural resonance—provide logics that can be taken in both critical and conservative directions. Take the paradoxical effect of the 1960s countercultural movements.[27] On the one hand, demands from the counterculture that the self be understood as a "project" enriched by a widening of social experience and interconnection were consolidated into a new mode of criticism epitomized in the lives and scholarship of radicals like Foucault, Derrida, and Deleuze.[28] However, management scholars understood these countercultural movements differently, and adopted a new capitalist hero that could fulfill the vision of the self they demanded: the hyper-mobile influencer that would later be reproduced in the management style of Silicon Valley.[29]

Thus, historical moments of debate about social life often produce enduring logics for thinking about the common good that continue to undergird future academic and public conversations. Aside from the 1960s movements, other historical critical moments have also left ambiguous traces on social life and theory. Adam Smith's critique of mercantilist price controls;[30] Friedrich Engels's criticism of family life under capitalism;[31] Max Weber's analysis of industrial efficiency;[32] postcolonialists like Frantz Fanon and Edward Said's exposure of the Eurocentrism and racism of social thought;[33] and feminists like Gloria Anzaldúa and Audre Lorde's rejection of the universalist pretenses of the social sciences[34] all captured and systematized the everyday sense of disillusionment in a particular age, and have been cited in diverse contexts.[35] Each repertoire provides one way to justify words and deeds in the present, and the overall diversity of tests serves as a resource for the adjudication of moral worth in ongoing empirical, methodological, and theoretical debates.

While we describe each repertoire as a distinctive measure of worth, actors may also apply repertoires sequentially or concurrently. For example, actors may invoke one repertoire under the assumption that another repertoire also holds. The case of the now retracted 2014 article by Michael LaCour and Donald Green, "When Contact Changes Minds," offers an instructive example.[36] The article claimed that conversations with gay canvassers positively affected voters' attitudes on same-sex marriage, with a broader, longer-lasting effect than a conversation with a straight canvasser. Critics widely praised the article for its *civic* contribution—namely, its demonstration that individuals can be convinced to support equality.[37] The campaign to legalize same-sex marriage in Ireland even called this study a "template" for canvassers engaging with conservative voters.[38] But this praise was contingent on the assumptions of the Efficiency Repertoire, particularly the assumption that the study was conducted with utmost rigor and meticulous enough methods to land it in the prestigious journal *Science*. A 2015 follow-up paper broke this assumption when it presented evidence suggesting that the research was fabricated.[39] Additional inquiry discovered that the first author, LaCour, had forged the entire study.[40] LaCour's contravention of the Efficiency Repertoire in misrepresenting research procedures pulled the rug out from under the *civic* claim. Moreover, some have argued that LaCour ultimately hurt the credibility of social scientific research on progressive causes by depicting scientific outlets as harboring such liberal bias as would blind them to obvious methodological errors or forgery.[41] One repertoire may thus serve as the base assumption for another repertoire. Additionally, certain repertoires may frequently cluster together and may be used concurrently to evaluate a study. Readers of a study like Elijah Anderson's hyperlocal study of the Black inner city, *A Place on the Corner*,[42] can value the book for its *civic* and its *anchored* virtues concomitantly (e.g., "by faithfully giving voice to this underrepresented population, this study supports their fight for equality"). A study like Michèle Lamont and her coauthors' multinational study of responses to microaggression, *Getting Respect*,[43] can be valued on both the *Efficiency* and the *Network* repertoires (e.g., "this study employs rigorous comparative methods with research teams from three different countries participating"). While each repertoire relies on a different logic, actors often apply them in creative combinations.

Let us return to the seminar room, where our colloquium presenter faces a roomful of colleagues whose questions attach entirely different stakes to sociological research. Each questioner is drawing on a different repertoire to define what good sociology is and how one knows it when they see it. We outline in table 1.1 the seven repertoires such questioners represent, including the key measure they prescribe for evaluating research and an example of a claim one might construe in its vein. We expand on each of these repertoires in the Afterword.

While many would maintain that claims consistent with the Efficiency Repertoire—focusing on scientific validity and industriousness—have nothing to do with morality, we argue that claims about the need for empirical validity employ a moral repertoire because they evaluate research practices in light of standards that are assumed to be universal, and adhering to these standards is further assumed to be essential for the common good (e.g., for informed policy making, for the advancement of sciences, etc.). This does not imply that claims about the need for methodological rigor are less warranted (or more valid); rather, it means that the logics such claims follow are based on a moral view of sociology.

Thus far, we have introduced moral repertoires in abstract terms. But how do moral repertoires unfold concretely in long-term scientific

TABLE 1.1 Moral repertoires commonly used in sociological meta-communication, along with their key measures of worth and hypothetical claims one might make based on each of them

Repertoire	Measure of worth	Hypothetical claim
Efficiency Repertoire	Productivity, efficiency, objectivity, expertise	"Good sociological work provides scientific tools to accurately measure social phenomena. Inefficient research practices undermine the discipline as a whole."
Civic Repertoire	Collective interest	"Sociology by definition promotes civil values that make this society a better one. Any research that does not promote civil values (e.g., by helping overcome inequality) is not good research."
Anchored Repertoire	Kinship, loyalty, tradition	"Sociologists are morally obliged to deeply understand and to give voice to local and familial experience, especially when it comes to underrepresented groups."
Creativity Repertoire	Originality, nonconformity, innovativeness	"Developing creative and significant theoretical advances is the purest form of sociology, which gives meaning to sociological research. Work that is not theoretically or methodologically innovative is insignificant."
Charismatic Repertoire	Reputation, deference to academic stars	"Scholar A is the most well-known and highly regarded expert in this area. Sociologists who critique scholar A are uninformed and often heinous."
Marketability Repertoire	Marketability, public attention, competitiveness	"Sociologists need to conduct research that draws donors to their university and wins grants, on topics that are in high public demand and appeal to public interest. This would be the best contribution to their institutions and to their fields, and would also make sure sociology remains publicly relevant."
Network Repertoire	Mobility, interconnectedness, boundary crossing	"Sociologists need to study the international networks, flows, and interactions that now characterize our world, and to cooperate with international scholars in doing so. Not doing so reinforces an old and pernicious world order." Or: "Sociologists need to engage with other disciplines, rather than stay confined to their own methods and assumptions. Interdisciplinary research is where real synergy happens."

Note: See Afterword for elaboration on each of these.

conversations? In the next section, we demonstrate this unfolding by look-ing at one of the most significant sociological debates of the last several de-cades, over the validity of the thesis that mass secularization will occur as part of the ongoing modernization process. The sociological conversation on this topic has branched in distinct directions since a wave of criticism started in the late 1970s, and each direction has employed a different reper-toire to justify research in light of a growing criticism of the secularization thesis. Thus, several different conceptions of how the sociology of religion ought to represent contemporary religious life evolved and became institu-tionalized over the past several decades. In what follows, we trace scholars' meta-communication[44]—in other words, their ongoing commentary about how their research contributes, what directions the sociology of religion ought to be taking more generally, and what constitutes good social out-comes for sociological research.[45]

THE SECULARIZATION THESIS DEBATES
AS DEBATES ON MORALITY

The founders of sociology understood religion in terms that forecasted its ultimate decline. The Marxian argument that religion is an opiate of the masses portrayed religious decline as a positive development that would do away with the superstructural legitimation of exploitation. Weber theorized that secularization would advance because the bureau-cratic state would always champion technological solutions favoring the "de-magification" of social experience. While Marx celebrated the end of religion, Weber bemoaned the loss of religious attitude. Up until the 1970s, the view that religion is antithetical to modernity, that mass secularization is underway, and that secularization would proceed undisturbed remained consistent throughout American sociology.[46]

However, the rapid growth of religious movements in the late twenti-eth century cast considerable doubt on the viability of the secularization thesis. As a response, scholarship started challenging the notion that mod-ernization inherently involves religious decline, and instead claimed that religious actors participated actively in multiple aspects of the transition to modernity.[47] Moreover, the emergence of new religious movements sug-gested to sociologists that religion should not be considered a thing of the past.[48] The 1970s global religious revival, the Moral Majority, and the high levels of American religious participation continued to challenge the no-tion that secularization was underway.[49] A growing number of sociologists claimed that the discipline's commitment to secularization theory in the face of these empirical developments was parochial.[50]

Crucially, this work also disputed the normative implications of traditional secularization theory by highlighting the positive, forward-thinking effects of religion and religious actors. Historical sociologists showed that religious movements provided revolutionary actors with counter-hegemonic ways of thinking and inspired democratizing social change.[51] Ample work in that era also pointed to the social capital gains religious affiliation provides.[52] Scholars criticized the general assumption among sociologists that new religious movements were cults and advocated that researchers treat them as legitimate forms of religion.[53] Overall, these scholars were criticizing secularization theory not only for its empirical failings, but also for its devaluation of the potential religion holds for social good. Articulating the general discontent of these scholars with the working assumption of their peers, Rodney Stark demanded that sociologists of religion "carry the secularization doctrine to the graveyard of failed theories."[54]

These critiques followed the logic of the Civic Repertoire, which ascribes value to social arrangements that promote equality, civic participation, and social welfare. It thus equates good research to research that promotes such values in all spheres of social life—the religious sphere included. Thus, what may have been an empirical criticism of existing sociological assumptions became a moral denunciation of research on religion as well. The ensuing debates, waged from the mid-1980s to the present day, took three distinct paths, each of which relied on a different definition of the common good and the ways research on religion should contribute to it.[55] These paths are summarized in table 1.2.

First Path: Religious Research as Civic Good

One vocal group of critics of the secularization thesis emerged in the 1980s and worked tirelessly to delegitimize the existing orthodoxy of the secularization thesis and to replace existing theories with a reworked model of religion and society. This new wave of sociologists of religion rejected the notion that the forces of modernization negatively impacted religious belief, and reconceptualized religious life using market models. According to these theorists, as state control of religious orthodoxy waned over time, market mechanisms became dominant and propelled religious innovation, thereby increasing religious participation.[56] While secularization theory had seen atheism as the final outcome of modernization, the failure of communist states to eradicate religious practice served as proof positive of the inability of states to enforce an anti-religious dogma.[57] In short order, the moniker "Religious Economy Model" (REM) cohered around market-based metaphors in religious life and proclaimed that it provided

TABLE 1.2 Critiques, paraphrased responses, and corresponding repertoires for meta-communication over the secularization debate

	Critique	Delegitimation	Partial Reform	Reconstitution
Claim	"The argument that religion is going to die with modernity ignores the potential for social good that religion holds."	"The secularization thesis is all wrong. The world is becoming more religious because different denominations have increased freedom to compete for adherents. Good research in the sociology of religion recognizes these trends and helps create better public policies."	"Religious identities are important because they challenge the norms of political power structures. Secularism must be understood as a political stance. "	"While the debate over secularization revealed the limitations of the field, the sociology of religion should take care not to paralyze itself in these debates. Sociologists of religion should create ways to move past this debate in order to remain relevant to funders and to the public."
Repertoire	Civic Repertoire	Civic Repertoire	Efficiency Repertoire	Marketability Repertoire
Definition of common good, morality	Equality, public welfare, solidarity	Equality, public welfare, solidarity	Equality, public welfare, solidarity	Marketability, public attention, competitiveness
Test—how does one determine moral worth based on this repertoire?	Does research take account of the potential for social good that religion holds?	Does research promote religious liberties and inform public policies on religion and society?	Does research recognize the historical variability and specificity of our notions of "religion" and "secularity"? Does research provide a sound depiction of the relationships between religion, politics, and society?	Does research appeal to funders? Does it draw public attention, to the scholar, to scholarly associations, or to universities?

a viable counternarrative that could easily explain why religion remained vibrant during the transition to modernity.[58]

The REM emerged at a time when rational choice theory was making inroads into a diverse array of subfields in the social sciences as an all-encompassing theory of human behavior. This particularly came under the almost unparalleled influence of the economist Gary Becker and, in sociology, of the growing popularity of James Coleman and his strand of rational choice theory.[59] Sociologists of religion certainly took their cue from these broader trends. In the context of religious participation, REM scholars linked competitive markets with just social arrangements, and thus saw free-market competition as a requirement for the social good. In this way, sociologists of religion linked the theoretical gains of the REM approach with a set of moral claims. REM posits that, much like the invisible hand Adam Smith said guides economic markets, a series of naturally occurring rules govern the religious market and constitute a modicum of self-regulation.[60] Thus, a society is headed toward the good when religious denominations are free to compete for adherents, and is headed toward disaster when religious "cartels" come to dominate in the marketplace of religions. Unsurprisingly, scholars like Anthony Gill developed REM-based models to demonstrate that the origin of religious liberty is tied to the way religious minorities organized to fight religious oppression and to create rules encouraging vibrant religious competition.

If their embrace of economic models suggested that they were useful for religious activists, market justifications also underlined a message of religious pluralism as a basic *civic* good that could justify ongoing research about religious market dynamics. For instance, Grim and Finke used statistical data to document the use of state violence to control religion, showing that it caused a decline in religious activity, but they justified their approach on wider civic terms:

> Using a wealth of new data, we have shown how denying religious freedoms so often leads to the physical abuse and displacement of individuals based on religion. But this relationship doesn't stand alone. Indeed, it is often embedded within a complex web of religious, social, ethnic, and political relationships. Religious persecution is often one part of a larger social conflict, and religious freedom is one of many freedoms denied. The relationship between religious freedom and persecution has implications that go far beyond the topic of religion.[61]

With numerous instances of oppression of religious groups across the globe, and with attacks on religious freedom persisting, Grim and Finke urged other scholars that these "remain topics in need of careful study."[62] Similarly, Gill's comparative analysis of regimes of religious freedom not only promoted the concept of a vibrant religious market, but emphasized the institutional legacy of "the separation of church and state" in the United States to conclude that "promoting religious freedom and the spiritual vitality that results from it would be desirable public policy."[63] Research on religious restriction was not merely a matter of promoting a free market in religious mission; it was also part of a larger scholarly project of building a society respectful of religious difference. This was presented as good policy that research could help inform. Using his presidential speech to the Society for the Sociology of Religion to present an overview of developments in this literature, Roger Finke drew on Alexis de Tocqueville's description of American democracy to argue that "ongoing attention to secularization has often diverted our attention from many interesting and important questions about restrictions,"[64] and claimed that research on restrictions placed on religious expression is justified because "religious freedoms have much in common with other human rights . . . the consequences of religious restrictions go far beyond social conflict and the origins are remarkably complex."[65] Scholarship on the persistence of religious vitality in the face of oppressive regimes was thus justified as serving an important civic role in exposing violations of civil liberties.

Second Path: The Need for Historical Nuance
in Rejecting the Secularization Thesis

While sharing with the previous group an orientation toward religion as central for civil life, a second group of scholars maintained that sociological research on religion cannot advance public goods without historical and methodological precision. Switching moral repertoires to the Efficiency Repertoire, this second group maintained that the critique of secularization needed to extend its empirical breadth and theoretical precision. While the REM was a good start, these researchers set methodological and historical validity as the moral marker of good sociological research, and posited that reforming the REM is a necessary step prior to sociologists making pronouncements on the public significance of religion in modernity. This approach to the critique of secularization theory appealed to scholars as concerns about religious politics became pertinent beginning in the late 1990s. In their diagnosis, both the secularization thesis and the REM had neglected the variability of religious life, thus misunderstanding its political significance.

Broadly, this second group of scholars adopted a theoretically collegial but morally oppositional stance in relation to the REM approach. In the American scene, Stephen Warner agreed with REM scholars who criticized European secularization theorists for assuming their own religious trajectory to be universal. However, Warner also chastised REM scholars for mistaking the institutional arrangements in one country (the United States) for universal laws. Proposing a "new paradigm" that centered questions on the institutional history of religion and on the different dynamics of religious adherence that emerged from the political regulation of religion, Warner ended an article in the prestigious *American Journal of Sociology* by noting that "it is conventional to conclude a paper with a call for more research, but this article—both a research review and a proposal—is such a call."[66] Asserting a view of sociology as dependent on empirical validity, he advocated for more research to resolve the issue: "Comparative institutional research, unburdened of the secularization expectations of the older paradigm, will serve to demystify the concept of American exceptionalism. Until that has been accomplished, the exception may well be taken as the rule."[67]

The concern about overgeneralizing from the US context expanded beyond questions of geographic comparison. Wherever secularization theorists and their REM critics saw laws, a new brand of reformer sociologists of religion saw historical particularity and the need for nuanced historical analysis.[68] Reflecting on "the stock arguments advanced by the four horsemen of the new atheism—Dawkins, Dennett, Harris, and Hitchens"—that religion generally leads to violence, Gorski and Türkmen-Dervişoğlu called a scientific foul:

> this moral reckoning requires some creative accounting. For example, the totalitarian atrocities of the twentieth century (i.e., fascist and communist) must somehow be cleared from the atheist balance sheet. Conversely, agents of peace who were people of faith (e.g., Gandhi and King) must be recast as closet humanists. . . . The relationship between religion and violence is far more complex and contingent than Hume and his modern-day followers realized, and sweeping distinctions between monotheism and polytheism or religion and reason give us little leverage over the problem.[69]

Conversely, to their peers advocating economic laws of supply and demand to explain the history of religious revival, theorists of political and religious mobilization insisted that

> cyclical theories of the return of the sacred or cyclical theories of religious revivals are ultimately flawed . . . the two best-known variants . . .

are both predicated on the assumption that functional need . . . is the mother of religious invention. If the assumptions were correct, the sacred should have returned and religious revivals or the birth of new religions should have occurred . . . where secularization had gone the furthest and the absence of religion created the greatest need . . . in highly secularized societies such as Sweden, England, France, Uruguay, and Russia. Yet the public resurgence of religion took place in places such as Poland, the United States, Brazil, Nicaragua, and Iran, all places which can hardly be characterized as secularized wastelands. What we witnessed in the 1980s was not the birth of new religions or the return of the sacred where religious traditions had dried up, but rather, the revitalization and reformation of old living traditions which both theories of secularization and cyclical theories of religious revival had assumed were becoming ever more privatized and irrelevant in the modern world.[70]

Similarly, Gorski leveraged neo-institutional critiques of rational choice theory to point out how "the idea that politics could itself be a source of ultimate values that compete with religious values, or that free markets are not natural occurrences but political constructions, is as foreign to them [REM proponents] as it is to their friends in economics."[71] Reformers insisted that both secularization theorists and REM scholars had failed because they had searched for universal laws in a world governed by contingency.

Historical criticism also allowed thinkers to extend the REM school's concerns about religious freedom to discussions about the importance of religion vis-à-vis secularism. Whereas REM scholars rejected secularization by seeing secular ideologies as groundless bids for power,[72] historical critics emphasized the independent force of competing secular-isms (e.g., liberal-ism, science-ism, etc.)[73] and their effects in the shaping of religious life.[74] Rather than defending religious pluralism in the name of "civic equality," they insisted that religious pluralism was valuable because "religious traditions are now confronting the differentiated secular spheres . . . [and] in many of these confrontations, it is religion which, as often as not, appears to be on the side of human enlightenment."[75] Here scholars expanded the claim to civic concerns their REM colleagues had raised by exploiting historical variation to demonstrate the civic possibilities and pitfalls of religious and secular engagement. For instance, sociologists in this mode compared contemporary Europe and the United States, revealing how aggressive forms of secularism (e.g., French or Turkish *laïcité*) may silence dissenting political voices by depicting them as mere religious fanatics.[76] Thus, calls like Charles Taylor's for a radical revision of the concept of secularism were not just appeals for academic reconsideration of a "failed" concept, but rather a normative demand to recognize that "we think that secularism (or laïcité) has to do with the relation of the state and religion . . . whereas in fact it has to do with the (correct) response of the democratic state to diversity."[77]

Third Path: Attention-Grabbing Religious Research

As the debate over the secularization thesis continued, a third group of scholars brought a new concern and a new metric for evaluation of research into play. According to this new wave of reactions to the secularization debate, the sociology of religion must integrate its critique of the secularization debate into new research directions that produce meaningful findings. Without devising new research directions that break away from the continuing debate over whether religion is in decline, the sociology of religion risks losing credibility, public interest, and "marketability" within academia. Thus, a new wave of sociologists of religion took a view of research drawing on the *Marketability Repertoire*, which emphasizes the ability of researchers to capture the public imagination as evidenced by attracting funding, citations, media interest, and other forms of public attention, and by the establishment of new research specializations. Indeed, recent sociology of religion has seen numerous attempts to reconstitute the sociological study of religion by asking how the critique of secularization has promoted or hindered publicly relevant scholarly research.

On the one hand, these scholars routinely acknowledge the criticism of the secularization thesis by noting in review articles that the field is consistently biased toward the concerns of evangelical Protestantism.[78] That is, the field has remained biased in terms of the groups researchers choose to study (white American Christians), the findings they report (those that show positive outcomes associated with religious participation), and the questions they ask ("is religious participation declining?"). These scholars conclude that such a bias results in an amplification of "positive socio-evaluative findings [in relationship to religion] and a focus on Christianity and the U.S. context."[79] In order to generate new research without becoming embroiled in debates about the empirics and normative implications of secularization, these scholars have advocated the study of religious boundaries within more generalizable frameworks of culture, power, and authority.[80] Others have turned toward ethnographic methods to underline the performative dimensions of "lived religion."[81] Rather than producing an "answer" to the secularization question, this work builds on the increased attention to power dynamics the secularization debate created in order to generate novel questions and critiques.[82] On the other hand, scholars of religion have tried to move past the debates about secularization by focusing on how the existing categorization of religious, spiritual, or nonreligious experience stalls the generation of new research.[83] Maintaining that "as theoretical tides began to shift and the focus turned toward the vitality of religion, those who were not traditionally religious were often neglected in the rush to study religious groups and individuals," Baker and Smith argued that such areas still "deserve concentrated inquiry and that such an avenue presents itself as a fruitful endeavor for social scientific study."[84] Such efforts resulted in large-scale projects to study secularists, atheists, "the spiritual but not religious," and the religious "nones"[85] and the role their metaphysical understanding plays in their lives.[86] Here a small group of sociologists rejected the old secularization research obsession with "emptying pews," and instead saw the growth of nonreligious persons as an opportunity for deeper research that could engage the public's curiosity about increasingly popular quasi-spiritual practices (e.g., mindfulness meditation at work[87]).

The converse also seems to hold. Where interest in secularization and market theories persists, scholars have turned to alternative frameworks to circumvent existing critiques and continue research. Thus, while some critics assailed the sociologists of religion for focusing on concerns central to their own (hegemonic) religious traditions, others worked to re-situate such studies as contributions to the "public sociology of religion."[88] Public sociology of religion seeks to make scholarly contributions to public debates pertaining to religion and civil society, and incorporates theological concerns and reasoning into research as a core feature of sociological inquiry. Rather than allowing critique to destroy research questions, scholars rebuilt their justifications for the contribution of their research. Similarly, Fenggang Yang took his presidential addresses at the Society for the Scientific Study of Religion to bemoan the definition wars surrounding religion:

> defining religion is not a simple matter in an ivory tower. For believers, a proper definition of religion has serious consequences for self-identification and sociopolitical classification that may affect the level of freedom or privilege one enjoys vis-à-vis others in society . . . the definition of religion sometimes can be a matter of life and death.[89]

While this appeal to the civic realm allowed Yang to urge his listeners to move beyond the debates about religion, he also couched his argument in his position as a working academic. For Yang, the debates around secularism had been important, but had become a distraction, and putting them to bed was of crucial significance for reasons of *funding.* As he put it, "why would your colleagues and administrators in the departments of sociology, psychology, political science, economics, and other disciplines want to allocate scarce resources to the study of the indefinable?"[90] Indeed, the concern over the marketability of the sociology of religion in the post–secularization debate era has remained salient. The sociologist of religion Samuel Perry announced on Twitter that his forthcoming book will argue "to both secular academics & devout citizens alike . . . that the rigorous, evidence-based, transparent, & accessible study of religion benefits ALL OF US." The book, according to Perry, will impress upon its readers "why we must prioritize it, fund it, & hire for it."[91]

DELEGITIMIZING, REFORMING, AND RECONSTITUTING: USING MORAL REPERTOIRES TO ADDRESS SOCIOLOGICAL CONTROVERSIES

The debates over secularization demonstrate three common types of responses to moral controversy where sociologists use moral repertoires to justify or critique research. The first group of responses to the secularization debate involved discounting any claim that religion is, in fact, in decline and depicting scholars who claim it is as malicious. In other words, this group of responses *delegitimized* former types of conduct and called sociologists of religion to completely replace their conceptual tools. The second group of responses agreed that the secularization thesis is too simplistic, but emphasized that a revised model needs to take into account the politically and historically variable nature of religious process and the capacity of religious groups to help bolster civic-mindedness. More abstractly, this group acquiesced to *partial reforms* of the secularization thesis, with the understanding that future critiques might be waged against this compromise. The third group agreed that debating whether secularization is truly occurring is important, but has also pushed for understanding religious experience beyond this debate. We term this third path the *reconstitution*[92] of the supposed problem, when scholars reformulate the issue under debate and thus direct the conversation toward new courses of research.[93] Scholars taking this route will acknowledge that the original debate is important, but will also employ a logic that moves past the debate into new (and perhaps more pertinent) areas.[94] All three groups of scholars thus assign very different logics of moral worth to their research, and as the chapters ahead will demonstrate, these patterns of responses recur across different debates in sociology.[95]

We opened this chapter by highlighting how moral positions sociologists take can often harden into belligerent attitudes toward their colleagues. This is certainly one possible result of sociology's inherent moral diversity. However, as we demonstrated in the debates around secularization, moral diversity can also be a resource scholars draw on to develop new research lines and to find ways to avoid overt warring with their peers. Indeed, the same actors can use different maneuvers in succession, leading to nuanced arguments about the nature of research, and its path forward. Take the work of Winnifred Sullivan as another example:[96] from declaring religious freedom "impossible" because both religion and politics seek to claim final hegemony over social action,[97] then moving toward a reconceptualization of law in the wake of secular critique,[98] her recent work with Lori Beaman has turned toward understanding the *Varieties of Religious Establishment*.[99] In their book of that title, Sullivan and Beaman aim to move beyond "a simple assessment of the existence of establishment and attendant assumptions about whether it is 'good' or 'bad' to refocus attention to what we consider to be more important and interesting questions and concepts." According to them, "if establishment is the default, it might be possible to set aside the freedom-disestablishment association that stifles more innovative and insightful analysis."[100] The critique of secularism was no longer on the side of innovation and insight, and as such, it was no longer useful for further exploration. Rather than carrying her moral commitments like dreadful obligations, Sullivan utilizes the diversity of moral repertoires to help push her thinking forward.

In the chapters that follow, we explore these types of productive moral maneuverings across various sociological subfields, with the working assumption that these moves between different moral registers are a common (if underappreciated) part of how sociology grows as a scholarly and a normative project. Thus, hypothetically, a group of sociologists studying income inequality may be faced with criticism about the use of the categories "white," "black," and "other" in their regression models: "Doesn't the category 'other' fold within itself dozens of different races, which may have variable outcomes?" "Shouldn't the category 'black' differentiate between African Americans and African migrants to the US whose experience is different?" And, most importantly, "Doesn't the use of such simplistic categories feed into public policy that then harms the same populations that these studies purport to represent?"[101]

One response to such criticism could be using a moral repertoire highlighting loyalty to one's research subjects in order to *delegitimize* the entire subfield of quantitative income inequality studies. This would involve tagging it as being oppressive to non-white populations, and advocating other research methods that involve a robust and reflexive engagement with the meaning of race and its relation to inequality. A second response to the critique might be using a repertoire that cherishes methodological efficiency to *partially reform* existing categorizations of race, for example by comparing three-race-categories research with more refined research using additional race categories. This way, scholars following this path accept the critique, but claim that their reformed models are those that best serve the populations in questions. Finally, a third response might be to agree with the claim that the use of three racial categories is pernicious, but to then use the question of racial categorization to launch a new type of research using a moral repertoire that values originality and inventiveness (for example, about how race categories are perceived by interview subjects, about how scientists use classifications, etc.). This path *reconstitutes* the emphasis on racial categorization by agreeing with the critique and expanding its basis of justification (through continued empirical and theoretical engagement). Scholars who opt for reconstitution acknowledge a critique's moral gravity and generate new research that incorporates it, rather than advocating a direct overturning of the previous paradigm or seeking to create compromise categories. Crucially, each approach demonstrates one way of balancing a concern about the moral implications of the research with a pragmatic orientation toward action.

With this conceptual framework in mind, chapters 2–4 will analyze three groups of responses to moral debate in which sociologists employ moral repertoires to address a controversy. The first will look at the demarcation of academic "no-go zones" through complete denunciation of streams of research; the second will focus on partial reforms of research practices in response to moral criticism; and the third will analyze the creation of new research trajectories that build on the existing debate but also change the repertoires that define what makes the research worthwhile in the first place.

CHAPTER TWO

Academic No-Go Zones

*On Social-Gene Interactions, Cultures of Poverty,
and Forbidden Knowledge Claims in Sociology*

In a 2017 podcast episode called "Forbidden Knowledge," the popular neuroscientist Sam Harris hosted the political scientist Charles Murray to talk about his 1994 best seller, *The Bell Curve: Intelligence and Class Structure in American Life*, coauthored with the psychologist Richard J. Herrnstein. The book argued that a combination of environmental and hereditary factors explains group-level differences in IQ by social class. Particularly appalling was the book's claim that genetics shape race-based unequal social outcomes like educational achievement and lifelong income by influencing intelligence, and thus that policy attempts to reduce inequality between groups (for instance, targeted school spending to level intelligence) are futile.[1] Scholars, professional associations, and public readers severely criticized the book, with the American Psychological Association and numerous genetics experts issuing statements disputing its factual basis.[2] Criticisms notwithstanding, many conservatives have cherished *The Bell Curve* because it depicts state interventions on behalf of the disadvantaged as useless.[3] Nevertheless, Murray became a pariah for many academics and his public talks were frequently disrupted. Indeed, a 2017 Middlebury College appearance ended in violence when students attacked both Murray and the moderator, a professor of political science at the college.[4]

Even decades after *The Bell Curve* appeared, Murray remains so controversial that Sam Harris himself was criticized for inviting Murray to his podcast. Harris explained his decision to a journalist, Ezra Klein:

> While I have very little interest in IQ and actually zero interest in racial differences in IQ, I invited Murray on my podcast, because he had recently been de-platformed at Middlebury College. He and his host were actually assaulted as they left the auditorium. In my view, this seemed yet another instance of kind of a moral panic that we were seeing on college campuses. It caused me to take an interest in Murray that I hadn't

previously had. I had never read *The Bell Curve*, because I thought it was just. . . . It must be just racist trash, because I assumed that where there was all that smoke, there must be fire. I hadn't paid attention to Murray. When I did read the book and did some more research on him, I came to think that he was probably the most unfairly maligned person in my lifetime.[5]

Assertions like Harris's about the need to recover discredited scholars in order to push against purported idea suppression are growing common in public discourse.[6] Some academics, too, have made far-ranging claims about a quasi-religious adherence of academic fields to liberal dogmas and about a wave of self-censorship overtaking academia.[7] While these scholars have hurled accusations at academia as a whole, one of the more common targets has been sociologists who allegedly demarcate "no-go zones" around the most pertinent topics of our times—race, gender, and class—and respond to research contradicting progressive party lines with threats, censorship, and public shaming. As proof, these critics point to controversial research like Murray's that is considered "uncitable" in sociological publications.

However prevalent these forms of censorship are, scholars—including sociologists—do publish on controversial topics. For instance, despite the long history of controversy surrounding the use of hereditary traits in social research, advances in DNA mapping have generated a new wave of sociological research that draws on (epi)genomics in order to analyze social phenomena.[8] As another example, the sociologist Rogers Brubaker published a monograph about the explosive public discourse comparing the famous transgender activist Caitlyn Jenner to the infamous transracial activist Rachel Dolezal. Brubaker argued that the topic's ability to incite anger on both the left and the right provided an "intellectual opportunity" for sociologists to explore the conditions under which equivalences can be made.[9] Such studies examining provocative topics challenge critical assertions that a culture of political correctness has paralyzed academia.[10] Without accounting for the myriad ways scholars venture into such controversial scholarly areas—academic "no-go zones"—research on the production of knowledge overlooks academics' agency in tackling disputed subjects and their ability to debate, ignore, or transcend controversy.

This chapter argues that sociologists often engage publicly with morally contentious research topics, rather than silencing entire research areas through threats or self-censorship. While sociology as a discipline has had a long history of contention over the ethics of research on race, class, gender, and colonialism, sociologists often tackle the moral puzzles at hand directly rather than shirking them. This chapter rejects the claim that discussions over topics as contentious as epigenomic sociology are closed off, and shows instead that numerous sociologists actively engage the ethical challenges those topics present. The chapter claims that scholars who do face ostracization for work on controversial topics are those who ignore, rather than address, the ethical problematics of conducting such research and pretend their work is mere "normal science." From this angle, "progress" in the social sciences not only includes opening new domains for empirical inquiry, but also tackling empirical topics that provoke moral controversy in ways that convincingly address ongoing moral criticism.[11] By no means do advances on such debates ever find complete resolution: the use of genetics in social research continues to be marred by its historical dalliance with eugenics. However, scholars find ways to publicly justify new research by arguing that it can contribute to the broader good (for example, by claiming that genetic data can be used to address health inequalities as long as practitioners recognize the risks associated with the technology) and advance the claims of justice more broadly.[12]

To demonstrate, the chapter delves into the history of sociological explanations of race-based inequality, and shows that sociologists have devised numerous modes of addressing the field's problematic past and the racist assumptions it has harbored. As is increasingly remembered across the discipline, the first decades of US sociology produced accounts of racial inequality by using Spencerian ideas about the cultural and biological "fitness" of different races to justify differences between groups.[13] As the twentieth century progressed, sociologists withdrew from such explicit social Darwinism, but have remained enamored, despite controversy, with the relationships between culture and poverty and between biological inheritance and inequality. Indeed, scholarly debate on these topics has resurfaced throughout the history of the discipline. This chapter tracks repeated attempts to study these controversial topics, and outlines how different scholarly perceptions about the morality of this research have shaped historic scholarly trajectories. The analysis highlights that the scholars who were publicly attacked for pursuing controversial research programs tended to be those who attempted to revive arguments about the role of genetics in shaping life outcomes or about cultural predispositions to poverty without addressing the long-acknowledged moral problematics of making such claims. Contrary to claims about academic censorship, sociologists have often recognized signs of progress by cultivating moral debate and diversity rather than by stifling conversation.

Sociologists and historians of science have given ample attention to scientific controversies—how they emerge and how scholars resolve them.[14]

Since policy and research institutions frequently collaborate, divergent forms of expertise are brought to bear on pressing problems of the day, often creating public strife around authority and proper policy implementation.[15] Sociologists of knowledge have shown that social scientific claims that capture the public eye through media exposure are similarly prone to controversy.[16] As the controversies over the sociology of race have demonstrated, contention can emerge not only by virtue of *what* is being claimed, but because of *who* is making the claims: while Black sociologists have offered poignant analyses of the social problems that plague Black communities,[17] public controversy will often only erupt when white commentators usurp the conversation (often ignoring the work of Black scholars altogether).[18] But in this chapter, rather than continuing the discussion of how a controversy emerges, we focus on how an academic community treats controversy once it has emerged, and what performative strategies sociologists who work in such areas develop to address the controversy. Through this, the chapter will show that while academic no-go zones deter some sociologists, other scholars find creative ways to engage with them directly by mobilizing moral repertoires that challenge or divert potential critiques.

ACADEMIC NO-GO ZONES: WHEN MORAL REPERTOIRES DON'T WORK

When do academics find a book controversial, perhaps even wrong, but still worthy of discussion? Conversely, when do they find an article so abhorrent it cannot be considered an acceptable (even if wrong) part of a discussion? Certainly, there is a difference between claiming that an article's approach is mistaken and its conclusions unwarranted and arguing that an article is so damaging that it should be unpublished and its author (and perhaps the journal) be sanctioned. The difference is between (1) academics' willingness to employ moral repertoires to debate the merits and failings of a scholarly work on the one hand, and (2) their decision *not* to debate it on the other. The decision not to debate could be expressed as (2a) an outright rejection of the place of the work in question within sociological conversations (i.e., refusing to discuss it to begin with), (2b) an attempt to ignore or minimize the controversy and proceed as though dealing with uncontentious normal science, or (2c) an attempt to transcend the controversy and to find broader criteria for inclusion and academic community-building.

Luc Boltanski suggested that actors' engagement with different social situations brings to light different human capacities, such as the capacity for logical debate, the capacity for violence, or the capacity to love others unconditionally. For Boltanski, modes of engagement with social situations differ on two axes.[19] The first axis distinguishes situations actors perceive as *conflicts* from situations they perceive as *non-conflicts*. The second axis distinguishes between situations where actors believe they can use logic to discuss the fairness of their interaction by *drawing equivalences* and situations where actors find such discussion *irrelevant*.[20] Based on these assessments of a social situation, actors will mobilize different capacities: in a conflict where no logical discussion is possible, the capacity for violence (direct or symbolic) will predominate; in a conflict where logical debate on justice is possible, so is the capacity to pursue justness; in a non-conflictual situation where logical discussions of fairness are irrelevant the capacity to embrace others unconditionally emerges;[21] and in a non-conflictual situation where discussion of fairness is possible the drive to assert normalcy reigns.

Looking at academic meta-communication, we can find similar patterns in the routes academics pursue in the face of highly controversial research (albeit with some differences from Boltanski's conceptualization). Academics can *disagree* and engage in a debate with other actors by using different moral repertoires, with the understanding that competing moral interpretations of the research exist and that logical discussion will allow actors to weigh the consequences for the research field of taking either approach; they can *ignore* the sensitivities and assume they are participating in routine practices requiring no particular moral justification;[22] they can try to *build solidarity* and assert that debate around moral interpretations of certain studies may never be resolved, but that such debate is a constitutive feature of scholarly community development; and they can *reject* the research and assert that one moral interpretation of the situation is the only valid one, thereby condemning all other views (see table 2.1). Importantly, where Boltanski saw examples of the last option (which he termed "violent") as situations where conversation comparing each party's views is impossible, in academic controversies some debate is possible in these situations, but the aim of the disputants is to remove the offending party from the academic conversation altogether. In such instances, rejecting

TABLE 2.1 Responding to academic controversy

	Conflict	Non-Conflict
Debatable	Disagreeing (1)	Ignoring (2b)
Non-Debatable	Rejecting (2a)	Building solidarity (2c)

certain types of discourse is a way for the academic community to harden disciplinary boundaries around what qualifies as acceptable research.

Thus, while working scholars have a capacity for adamantly rejecting controversial research, they also have a capacity to debate the moral value of research, to strive for solidarity between scholars, and to push away controversy and treat the research as noncontroversial. Our analytical perspective is that we cannot, as outside observers, predetermine which controversies will emerge or how actors will respond to them. However, we highlight that *responses* to controversy will draw on diverse situational framings to make their point. Our historical analysis of the decades of academic debate over the uses of culture and genetics in the study of racial inequality shows that *some* critics have demanded that such research be abolished, but others have devised nuanced strategies to propose ethical ways of conducting such studies.

In what follows, we first provide a brief history of the long-standing moral contention over research on race and poverty in sociology, a history that goes back to the nineteenth-century writings of Herbert Spencer. Then, we turn to our two parallel controversy study cases, one over the use of genetics in the sociology of race and the other over the assumption that certain cultures promote poverty. For each study case, we trace four different modes of engagement with the controversy—disagreeing, rejecting, ignoring, and solidarity-building—and show that the scholars who were ostracized for work on controversial topics ignored the moral ramifications of their research.

HISTORICAL BACKGROUND: RESEARCH ON RACE AS A QUESTION OF MORALITY

Social Darwinism and eugenicism were foundational perspectives in American sociology's early days. Published in the top journals, taught in the first sociology courses, and endorsed by some of the first presidents of the American Sociological Association, ideas outrageous by contemporary standards circulated as core sociological truths at the turn of the nineteenth to the twentieth century.

For instance, in 1904, the prominent eugenicist Francis Galton published "Eugenics: Its Definition, Scope, and Aims" in the *American Journal of Sociology*, in which he insisted that the new science of sociology could be directed to promoting "a considerable list of qualities . . . includ[ing] health, energy, ability, manliness, and courteous disposition" through attention to selective human breeding.[23] A consummate scientist, Galton argued that eugenicists "must . . . leave morals as far as possible out of the discussion."[24] Nevertheless, many thinkers quickly proclaimed him a new torchbearer of modern morality. In some commentaries, admirers portrayed Galton as nothing less than messianic. Indeed, his star student Karl Pearson (as in Pearson's Correlation Coefficient) noted,

> he [Galton] attacks the gravest problem which lies before the Caucasian races "in the morning." Are we to make the whole doctrine of descent, of inheritance, and of selection of the fitter, part of our everyday life . . . ? It is the question of the study now, but tomorrow it will be the question of the marketplace, of morality, and of politics. If I wanted to know how to put a saddle on a camel's back without chafing him, I should go to Francis Galton; if I wanted to know how to manage the women of a treacherous African tribe, I should go to Francis Galton; if I wanted an instrument for measuring a snail, or an arc of latitude, I should appeal to Francis Galton; if I wanted advice on any mechanical, [or] any geographical, or any sociological problem, I should consult Francis Galton.[25]

Galton had other devotees. George Bernard Shaw announced that "there is now no reasonable excuse for refusing to face the fact that nothing but a eugenic religion can save our civilization from the fate that has overtaken all previous civilizations,"[26] and G. A. Archibald Reid proclaimed: "at the root of every moral and social question lies the problem of heredity. Until a knowledge of the laws of heredity is more widely diffused, the public will grope in the dark in its endeavors."[27] Nor were his admirers confined to the *AJS*. The first four presidents of the American Sociological Association[28]—Franklin Giddings, Albion Small, William Graham Sumner, and Lester Ward—all saw promise in eugenics.[29] Even today, Galton's pithy distinction between "nature and nurture" remains in regular usage.[30]

The era's most influential sociologist was Herbert Spencer, who reduced Darwin's theory to the motto "survival of the fittest" and turned that logic on social policy—for instance, by suggesting that poorhouses were merely a way of "helping the worthless to multiply at the expense of the worthy."[31] Mainstream publications did not commonly cite Marx, Weber, or Durkheim until years later because Spencerian notions of social evolution fit better with then dominant views of sociology as a universal science of natural laws. Spencer's ideas thrived in the era of laissez-faire policies that quashed social supports for the disadvantaged—particularly Black Americans, immigrants, and women.[32] Indeed, early publications on inequality in flagship journals were given titles like "The Mind of Woman and the Lower Races"[33] and were riddled with biologically reductive assumptions.

Journals effectively ignored the few active empirically minded American sociologists of the era, such as Anna Julia Cooper, W. E. B. Du Bois, and Ida Wells-Barnett.[34]

US sociologists only turned away from explicit Spencerianism in the 1930s. As the economic downturn of the two preceding decades morphed into fascism in Europe, Talcott Parsons urged his peers to abandon evolutionary models by posing a famous rhetorical question, "Who now reads Spencer?" in 1937.[35] Although Parsons shifted American sociology away from some of its most embarrassing assumptions, the discipline had hardly rid itself of its racist underpinnings.[36] Parsons sought to erase Spencerian sociology from the discipline's collective memory, but he did little to rewrite its assumptions about race. Instead, Parsons primarily analyzed racial inequality as one out of the many ways modernity caused strain between social roles:

> the white man has in his role as American Citizen internalized participation in the universalistic values of the wider society, the "American creed," but also as a Southerner in the pattern of "white supremacy." . . . He deals universalistically in some contexts for example vis-à-vis white colleagues in his occupational sphere, and particularistically vis-à-vis the negro-white situation. This segregation [between races] is essential to minimize the strain.[37]

This stance allowed Parsons to acknowledge the importance of race in social relations in the United States, while at the same time avoiding the dubious legacy Spencer had left. For Parsons, race constituted a cultural system like all others, and did not merit unique inquiries on its own terms. By treating racial discrimination as an example of functional strain particular to the United States,[38] rather than as only one aspect of systemic racism, Parsons left two Spencerian assumptions open for reinterpretation by future sociologists. Both assumptions construed inequality as a result of unchangeable characteristics, with racialized groups inherently predisposed toward differential social fates.

The first—the "nurture assumption"—was the idea that culture is an intrinsically orienting force predetermining social groups' ability to thrive in modern society. As the sociologist Ruha Benjamin describes, this kind of "culture talk" transforms biological patterns into "discrete biological entities [by which] distinct ethnoracial groups are managed and manufactured."[39] Examining how actors co-produce culture talk in medical labs, Benjamin demonstrates how this assumption persists in medical settings where the notion of cultural inheritance "shapes and grows out of health policy in a dynamic feedback loop that changes dramatically depending on how target populations are represented."[40]

The second—the "nature assumption"—was that genetic common-alities define social groups, predisposing group members toward certain capacities that affect their likelihood of socioeconomic success. This assumption is another feature of what the sociologist Alondra Nelson describes as the social life of DNA—namely, the ways notions of heritability function outside their proper scientific context, particularly where actors reformulate the notion of heritage through the language of genetics.[41] As Nelson concludes from an analysis of DNA "reconciliation" projects (i.e., legal cases that use DNA evidence to establish genetic ancestry, and thus rightful reparations), such "a genetic framing of history, ethnicity, and the past ... presents a barrier to mutual understanding."[42] While both assumptions are deeply controversial, sociologists have revisited and debated the ethics of each in diverse ways over the past century.

NURTURING INEQUALITY: THE LONG "CULTURE OF POVERTY" LEGACY

The Truman administration's late-1940s investment in international development drew social scientists to research modernization in so-called "traditional societies." What came to be known as Modernization Theory developed a simplified version of Parson's general model and applied it to international development.[43] Cohering in the work of Shils, Lerner, and their colleagues, Modernization Theory posited that adaptation to modern societies is gradual, where groups "lagging behind" are destined to "catch up" as they transition from particularist to universalist values.[44] Culture, for these scholars, was the key marker of modernization, and is thus assumed to be a *moral good*: the more "traditional" a society's culture, as measured by kinship-based social hierarchies and adherence to religious values, the more resistant it will be to processes like democratization, bureaucratization, and development.[45] While empirical disagreements about the accuracy of different models of ethnic relations existed, the dominant assumption was that certain "cultures" hindered socioeconomic growth.

This model set the backdrop for a US Department of Labor report, authored by the researcher Daniel Patrick Moynihan, which claimed that ongoing discrimination, lack of work opportunities, and the legacy of slavery were to blame for the erosion of family structures in the Black community during the 1950s and 1960s. Notably, the report claimed that the increasing prevalence of female-headed Black households exacerbated preexisting social problems in the community, thereby perpetuating Black poverty.[46]

Moynihan infused this internal document—written specifically for Department of Labor policy making—with boldly racialized statements and sexist language. Particularly attention-grabbing was Moynihan's claim that the increasingly matriarchal African American family undermines men's authority and thus contributes to widespread social disintegration.[47]

The Moynihan report was leaked to the press, and the ensuing controversy left a lasting mark on sociologists' approach to race and inequality. Over the decades that followed, sociologists responded in several different ways to the conjuncture between the already existing public and scholarly dissatisfaction with "culture of poverty" literature and the publication of the Moynihan report. Many have treated the report as an iconic example of victim-blaming explanations. But there were other responses: some scholars ultimately worked to recover culture in the analysis of poverty, others held—despite controversy—on to a classic modernization approach, and others still encouraged conversation and community-building around this research area (see table 2.2).

First Response: Rejecting—Denouncing Moynihan's Report (and the "Culture of Poverty") as Racist

By the time the Moynihan report appeared, discontent with Modernization Theory's model of culture had already been brewing. Scholars saw the model's blindness to power relations and inability to account for

TABLE 2.2 Responses to the controversy over the "culture of poverty" assumption

	Conflict	Non-Conflict
Debatable	Disagreeing—claiming that, while the original form of the "culture of poverty" argument is harmful, studies of poverty must account for the various ways culture and poverty are intertwined.	Ignoring—making public claims based on the "culture of poverty" assumption without acknowledging that they are problematic or subject to controversy.
Non-Debatable	Rejecting—identifying "Culture of Poverty" arguments as a way of "blaming the victim" and as hurting already marginalized communities.	Building Solidarity—calling for renewed debates about culture and poverty in order to increase cooperation between scholars and promote common knowledge about the sources of and solutions to inequality.

exceptions as fundamental problems.[48] Despite numerous attempts at revision, Modernization Theory became morally polluted in the 1960s because, as Jeffrey Alexander claimed, "the emerging younger generation of intellectuals could not believe it was true."[49] New social movements, under the banner of liberation, worked to flip the *zeitgeist* so that "modernization"—until recently considered the worthiest value—came to signify colonialist oppression. Critics placed the Moynihan report in the same camp as Modernization Theory and censured it as the policy implications of a flawed theory.[50] Early on, the Moynihan link was part of the larger controversy around the cultural anthropologist Oscar Lewis's work on Latin American poverty, where Lewis had coined the term "culture of poverty" to describe the way cross-generational values hindered lower socioeconomic classes from moving out of poverty.[51]

Thus, a prominent wave of commentators—civil society actors *and* sociologists—denounced the report and Moynihan himself as worthy of nothing less than ostracization. Civil rights groups (such as the NAACP) censured the report for perpetuating stereotypes of African Americans and placing the blame on the community instead of on the root cause, structural racism. *The Nation* published a now famous pronouncement by the psychologist William Ryan that the report "seduces the reader into believing that it is not racism," but the characteristics of African American society in themselves, that explain poverty.[52] Ryan's damning label for the Moynihan report (and the sociological genre it represented), "victim blaming," captured poignantly the moral sin critics saw in the report. Others emphasized how it lay the blame on Black women. Feminists criticized the report for its gendered assumption that women depend on a male breadwinner.[53] Journalistic accounts focused their ire on the repeated references to the "failure" of Black men to gain employment and highlighted Moynihan's individual faults, without making much of his attention to the historical and structural causes of racial inequality.[54]

Moynihan's "culture of poverty" argument, publicly denounced by its critics who called for its complete exclusion from acceptable discourse in sociology, has left an enduring mark on the sociology of race and inequality. Sampson and Massey claimed that Moynihan paid a "high reputational price," causing "a decided chilling effect in public debate and social science research."[55] As the strong backlash against the Moynihan report combined with a general retreat from Modernization Theory in sociology, scholars like Orlando Patterson and William Julius Wilson lamented what they saw as an unwillingness to research the intersections of culture and poverty.[56] Wilson argued that the Moynihan report blamed the long-lasting effects of slavery, and not contemporary families, for the social problems Black communities were experiencing, and that leading Black public figures endorsed the report before the onset of controversy.[57] Furthermore, Wilson pointed out that Black scholars like Bayard Rustin, E. Franklin Frazier, and Kenneth B. Clark had published related arguments before the Moynihan report.[58] Even after finding success in the field, and decades after the controversy, Wilson complained that "many liberal social scientists tended to avoid describing any behavior that could be construed as unflattering or stigmatizing to people of color."[59] According to these critics, all of whom held positions in top-ranking sociology departments, public reaction to the Moynihan report had ongoing scholarly consequences. This claim in itself has critics like Philip N. Cohen, who claimed that it was a substantive disagreement with Moynihan, rather than fear of backlash, that kept researchers away from investigating the role of culture in poverty.[60] It is not our task here to adjudicate between these two positions; rather, our purpose is to examine how the claims *about* the "Moynihan effect" influenced the shifting boundaries of moral acceptability in scholarship on culture in poverty research in the decades that followed.

Second Response: Disagreeing—How Race Scholars Brought Culture Back In

While sociologists initially withheld comment about culture following the controversy, they did not stay quiet for long. A second wave of responses to the Moynihan report chose *not* to exclude the report and its author from acceptable discourse, but to engage in conversation that—while often critical—acknowledged that the role of culture in the phenomenon of urban poverty is part of a legitimate discussion. These scholars mobilized the *Anchored Repertoire*, which focuses on deep experiential understanding of one's research subjects, to call for research on how the structural bases (e.g., economic and political) of social life give rise to specific forms of local culture.

In 1987, Wilson published *The Truly Disadvantaged* and spurred renewed interest in and controversy over the role of culture in poverty. Wilson pointed to what he called the "ghetto-specific culture" that emerges in "response to [the] structural constraints and limited opportunities" in inner-city communities. For Wilson, "a ghetto subculture is not to be equated with the popular conception of *culture of poverty* . . . [where] these traits assume a 'life of their own' and continue to influence behavior even if opportunities for social mobility improve."[61] According to Wilson, relying on this alternative view of "ghetto-specific culture" produced a "key conclusion from a public policy perspective . . . that programs created to alleviate poverty, joblessness, and related forms of social dislocation should place primary focus on changing the social and economic situations, not the cultural traits, of the ghetto underclass."[62] In other words, for Wilson, policy should focus on the structural factors that give rise to "ghetto-specific culture," rather than assault that culture itself. Dusting off the Moynihan report, Wilson insisted that "aside from some problems in historical accounting, Moynihan's analysis . . . proved to be prophetic."[63] Wilson's book coincided with an efflorescence of cultural theorizing in sociology that contributed to a resurgence of cultural studies of poverty in the following decades.[64]

However, the new wave of cultural scholars of poverty worked in an environment where many readers understood claims about "ghetto-specific culture" as yet another form of victim blaming and thus as morally unacceptable. Consequently, working on culture and poverty demanded alternative framing strategies. For instance, Orlando Patterson pointed out that while Clinton-era reforms provided millions of new job opportunities, "the jobless black youths simply did not turn up to take them. Instead, the opportunity was seized in large part by immigrants—including many blacks—mainly from Latin America and the Caribbean."[65] This confounded economists' expectations that employment opportunities would address a host of social problems plaguing African American communities. Sociological silence on the matter was, for Patterson, the evidence of a deep misunderstanding of the "culture" concept that was an aftereffect of the Moynihan debates. According to Patterson, such sociologists made three incorrect assumptions about cultural explanations of poverty: that they unavoidably blame the victim; that they lead to deterministic claims about groups being incompatible with modern society; and that they depict unchangeable patterns of customs and beliefs that influence group behavior indefinitely. Patterson claimed that sociologists have limited themselves to thin accounts of culture, and have in turn allowed conservatives to dominate the discourse on culture and poverty:

> it was and is still too often the case that cultural explanations are employed by reactionary analysts and public figures who attribute the social problems of the poor to their "values" and thereby wash their hands and the hands of government and the taxpayers of any responsibility for their alleviation. Indeed, perhaps the main reason why cultural explanations are shunned by anthropologists and sociologists—both very liberal disciplines—is the fact that they have been so avidly embraced by reactionaries or simple-minded public figures. Culture as explanation languishes in intellectual exile partly because of guilt by association.[66]

Patterson thus maintained that sociologists' silence on cultural explanations of poverty was deeply consequential. For Patterson, by ignoring culture as an explanatory factor for poverty, sociologists have inadvertently allowed welfare opponents to co-opt simplistic accounts of poverty among Black communities to their own ends. In response, Patterson reconstructed the concept of culture for sociological thinking about inequality, incorporating both historically constituted cultural legacy and its reception under present circumstances. Here, Patterson also provided a way around problematic assumptions about culture-of-poverty studies by drawing on historical reconstruction of cultural forms, the analysis of the transformation in cultural structures, and the contemporary conjunctures that shape specific exposures to culture norms, to address specific behavioral outcomes. In Patterson's model, culture is neither innate to a social group nor unchanging; once his model was available, research on cultural poverty could now avoid the shameful mistakes of its past.[67]

Studies of culture and poverty resurfaced around the turn of the century with a cautious but productive rethinking of the concept. David Harding, Michèle Lamont, and Mario Small's 2000 edited issue of the *ANNALS of the American Academy of Political and Social Science* was an important marker of this revival. The challenge for them was twofold: on the one hand, Marxist analyses of poverty have tended to see culture as a byproduct of material arrangements, and on the other hand, some "remain suspicious of the political intentions of the new culture scholars [in the study of poverty], and charges of 'blaming the victim' have not disappeared."[68] For the editors, "the judicious, theoretically informed, and empirically grounded study of culture can and should be a permanent component of the poverty research agenda."[69] Another important marker was Elijah Anderson's influential book *Code of the Street*, which refocused attention on the grounded norms inner-city communities generate to address the harsh realities they face. For Anderson, the distinctions inner-city Black communities make between their members and the exacting norms they develop as "cultural adaptation to a profound lack of faith in the police and the judicial system."[70] Thus, far from being silenced in the discipline, studies of culture and poverty persisted, with scholars largely acknowledging that reviving "culture" as an explanatory force requires addressing mistakes from past generations and insisting that new research serve morally justified ends. By weighing the utility of various theories of culture in understanding poverty, these scholars offer a defense against allegations that they are naively resuscitating a Moynihan-era "culture of poverty."

This renewed scholarship has seen its own critics. Younger scholars mobilized the *Civic Repertoire*, which emphasizes equality, to highlight the failures of revised approaches to culture and poverty. Michael Rodríguez-Muñiz argued that the new cultural sociology of poverty retains a problematic assumption that "the 'poor' . . . should constitute the *principal* empirical object of poverty knowledge" rather than focusing on how the nonpoor help maintain poverty.[71] Scholars have criticized Wilson's approach as downplaying the structural racism that critical race theory has uncovered.[72] Crystal Fleming has referred to Wilson's argumentation as *"post-really-bad racism,"* arguing that his approach was based on the unfounded assumption that racism in itself is decreasing in explanatory power for poverty research.[73] Yet, unlike the early responses to the Moynihan report, this criticism was focused on improving existing forms of research on culture and racial inequality rather than excising entire subfields from the discipline.

Third Response: Ignoring—Treating the Relationship between Culture and Poverty as Unproblematic

Despite attempts by cultural sociologists to rethink their background assumptions, some of the staunchest supporters of the "culture of poverty" argument preferred its original form and chose to ignore well-known criticisms. In other words, while sociologists have shown the capacity to argue about the role of culture in the creation of poverty without exiling their interlocutors from the conversation, some scholars sought to dismiss the entire conversation and to act as though "culture of poverty" arguments are unproblematic.

The political scientist Lawrence M. Mead, whose 2020 *Society* commentary article caused a maelstrom, is a prime example. Mead's piece argued that Black and Latinx Americans are overrepresented among lower-income Americans because they originate in collectivist cultures ill-suited to contemporary US individualist culture. The article presented no new evidence in support of its claim; instead, Mead limited himself to a short passage summarizing his complaints about existing scholarship,

> Some have thought that the seriously poor simply rejected middle-class values. They tried to live liberated lives like some movie stars in Hollywood—abandoning families or getting high on drugs—to their own cost. But their professed values do not appear to differ from the mainstream. Many experts also thought that "social barriers" of some impersonal kind were preventing adults from working—such as racial bias, absence of skills or child care, and so on. But no such clear impediment has been found. True, government benefits can raise income

among the poor or help them cope—but none causes them to do much more to help themselves. External impediments are not their main problem.[74]

What policy implications does Mead say we should draw from his analysis?

External order must at least be restored in poor areas. . . . Recent work, education, and training programs have become more paternalist, or directive, telling clients what they must do to get ahead. . . . One reason this approach works is that non-Western culture is strongly deferential to authority. Once society shows a willingness to enforce norms, the poor generally comply.[75]

While Mead did not attempt to defend his thesis from potential objections and wrote as though these were unproblematic grounds, his readers fought back. Beginning with social media posts and continuing with a petition calling on the journal to retract the article, scholars expressed outrage at the racist stereotypes Mead perpetuated and at the xenophobic assumptions underpinning his article. Within weeks of publication, the journal retracted the piece, stating that the "article was published without proper editorial oversight" and that the "Editor-in-Chief deeply regrets publishing the article and offers his apologies."[76] According to the journal's statement, Mead did not agree to the retraction.

Unlike most empirically flawed articles, where critics might respond by publishing a comment in the following journal issue, here critics suggested that the article's publication was a form of violence that must be redressed. Drawing attention to the moral consequences of the research Mead was promoting, one petition reasoned:

As a community, granted the power to educate and inform, who have worked diligently to become experts in our own respective ways, we have the responsibility to do so in a manner that progresses equity for those communities historically and consistently oppressed. We have a social and professional responsibility to help mend the wounds of racial violence and oppression. We have a responsibility to dismantle structural barriers while creating new systems of resistance and acceptance that celebrate and promote justice.[77]

To rectify this failure of editorial oversight, the petition asks that the journal "immediately retract the commentary . . . issue an apology to the BIPOC [Black, Indigenous, and People of Color] community, and the communities negatively impacted by these narratives," and respond to questions such as "How many BIPOC serve on the journal's editorial board? How many BIPOC scholars were asked to peer review the commentary? Were BIPOC scholars offered an opportunity to present a counter to the commentary?" For the authors of the petition, answers to these questions will "help elucidate the ways that academia in general and academic journals specifically serve to strengthen white supremacy."

Unsurprisingly, scholars critical of the article invoked a notion of justice to support their denunciation. However, they also highlighted the meaning of the scholarly community's response to Mead. Indeed, the criticism intertwined two different claims to justice: a factual objection to the claim that innate cultural traits determine predispositions toward work, and an ethical concern over the results of entertaining this idea. Critics contended that, in both situations, the scientific community risks contributing to scholarly justification of white supremacy. Thus, such critics concluded, ejecting such claims from the conversation and remedying them through strengthening BIPOC representation in the journal was necessary.

Fourth Response: Solidarity-Building—Encouraging Conversations in a Contentious Field

But a fourth response to the ongoing controversy, emerging primarily in the early 2000s, called on scholars to embrace the livelihood of the debates around the study of culture and poverty in order to build a scholarly community that cherishes academic debate.

In the years since the publication of Wilson's *The Truly Disadvantaged*, calls for cooperation, while acknowledging the contentious past and potential pitfalls of culture and poverty research, stressed how scholarly disagreements are in themselves important for the field to develop. The entire field of poverty research would benefit from discussion around such possibly controversial matters. Scholars calling for renewed conversation included Mario Small and Katherine Newman, who insisted that "the cultural literature in urban poverty, still in its infancy (or early re-incarnation from the 1960s), is in dire need of conceptual work." Rather than bemoan past failures, here they argued that the way forward was *more* cultural studies of poverty, in particular comparative and historical studies that can "assess the origins and development of urban cultures." In this, "the existing ethnographies have provided critical insights, but because so few of them have been comparative, they have not taken us far enough on the cultural front. If anything, these ethnographies, and the new work in urban poverty as a whole, has laid the groundwork for the important work to come."[78]

In advocating for a platform for discussion, scholars highlight the joint mission sociologists have in advancing knowledge, and contend that despite disagreement, they form one continuous field of knowledge. As Brunsma and Embrick, in a call for contributions for an edited journal issue on the "Sociologies of Race/Racism/Ethnicity and Culture," write: "There are many areas of sociology that do not 'talk' to each other, or whose concepts, analyses, and questions seem fundamentally related, but continue to remain in their proverbial 'silos,' ultimately engaged in parallel conversations that rarely, if ever, meet. One of the most surprising of these 'silences' is the consistent disciplinary boundary between the sociologies of race/racism and ethnicity and the sociologies of culture. We seek scholarship whose theoretical, epistemological, methodological, and substantive approaches actively suture these areas—the cultural (e.g., social structures of meaning-making) and the racial (e.g., racialized social structures) together."[79]

Treating the field as one where disagreements can be brought into productive conversation, solidarity-builders provide platforms for continuing exploration of the intersections of race, inequality, and culture. Indeed, such solidarity-building is particularly important in a field where scholars have historical and institutional reasons to worry about each other's moral inclinations.

———

The long history of the study of culture and poverty contradicts the claim that sociologists are either too blind or too scared to address such topics. While self-censorship certainly exists, public conversations in sociology show that sociologists *also* engage in lively discussions over the repercussions of simplistic accounts of the role of culture in creating poverty. Indeed, our analysis highlights two intertwined aspects of the production of social science knowledge. First, it shows that moral limitations to entry into the social sciences exist, and that scholars react both to the empirical validity and to the moral ramifications of their peers' arguments. Second, it shows that these moral limitations do not block off entire research areas, and that the study of culture and poverty has continued—as long as scholars acknowledged and debated the ethical grounds on which they delve into this topic. To maintain legitimacy in the field, sociologists studying culture and poverty must balance and integrate both the empirical validity and the moral value of their research. As the next section shows, this balancing act is even more pertinent for researchers wishing to use genetic data in sociological research.

THE NATURE OF RACE: ADVANCES IN
THE GENETIC SCIENCE OF RACE

Like cultural essentialism, the echoes of early-twentieth-century eugenicism have continued to haunt sociology. After the collapse of eugenics in the aftermath of World War II, scholarship on human biodiversity rebuilt itself at the molecular level by turning attention to the science of genetics, culminating in a 2000 White House Press Meeting. There, President Bill Clinton himself marveled at the pace of the project to map the DNA molecule, noting that "[i]t was not even 50 years ago that a young Englishman named Crick and a brash even younger American named Watson, first discovered the elegant structure of our genetic code." Yet, at this very meeting, Clinton formally announced the completed mapping of the human genome, creating something of a "post-genomic" historical rupture, a period after which society, life, and politics will be characterized by their response to effective mapping and manipulation of genomic data. While language describing how nature influenced social outcomes had never left the social sciences entirely—for instance, studies of twins have always been a popular means to understand the influence of genetic inheritance[80]—advances in genetic research have marked a stunning return of biological thinking across the human sciences (including sociology).[81]

Moreover, the age of the genome has been beset by conflict around what such "maps" mean for the future of racial (in)justice. Initially, it seemed advances in genetics would legitimate a new anti-racist society. Indeed, Clinton repeated the standard claim genetic scientists have forwarded to sidestep accusations of pedaling a new eugenics: that "in genetic terms, all human beings, regardless of race, are more than 99.9 percent the same." Yet the problem became gradually harder to ignore, leading to a variety of typical responses by scholars (see table 2.3). As this section will show, sociologists embracing the new genetic science have situated their research on race, genetics, and inequality as justified by the new norms of genetic science, as a source of dispute within the scholarly community, as a way in which unseen violence sneaks into sociological reasoning, and as a means to generate new forms of scholarly collaboration.

First Response: Ignoring—Am I Doing Something Wrong?

Social thinkers have adopted genetic data in recent decades for a myriad of reasons. Perhaps the most obvious argument has been that advances in the biological sciences are part of the normal advance of knowledge, and it is now time for sociologists to recognize the paradigm shifts that

TABLE 2.3 Responses to the controversy over the Genes-Race-Inequality assumption

	Conflict	Non-Conflict
Debatable	Disagreeing—arguing logically over whether and how genetic data can be used ethically to advance our knowledge on inequality.	Ignoring—making public claims that contemporary accounts of inequality are flawed when they ignore clear evidence of the utility of biogenetic data in various forms of social reasoning, without acknowledging historic uses of eugenics in sociology.
Non-Debatable	Rejecting—identifying the use of biogenetic data to talk about racial difference as a way of reinforcing racist narratives that risks the same mistakes of the eugenics era.	Building Solidarity—claiming that scholars who disagree should debate the uses and importance of biogenetic data and arguing that this debate itself is a valuable way sociologists and scientists can clarify their understanding.

have occurred in the biological sciences. Here, scholars assert that their research is a routine feature of scientific updating, and unworthy of continued moral debate. For instance, scholars regularly express concern about the "specter of eugenics"[82] but still argue that "if the received findings from behavioral genetics are even approximately correct, then conventional sociological techniques for estimating effects of social environment causes likely yield pervasively biased results."[83] Such refrains have become commonplace in *Annual Review of Sociology* pieces where scholars who blend research on genetics with new sociological insights argue that

> the methodological issue is how to design meaningful experiments to explore the interaction of the environment and gene regulation; and the political and economic issue is about priorities for national biomedical and public health funding and potential policy outcomes. It is not the time for sociologists to stand back and watch as these contests play out in other research areas. . . . This is literally a "critical window" for engagement. It is our hope that readers will take from this overview a range of possibilities for how to engage and shape—and be shaped by—this emerging field of knowledge as it attempts to redefine the social.[84]

In this view, the natural goals of the biological and social sciences—to sustain, support, and foster life—and the unrelenting speed of recent advances present a "critical window" in which sociologists must act to ensure that their voices are heard. Certainly, sociologists' embrace of genetics is not without risks, but it is held by many to be part of a larger project of social good promised by the routine workings of different forms of science.[85] For instance, Goosby, Cheadle, and Mitchell note that "the a priori rejection of genetic information based on the key (and well documented) distinction between genetic ancestry and the social attribution of race impairs our understanding of how life in a racialized social system affects health through genetically influenced pathway."[86] Here, sociologists' ability to agree on the use of genetic data impacts the future of science itself.

Nor are those leading the charge in the name of science the only ones willing to readopt the once polluted ideas of genetic inheritance by reference to the new science of DNA. For instance, some have advocated that Indigenous populations adopt a "strategic biological essentialism" when it comes to the question of race[87]—suggesting that Indigenous populations use genetic information to acquire legitimacy in the public sphere (for instance, by using biology to demonstrate ongoing epigenetic trauma). Similarly, Ifekwunigwe et al. survey how anthropologists conceptualize race and demonstrate that a new wave of scholarship seeks to reconcile constructivist and biological arguments by focusing on how "race is a social and cultural construct that, when applied, acts as a self-ascribed badge of affiliation while also having lived and ideological consequences as different forms of racism."[88] Here the notion of self-ascription reveals that race can be used as a tool for both dividing *and* uniting groups in the name of justice. In both these instances, the hope to promote civic equality legitimates adopting new biological understandings of race. These scholars justify their research by urging that new forms of genetic science produce an opportunity for innovation through routine sociological engagement.

Second Response: Disagreeing—What Makes Genomics Good?

Competing claims about the uses of biogenetic data have inevitably led to debates over the moral appropriateness of different scientific understandings of race. Here, scholars mobilized the Civic Repertoire to debate the appropriateness and potential harm that the use of biogenetic data can cause. While some anthropologists have advocated the strategic use of biological data to support projects of racial justice (see above), others have pointed out that the discipline's historical dalliance with eugenics has led to significant traumas for Indigenous populations. According to this critical view, recourse to biological anthropology merely recapitulates the ugly past of the social sciences. Such scholars point to the repeated attempts by Indigenous populations to avoid DNA collection, and scientists' unwillingness to honor the wishes of their research subjects, as proof of a trauma reworked in the age of DNA. Reviewing a legal dispute between Arizona State University geneticists and members of the Havasupai tribe, Reardon and TallBear conclude: "while in the nineteenth century, Europeans sought to tame American wildernesses and the 'savages' that inhabited them—a so-called civilizing project now generally viewed as racist—in the twenty-first century, self-proclaimed Europeans continue to make a claim to indigenous peoples and their resources, only this time they do so in the name of the civilizing project of antiracism."[89]

Sociology has also seen such disagreements. For instance, in the early 2010s two prominent sociology journals—*Sociological Theory* and *Demography*—published articles advocating the use of biogenetic data to help foster civic equality (particularly relating to health inequalities amongst racial minorities).[90] However, numerous sociologists quickly objected, noting that "the view that our constructed racial groupings, like those on the US census, spring from underlying biological characteristics reflects a profound misunderstanding of the history and nature of race." Deeming this view "completely backwards," scholars urged others to expose how "racial groupings are rooted in political and social rumination" rather than to see them as "the product of laboratory discoveries that only later get caught up in power relations."[91]

In a similar attempt to reassess the moral status of such projects, Fullwiley documented the collaboration between a biogeneticist and a sociologist that resulted in students of a Sociology of Race and Ethnicity course undergoing a DNA test and discovering their "racial admixture" in the hopes of promoting anti-racist sentiment. Fullwiley concluded that such tactics are another example where "the organization of protocols by race too often reduces biological outcomes that have social origins to genetic explanation."[92] In both instances, the variety of understandings of the situation demands that actors judge the relative value of each form of moral reasoning.

Third Response: Rejecting—Genetics as a Threat

When scholars disagree in the extreme, they move beyond a debate about the relative merits of different moral frameworks, and instead treat the situation as a zero-sum game. In the debate around racial genetics, this mode can be seen in the ways scholars underline the "slippery" nature of the harm careless science could cause. For instance, Roberts and Rollins urge that "the problem [with such research] is not technological usage per se, but its ability to obscure ethical uncertainties and structural forces and to reconstitute problematic sociocultural assumptions that researchers relied upon uncritically to execute biosocial research and/or biometric surveillance."[93] Of particular concern has been the uncritical use of self-identification of race and ethnicity (SIRE) survey responses as a proxy for genetic differences. Scholars have criticized SIRE responses on multiple fronts,[94] and yet bio-sociological researchers have increasingly used them (although they remained less common in sociology journals).[95] Indeed, recent scholarship includes warnings not to "conflate biological and social identities,"[96] as such tactics will leave one stuck between "two contradictory magnetic poles . . . producing a tension that will never be resolved"[97] and will ultimately doom the researcher to "viewing life through race-colored lenses."[98] For these scholars, genetics-based research on race is unacceptable, and must be actively fought.

Often, scholars invoke the historical trauma associated with genetic claims-making to confer a sense of urgency on their fight against introducing genetic data to sociology. Describing the growing clash between social and biological visions of race, Duster notes,

> because the rate of prostate cancer in African Americans is more than double that of white Americans, it was inevitable that some would attempt to explain this through the lens of genetics. This in turn would lead down the path that would serve to rescue old racial taxonomies and their relationship to genetic profiles and genetic conditions. It was not expected that, in so doing, this strategy would inadvertently resuscitate the idea that genetic differences between those we place in racial categories might well explain different health outcomes. This is territory fraught with minefields for obvious reasons, dating back to the eugenics movement in the USA and its promulgation and extension into Nazi Germany.[99]

For Duster, science no longer has the right to claim that the pursuit of knowledge trumps morality, as it has participated knowingly and unknowingly in extreme violence in the past. Duster is not alone in his view that history proves such areas are dangerous for sociologists. Invoking the legacy of social Darwinism, Byrd and Hughey have warned that the new "biological deterministic approaches of today echo similar approaches of decades ago by 'naturalizing' inequality."[100] Highlighting the propensity of the human sciences to forget its own past, Ann Morning has argued that new scientific claims are "simply another handmaiden recruited to bolster an eighteenth-century European world view: the notion that there 'really' are black people and white people, yellow people and red people, independent of any cultural biases or proclivities that we might have."[101] Surveying understandings of how environmental conditions shape the expression of genes associated with obesity amongst Indigenous populations around a Mexican Public Health initiative, Saldaña-Tejeda and Wade distinguished an older discourse of eugenics from a new "post-genomic" discourse. They warned that

> in [nineteenth-century] eugenics, the relative roles of heredity and the environment were not clear even as together they were seen to determine the moral and physical qualities of la raza [the race]; in post-genomics, the relative roles are more clearly defined, but the reductionism that still inflects (and racializes) genetic research encourages similar styles of thought in the realm of epigenetics.[102]

In all three cases, critics referenced the historical legacy of violence to warn that past moral failures may return under a new guise, and that advocates of polluted research are ignorant of the past or of the moral consensus. Indeed, Dorothy Roberts closed her influential book *Fatal Invention: How Science, Politics and Big Business Re-Create Race in the Twenty-First Century* by noting, "American is *once again* at the brink of a dangerous biopolitics of race, fueled by a new racial science based on cutting-edge genomics, a staunch refusal to acknowledge enduring racial inequality, and a free-market fundamentalism that, having virtually eliminated the social safety net, relies instead on technological solutions to social problems."[103]

Fourth Response: Solidarity-Building—Together We Can Overcome

Despite the threat of rejection, some still see work on genetics and race as an essential next step for sociological advancement. Moreover, unlike scholars who use existing moral frameworks to justify genetic sociological research, here scholars admit that moral risks are inevitable but maintain that actors of good faith can overcome them together. For instance, in his introduction to a special issue on the topic for the *American Journal of Sociology*, Bearman asserts that "the focus on the supposed genetics of behavior is a eugenicist's project in (not so veiled) disguise"—is in fact a misnomer.[104] Instead, Bearman contends that by collecting open-minded scholars, "the special issue should be a 'big tent' in which all of the various modalities in which relevant work was undertaken would have a shot at publication."[105] Consequently, such efforts at building community tend to include scholars justifying their research according to well-known scientific-cum-moral rhetorical moves—e.g., claiming that knowing certain gene associations can improve estimates of disease or that heritability plays a role in particular social outcomes such as happiness—but also more ethereal discussions like "whether 'genes' are things to think with and in what ways they are useful to think with."[106] In such spaces of solidarity-building, a collective search for new forms of academic community identity opens up.

This refrain frequently turns to an explicit recognition of how differences in *method* result in confusion that can only be overcome by a concerted effort across divides. A *Nature* editorial noted,

> Many sociologists . . . are still immured in their fortress, struggling to catch up with a debate that has shifted from nature-or-nurture to nature-and-nurture, or are unable to shake off their distrust of scientists, worrying that scientists will force them to play second fiddle in their own territory: the environment. That is a shame: both academia and society still need their engagement at many levels. Now is a perfect time for a reconciliation of the two cultures.[107]

Rather than place blame on any particular constituency, the writers contend that the only road forward is through a communal effort respecting differences in method, understanding, and scientific principles. As the *Nature* team put it,

> Sociologists have been studying human environments for decades, and have tallied the social damage that stresses such as poverty or child abuse can cause. Biologists are now in a position to benefit from their insights, although they will need to learn the language of sociology. And sociologists stand to benefit from the understanding that biology will bring to their own, vindicated, empirical research.[108]

Here, the collaboration between two traditional antagonists sustains particularly worthy actions: *Nature* emphasizes the role of collective reasoning in improving society "in general" and through future efforts at solidarity-building. Ironically, such bids toward collaboration are necessary even in fields that are not so classically antagonistic. For instance, in an introduction to a special issue of the *International Journal of Epidemiology* on new epigenetic research, the editors noted, "the field of epidemiology has much to offer the field of epigenetics by providing a framework for population-based studies with well-established methods for circumventing fundamental issues such as confounding and reverse causation as well as more recent developments of approaches to strengthen causal inference."[109] While to outsiders the fields appear interchangeable, as with all things in academia the neurosis of small differences means that efforts at community-building are twice as essential as in other domains.

A host of public critics have blamed social scientists for allowing their liberal values to blind them to the supposed truths that epigenetics hold. But based on this review of the lively sociological conversations on the topic, such claims are not only factually wrong, but also insulting to the intelligence and critical capacities of working academics. While sociologists *may* reject the use of genetic data wholesale, this response has hardly been the only one, and even said rejection is not a knee-jerk reaction but a response rooted in the long history of misuse of genetic data in the discipline.

CONTROVERSY AS AN OPPORTUNITY RATHER THAN A CRISIS

Public observers have depicted a variety of social science controversies as crises.[110] Some critics have touted such controversies as evidence that liberal academia cannot withstand new perspectives on social problems.[111] Others have seen controversies over methods and ethics as uncovering the shaky grounds on which contemporary sociology stands.[112] But our analysis of controversy invites different thinking: seeing academic controversies not as crises or as evidence of unsound intellectual foundations, but as a constitutive feature of knowledge production communities. As we have shown, academic no-go zones are not shut off from disciplinary conversations. Quite the contrary—academics mobilize a variety of resources to address "hot potato" topics, and engagement with such issues is an endemic part of routine sociological debate. Many academics would call *all* of the disputes covered in this chapter a form of "disagreement." However, we have underlined that scholarly discord entails not only overt rejections, normalizations, and coalition formations, but also explicit disagreements about how and why research is morally justified. While the cases we reviewed in this chapter are extreme examples, lower-intensity controversies punctuate sociological conversations and provide academics with opportunities to negotiate the boundaries of acceptable research in the discipline. This chapter showed that controversies are also sites for scholarly creativity, as sociologists devise ways to address the existence of an academic no-go zone in their research area.

If confronting or addressing controversy is a common rhetorical way to frame the need for theoretical growth, then recognizing controversy as a legitimate form of disciplinary boundary questioning allows sociologists to respond to public critiques of sociological knowledge production more holistically. Those critiquing sociology for "silencing" unpopular ideas rarely consider a much simpler narrative than liberal tyranny—namely, that actors like Mead and Murray who revive lost causes are attempting to assign moral worth to their research on grounds that are incompatible with disciplinary standards for knowledge production.[113] While eugenicists like Galton presented his pseudo-science as a contribution to the common good of the human race, scholarly debates have revealed that the bases of the common good it promised were ill-conceived. The problem was not closed-minded sociologists unable to deal fairly with the "truth" of eugenics. Rather, it was that the moral goods eugenics purported to offered were axiologically indefensible—they lacked a vision of common humanity strong enough to justify a claim to universal moral authority.

Although some sociologists continue to discuss the potential uses of genetic data for the discipline (for instance, as it relates to health inequalities), these sociologists are also demanding a "renegotiation and reconfiguring of the biological, the social, and their interrelation" where sociologists will not only be the passive consumers of biological knowledge, but will also inform epigenetic research with methodological and theoretical innovations from their discipline.[114] Dorothy Roberts, for example, concludes her historical account of biogenetic science by applauding scholars investigating "the biological pathways through which racism is translated into poor health and devising strategies to end racial inequalities in health by changing social policies," but only to the extent that these studies use the race concept "defined properly as a social category."[115] These scholars do not demand a head-in-the-sand approach to the rise of racial genomics; rather, they insist that social forces be consistently brought into the conversation as a means of rectifying genetic arguments.

Those blaming social scientists for censoring and encouraging self-censorship similarly misunderstand the academic dynamics at play. We have only analyzed the debates around Charles Murray in ancillary fashion here, but by addressing his claims from the viewpoint of a sociology of critique we demonstrate that his claims are not only groundless, but a way of overlooking and undoing the creative moral debates at the forefront of the social sciences. While sociology as a discipline may designate certain areas as off-limits, it does so to counteract research assumptions that contradict the common humanity of its research subjects. Even then, as this chapter has shown, sociologists continue to explore new ways of conducting controversial research while correcting its problematic presuppositions. Controversy not only hinders knowledge production, but may also stimulate it and turn it in directions that are more conducive for the common good.

Understanding that scholarly "no-go zones" are a collective product of scholars' critical ethical sense, rather than proof of an academic liberal bias, is doubly important when it comes to debates on inequality, because of their direct bearing on social policy. Studies touting genetic and cultural essentialism have historically argued that systemic efforts to counteract inequality are futile. Their approaches have indelibly harmed those experiencing poverty—particularly Black, Indigenous, and People of Color—by advocating for a decrease (or even elimination) of state welfare policies.[116] Morning shows that policies based on racially essentialist ideas remain prevalent, but are normally attributed to either genetic variances or thinly veiled claims about cultural differences.[117] By showing that sociologists evaluate and debate the ethical appropriateness of research into these contentious domains, this chapter pushes against claims that a supposed hegemonic "liberal academia" silences entire research fields wholesale. Instead, it demonstrates that the discipline has the capacity to reject scholarship that relies on dehumanizing assumptions about race, gender, or class, and that this capacity is far from a knee-jerk reaction.

CHAPTER THREE

Moral Highways and Byways

Connecting New Critiques with Old Insights in the Study of Nationalism

Few sociologists foresaw the election of Donald J. Trump as the forty-fifth president of the United States. While some scholars had pointed to presidential candidate Trump as yet another concerning sign of the decline of respectable politics,[1] the election result shocked many who believed the Obama presidency signified a long-term change of direction in American political beliefs.[2] While the Brexit referendum had taken place just five months earlier, and could have been a wakeup call to political thinkers worldwide,[3] most dismissed the idea of a rising nationalist tide as the last gasps of a waning demographic.[4] Many commentators simply assumed that unabashed patriotism was a thing of the past. Yet, an election campaign touting the slogans "Make America Great Again" and "America First" won the day.

Trump's victory brought to light a growing tension around the ways sociologists have dealt with nationalism as a phenomenon. On the one hand, Trump's election confirmed the claims of students of US white nationalism[5] and Christian nationalism,[6] that the progressive turn in late-2000s US politics masked simmering conservative currents nationwide. On the other hand, the elections confounded the late-twentieth-century turn to cosmopolitan thinking among sociologists—in particular, the widespread idea that the world is moving toward intercultural openness, and that nation-states and nationalism are in global decline.

Indeed, the sharp nationalistic turns in the US, the UK, and many other countries over the past decade has raised a question mark over some of the most influential ideas within the discipline. Starting in the 1980s, scholars like Ulrich Beck, Manuel Castells, and Scott Lash had made passionate claims (and successful careers) suggesting that a new world order was emerging: one where national boundaries matter far less than international cooperation, universal ethics, and worldwide responsibility on global risks. As Beck put it, with the global risk climate change poses, the world is undergoing "a fundamental shock, a sea change which explodes the anthropological constants of our previous existence and understanding of the world." This metamorphosis, for Beck, "means simply that what was unthinkable yesterday is real and possible today."[7] This new wave of intellectual thinking saw the social sciences as having a key role in simultaneously documenting and promoting a new world, seeing the nation-state as a central cause to the most pressing social problems. By 2016, numerous scholars had spent decades insisting that traditional nation-state boundaries and national sentiments were morally questionable, socially damaging, and politically doomed, and celebrating—often uncritically—what they saw as a post-national reality. From this perspective, scholars researching topics like immigration, nation-state establishment, domestic politics, or any other topic taking national boundaries for granted had to tread lightly. The danger for such scholars, now, was appearing to endorse pernicious, outdated methodological-nationalist views legitimating the nation-state system. The study of nations and nationalism in sociology has become morally contentious over the last quarter of the twentieth century.

Chapter 2 showed how sociologists delegitimize certain research areas as immoral—areas we called *moral no-go zones*—and how they continue engaging with a topic despite deep controversy. As we showed, while one pattern of response to morally polluted scholarship rejects the research and its authors outright, another pattern debates the nature of the research and justifies it using different moral conceptions of the goods sociological research provides. The current chapter delves deeper into the messy work of renegotiation of what counts as acceptable research, looking specifically at how scholars persevere in pursuing research in areas that have come under scrutiny. How do specific notions of good research persist when they come under attack on moral grounds? We argue that, when a complete delegitimation is not considered a viable or desirable option, scholars draw on alternate notions of worth to address and confront moral challenges to their work. We develop the notion of *partial reforms*: justification techniques that respond to a moral criticism by reformulating the moral framing of the conversation to justify research in contentious fields.

Thus, where cosmopolitan critics have claimed that good social research should focus on the porousness of national boundaries and on transnational cooperation—a claim typically associated with what we call the *Network Repertoire* of moral worth[8]—we show how other scholars used alternate conceptions of worth—those associated with local traditions, political civility, and academic efficiency—to address potential criticism from cosmopolitan-minded scholars without radically altering their own research programs. Unlike the moral no-go zones we profiled in chapter 2, here critical assaults on old theories succeed partially: they help change the configuration of a moral debate, but they do not manage to delegitimize an entire research area.

The critique of the "nation" as an analytic and empirical category has preoccupied social scientists for decades. Indeed, some of the grandest claims about international relations in the recent history of social thought, such as Frances Fukuyama's *End of History* and Samuel Huntington's *Clash of Civilizations*, have been highly controversial. This decades-long debate has also produced durable and nuanced middle positions that have emerged to reconsider the significance of the co-constitution of the global and the local. While our focus on some of the most polarizing claims in this debate in our retelling of this intellectual history is in itself consequential,[9] the aim of this chapter is not to capture the entire debate, but rather to demonstrate that even in the context of polarizing moral claims about where the discipline should go, intermediate positions persist and sustain innovation. Thus, rather than promoting a view of the cosmopolitanism movement in sociology as one-sided, this chapter highlights its multivocality and its ultimate contribution to the livelihood of the discipline.

POLLUTING NATIONS AND NATIONALISM

Although some scholars have identified cosmopolitan sociological thinking in classical theorists' work—like Durkheim,[10] Du Bois,[11] and Simmel[12]—most sociologists have used nationally bounded states unproblematically as exemplars of distinct societies until the late twentieth century. At that point, intellectuals across disciplines increasingly identified nationalism as the root cause of warfare, xenophobia, and social suffering, and attributed pernicious qualities to national boundaries. What happened in the late twentieth century that turned nations and nationalism into a morally loaded topic in social science research?

Sociologists, cultural anthropologists, and other social scientists had certainly noted the growing influence of transnational processes on their field sites in the late twentieth century, but two 1983 books significantly impacted scholarly conversations on the nation-state and provided a moral framework to interpret these accumulating empirical observations in a new light. In political science, Benedict Anderson's *Imagined Communities* attributed the appearance of nation-states to cultural changes associated with the invention of the printing press. In history, Eric Hobsbawm and Terence Ranger's edited volume *The Invention of Tradition* claimed that many of the legitimating traditions nations uphold were introduced through the various nineteenth-century state-building projects. Both books historicized nations and nationalism as new cultural phenomena, countering scholars like Anthony Smith who maintained that the nation-state is the ultimate expression of group-level collective history.[13] Given their newness, scholars like Liah Greenfeld contended that ethnic nation-states could be jettisoned as an analytic framing device since nations fulfilled no innate human need.[14] Collectively, these works depicted nationalism as standing in the way of human flourishing.

While social historians were questioning the durability of the nation-state, philosophers developed their own moral critiques of national distinction and, in particular, of national*ism*. One of the strongest voices against nationalism in the United States in that era was that of the philosopher Martha Nussbaum. In her 1994 article "Patriotism and Cosmopolitanism" she contended "that to give support to nationalist sentiments subverts, ultimately, even the values that hold a nation together, because it substitutes a colorful idol for the substantive universal values of justice and right."[15] Urging instead an embrace of the Stoic ideal of cosmopolitanism—a "primary allegiance . . . to the community of human beings in the entire world"[16]—Nussbaum proclaimed that "*only* the cosmopolitan stance"[17] could provide the ethical resources to supersede the old system of nation-states. The article became a rallying cry for big-name intellectuals like Judith Butler, Hilary Putnam, and Amartya Sen, who were all working to identify the social good that marked their time.[18]

For many, the transition from an academic conversation about de-nationalized research practices to a full-fledged movement to change research norms was most directly associated with the German sociologist Ulrich Beck. His works argued that the transition to late modernity—with its scientific and communicative advances—had transformed perceptions of risk worldwide. From being tangible, manageable, and containable within national borders (e.g., wars, economic downturns, floods, accidents), risk has transformed into an abstract, all-pervasive force that transcends national interests (e.g., climate change, pollution, radiation). In a 2000 interview, Beck recalled how his motivations derived from the historical events he lived through, and the theoretical fashions with which he grappled: "[The nuclear disaster at] Chernobyl happened just as I was finishing the proofs of *Risk Society*. One thing that made it so dramatic was that German contingency plans for nuclear accidents at that time foresaw a maximum possible radius of 28.5 kilometers. The idea that an accident in another country could affect us in Germany had never come up during planning."[19]

So, when news rolled in about the nuclear disaster, Beck could not help thinking his ideas had touched on something significant:

[in Germany] we were having a wonderful spring that year, the weather was just fantastic. And then through the media spread this news that there was this deadly danger. . . . We were suddenly exposed to a danger that was physically imperceptible and which could only be experienced through mediation, through the media, which meant through the contradictory statements of experts.[20]

The Chernobyl disaster, then, fulfilled Beck's prophecy to the letter: as radiation alarms sounded off in Sweden, Germany, and then elsewhere across the continent, Europe became starkly aware that traditional nation-states could no longer protect territories, societies, and citizens.[21] Existential risks now defied national borders, and thus required global awareness to address them. Instead of rigid, territorially bounded institutions, scholars now assumed a fluidity in which old certainties of nation and nationality were in flux (which, at the same time, contributed to increasing uncertainty and ambivalence[22]). For sociologists like Manuel Castells, Alain Touraine, and John Urry, the concept of society as traditionally presupposed in sociology no longer described contemporary social arrangements, and had to be replaced by new analytic tools: *flow* rather than locality, *mobility* rather than stability, *network* rather than boundaries.[23]

Beck's intervention struck at the conjuncture of accumulating scholarly discontent with existing treatments of nations and nationalities on the one hand, and the public recognition of new global threats on the other. In terms of his career, the timing of the disaster could not have been better. Beck's interviewer, Johannes Willms, later diagnosed that, for the social sciences, Chernobyl "was a great turning point. It was like a flash of lightning that made several things clear at once."[24] *Risk Society* also helped rocket Beck further into international public intellectual status. Beck and his colleagues' writings sparked a movement to radically transform the social sciences to fit a cosmopolitan, post-national vision of society. While the United States had not experienced the same type of existential threat as Chernobyl, it developed its own strand of cosmopolitan sociology in the form of "world polity" research, focusing on the global diffusion of organizational forms and the growing similarity between seemingly independent states.[25] Such reforms involved discarding what Beck called *methodological nationalism*—the fundamental assumption that social phenomena are bound by national contexts. This new wave of scholarship—known as *cosmopolitan sociology*—included a strong normative injunction to discard old ways of thinking and to support a purported new world order—both scientifically and in everyday life.

THE SUCCESS OF COSMOPOLITANISM THOUGHT

Why did cosmopolitan thinking spread so widely among sociologists? Cultural sociologists have shown how ideas that accrue moral salience fulfill several conditions, all of which apply to the drive toward cosmopolitanism in sociology. First, ideas that achieve prominence usually articulate concerns over a common, often inchoate social tension that preoccupies a society, helping make sense of new conditions such as economic downturn or population growth.[26] Indeed, the wave of cosmopolitan theorizing directly addressed the new conditions of boundary-crossing risk that characterized late-twentieth-century Europe and made sense of the shock of Chernobyl and the collapse of the Berlin Wall. It also captured the public interest in the expanding transnational relief projects of the 1980s, which drew media attention to the heroic efforts of humanitarian groups like Médecins Sans Frontières traversing national boundaries under the banner of common humanity.[27] Most importantly, cosmopolitan theorizing helped make sense of the findings of 1980s and 1990s sociologists working in field sites around the world—namely, that local actors increasingly draw on transnational concepts.

Second, ideas that reach moral prominence circulate widely through social, professional, and scientific networks, and accumulate moral significance through attachment to key institutions.[28] Indeed, over the turn of the century, key institutional hubs for sociology and adjacent disciplines like political science became focal points for cosmopolitan research. For example, the London School of Economics' Centre for Global Governance brought together scholars like David Held and Mary Kaldor, key proponents of political cosmopolitanism;[29] and prominent journals like *the British Journal of Sociology* and *Theory & Society* published symposia on related topics.[30] Professional academics in positions of power echoed Beck and Nussbaum, calling for an overhaul of sociology so as to attune social scientific inquiry to transnational flows, hybrid networks of association, and other forms of social-spatial change that defied nation-centric definitions of society.[31]

Third, widely adopted ideas provide specific guidance on how to solve preexisting social problems.[32] Research on cosmopolitanism had specific guidelines for how to transform social research to facilitate the deepening of a global (or cosmopolitan) consciousness. Cosmopolitan scholars worked out specific blueprints for the post-national world: the Italian political theorist Daniele Archibugi, for example, advocated the expansion of democracy into international relations in order to give states equal representation in global politics, and even the establishment of world citizenship, giving citizens of all countries an opportunity to influence local, national, and global politics.[33] Other studies in the same vein examined global interventions in war-ridden areas,[34] the characteristics of transnational political institutions such as the European Union,[35] and other facets of what authors saw as an emerging transnational political entity. In all, these authors combined a negative normative view of the state with a positive view of transnational activism, global justice, and international humanitarian intervention. Empirically, these scholars highlighted how the global interconnectedness between different sub-national locales and between world institutions was crucial in the construction of local needs. A scholarly intervention became a moral imperative to reshape sociology, the social sciences, and global politics according to the cosmopolitan vision.

Thus, by the turn of the century, a wide swath of philosophers, social scientists, journalists, and policy makers became critical of the nation-state idea, and of nationalism in particular, describing them as regressive and belligerent, and treasuring cosmopolitanism as a moral order. While as an academic movement it sought to reshape social scientific thinking, cosmopolitanism was also a political movement with an explicit aim to strengthen international networks and organizations at the expense of national sovereignty, to the point of achieving global democratic transformation. This was certainly evident in the title of Daniele Archibugi and David Held's 1995 coedited book, *Cosmopolitan Democracy: An Agenda for a New World Order.*[36]

A COSMOPOLITAN SOCIOLOGY: THE NATION AS AN IMMORAL CATEGORY

The growth of cosmopolitanism coincided with a new way of defining moral worth that emerged over the late twentieth century.[37] The Network Repertoire attaches worth to networked relations that cross traditional borders and converge arounds areas of joint interest. Thus, the worthiest actors—scientists, executives, artists, or any others—create networks across traditional boundaries, hierarchies, and norms. In academia, these would be the scholars who find new ways to address global processes, who conduct projects in collaboration with international colleagues, and who gather people from different locations and disciplines around a common topic of inquiry. These actors treat effacing boundaries as a moral good by claiming it promotes innovation, global equality, or inclusion in the "global village."[38] Based on the Network Repertoire, scholars identifying as "cosmopolitan" have tended to make two intertwined assumptions about the moral significance of nationalism.

The first assumption was that national boundaries were fast eroding due to globalization providing easier travel means, faster international communication, and greater exposure to different cultures,[39] transforming people's lived experience regardless of whether they themselves subscribed to the philosophical ideas of cosmopolitanism. Writing in *The New Left Review*, the economist Daniele Archibugi noted that "the external threats to the state from the process of globalization and the internal demands for greater autonomy give new force to the old aphorism that the state is too large for small issues, too small for bigger ones."[40] The second assumption was that national boundaries *ought* to disappear (or at the very least, weaken considerably). Since network frameworks emphasize how boundaries constrain the formation of new connections, the idea that many evils of our times were rooted in nationalism seemed second nature. Indeed, cosmopolitans celebrated the decline of nationalism because, as Nussbaum had it, "only this [cosmopolitan] stance asks us to give our first allegiance to what is morally good—and that which, being good, I can commend as such to all human beings."[41]

Thus, as the Network Repertoire rose, so too did claims that sociologists must shift their practices to capture, endorse, and lead a cosmopolitan research strategy in order to grasp and help bring about a new global order.[42] Pointing to "the global economy of signs, of globally circulating information and images . . . transforming the public sphere into an increasingly de-nationalized, visual and emotional public stage," the British sociologist John Urry proposed a "mobile sociology" to address the "many social groupings [that] are appearing, developing partially, imperfectly and contingently, [as] a kind of globalizing civil society."[43] Writing about this intellectual trend, the British sociologist Robert Fine observed that cosmopolitan theorists were like other "radical intellectuals [who] like to think of themselves as living in a critical moment of history and playing a pivotal role in its outcome." For Fine, this emerging generation of sociologists, with their certainty that old structures of class and nation were radically eroding, were making "a contribution to the social sciences that is at once theoretical, empirical and normative."[44]

DIFFICULT IMPLEMENTATIONS OF THE CRITIQUE: CHALLENGES TO COSMOPOLITAN SOCIOLOGY

However, scholars rejecting nations and nationalism began encountering significant challenges in the 1990s, as historical circumstances made the application of the cosmopolitan critique more difficult. Rogers Brubaker captured the distance between the idea that nation-states are (and ought to be) defunct and the existing political realities of that decade. For instance, he noted that while 1992—when the Maastricht Treaty which founded the European Union was signed—signified to many an end to the old nation-state system,

> [T]he first half of the 1990s has seen not the anticipated eclipse but the spectacular revival and rebirth of the nation-state and the national idea in Europe. . . . Not only was "Europhoria" shattered by the unforeseen resistance to the Maastricht treaty, by the currency crisis of 1992–93, and by the ignominious failure of a common European response to the Yugoslav crisis. Not only has immigration sparked a major revival of nationalist rhetoric in most European countries. Not only has German unification . . . engendered concern about a revival of German nationalism. Most important, the spectacular reconfiguration of political space along national lines in Central and Eastern Europe and Eurasia has suggested that far from moving *beyond* the nation-state, history . . . was moving *back to* the nation-state.[45]

More broadly, repeated examples of resurging nationalism led turn-of-the-century historians and sociologists to criticize cosmopolitan scholarship on empirical and conceptual grounds. Craig Calhoun, for example, criticized cosmopolitans for "imagin[ing] the world from the vantage point of frequent travelers, easily entering and exiting polities and social relations around the world, armed with visa-friendly passports and credit cards."[46] Calhoun's book *Nations Matter* pointed to the ways—globalization notwithstanding—that national belonging continues to serve as a key mediator for social activism.[47]

Critics contrasted the experience of global elites with that of most citizens,[48] and pointed to attitude surveys showing the enduring salience of the nation as an identifying category across the world, with Western Europe being only a partial exception in the post-Brexit era.[49] Soon after, the London School of Economics (LSE) Centre for Global Governance was embroiled in scandal surrounding the granting of a PhD to and receiving gifts from the son of the controversial Libyan leader Muammar al-Gaddafi. Facing severe criticism from Human Rights Watch and other groups for endorsing a repressive regime, and with LSE students demanding that funds be returned to the Libyan people, the center claimed it had formed strong links with the Gaddafi regime in the hope of aligning Libyan policy with global human rights norms and thus promoting a cosmopolitan mission.[50] The association between LSE and Gaddafi raised additional skepticism about the aspirations of cosmopolitan intellectuals.[51]

Scholars also pointed to inconsistencies in the depiction of cosmopolitanism and nationhood as opposites. For one, the sharp contrast between cosmopolitanism and nationalism did not hold up to historical scrutiny, as critics pointed to their co-constitution in the context of the expansion of the capitalist world system.[52] Second, scholars noted that contemporary cosmopolitan thinking originated from a particular European vantage point, and they have highlighted its inherent contradictions. In particular, policy makers and intellectuals deployed cosmopolitan ventures in colonial contexts, paying lip service to the ideal of nation-transcending embrace of humanity while at the same participating in an oppressive project.[53] Third, critics noted that Western nations were those entrusted with pushing forward the global transformations that liberal cosmopolitan scholars envisioned onto the non-Western world. As Vivienne Jabri put it,

> We . . . see significant transformative agency attributed to specific societies that are deemed to possess the "moral resources" . . . that drive progress towards a cosmopolitan order, namely societies that exhibit constitutional modes of governance, democratic accountability, and "sophisticated" understandings of dialogical communicative practices. However, given the focus on intervention, the liberal cosmopolitan project is not merely confined to dialogical practices but seeks the juridical transformation of the international order, so that those in possession of the above resources are also accrued the political authority to intervene in the name of cosmopolitan right . . . the overwhelming capacity that defines transformative agency is military and each intervention accrued legitimacy by liberal cosmopolitan authors is one that has involved the use of armed forces, including in the cases of Kosovo, Iraq, Afghanistan, full-scale warfare.[54]

Through such critiques, the initial impetus to deny the nation-state's primacy in organizing social life—politically, economically, culturally—was thus increasingly called into question.

With these shortcomings becoming more apparent, a tension emerged between acknowledging the limitations of viewing societies as nationally bounded, and trying to explain processes in which nations constituted a key force, such as immigration, politics, state-building, and welfare policies. For scholars researching any of these substantive phenomena, decentering nation-states as a salient factor entailed ignoring the obvious, and causally significant, impact ideas of nationhood have had on social processes. These social scientists needed to devise new ways to address nations and nationalism—ways that allowed them to continue research while displaying appropriate awareness of the shifting moral climate.

PARTIAL REFORMS

In response to the tension between the call to discard methodological nationalism on the one hand and the growing critique of cosmopolitan thought on the other, numerous scholars researching nations and nationalism devised new ways to justify their research morally. Their maneuver—which we call partial reform—switched between different logics of justifying research to reframe the study of a morally contentious topic in a positive light. Thus, rather than discard research on nations and nationalism, as Beck would have it, these scholars drew on alternate moral logics to frame research on nations and nationalism as contributing to the common good. Two strands of work exemplify this shift. In the first, scholars drew on a logic that highlighted the moral goods national belonging can supply, and in the second, scholars drew on a logic highlighting the role of science in generating useful knowledge for the social good.

The Anchored Repertoire: Nations as Moral Communities

For one group of sociologists, the way scholars have been delegitimizing nations and nationalisms wholesale not only misrepresented contemporary global geopolitics, but also ignored the moral goods that nations have produced across history and thus dismissed an important public resource. While not denying that certain types of patriotism could lead to violence and xenophobia, scholars urged their peers to continue investigating the ways both nations as categories and nationalism as a cultural framework held the potential to promote moral aims. The sociologist Liah Greenfeld, for example, distinguished between morally suspect nationalisms that privilege ethnic solidarity (and are more attractive to many citizens) and morally laudable nationalisms that ensure individual rights and civic equality.[55] The question shifted from "whether nationalism leads to violence" to "why nationalism leads to violence under certain conditions." Conversely, nationalism has also served as the basis for egalitarian thought, for the notion of human dignity, and for modern economy.

Thus, for Greenfeld, research needs to recognize the benefits collective belonging offers, as she herself outlined in her work. "I was sustained in my determination," Greenfeld wrote, "by the firm conviction in the absolute centrality of nationalism in our experience and the vital importance of its understanding today."[56] Greenfeld's view, that research should highlight the goods national belonging provides, is akin to what we call the *Anchored Repertoire*. This repertoire identifies community ties as constitutive of social experience, with the community defined broadly to include units as small as nuclear families and those as large as entire nations.[57] The Anchored Repertoire sees collective belonging and tradition as the values that define moral worth.[58] Scholarship relevant to nations and nationalism can thus be morally justified because some moral codes are uniquely expressed through the language and practices associated with particular collectivities. For scholars relying on this framing, research on nationalism taps into a source of the moral good for one of two reasons: (a) this research can show how nationalism provides a broad ethical framework legitimizing universal goals, such as promoting global human rights, addressing climate change, or organizing humanitarian interventions; or (b) this research can identify ways to foster group-level moral self-efficacy through collective belonging—i.e., a group's confidence in its capacity to achieve broad moral goals, allowing it to counteract pressures toward transgressive attitudes amongst its members.[59]

When appealing to the logic of the Anchored Repertoire, sociologists demonstrated how national cultural frameworks can empower benevolent projects, and thus defended research on nations and nationalism as identifying ways to promote progressive projects. For Calhoun, for example, the idea of the nation "represented the 'people' of a country as an internally unified group with common interests and the capacity to act." This way, "the idea of nation not only laid claim to history or common identity. It purported to describe (or construct) a collective actor."[60] Thus, nationalism empowered polities to recognize themselves as political actors and to make demands of the government whose role is to represent them. The rise of nationalism across Europe throughout the nineteenth century allowed progressive social movements to form and to advocate for causes like workers' rights and public welfare.[61] In a different way, sociologists working on humanitarian interventions showed how forms of nationalism served as justification for international relief projects. As Dromi showed, both relief workers and national leaders have taken intense pride in providing humanitarian relief to non-nationals and have inferred a sense of national moral superiority from helping others.[62] Thus, research on nationalism was justified as identifying means for organizing collectively for the common good, both within and beyond national boundaries.[63]

When appealing to the Anchored Repertoire, sociologists acknowledge that some contemporary forms of nationalism are regressive, but refuse to let these ugly instances define a broader phenomenon that has also been central in the thinking and practice of progressive activists and organizations. One example of this kind of thinking about nationalism is Philip Gorski's work on American exceptionalism and American civil religion. Conservative interpretations of American exceptionalism had envisioned the United States as an inherently religious, democratic, and capitalist nation whose foreign relations—whether diplomatic, business, or military—act as a force of good in the world, sharing the country's gifts with the rest of humanity. But Gorski and McMillan highlight another interpretation of American exceptionalism, evidenced by Barack Obama's political outlook: a view of the United States as a nation that reflects upon its sins and works to self-improve through increasing solidarity, striving for equality, and enhancing inclusivity. In this view, America undertakes these commitments to serve as a role model for other countries.[64] The question scholars should pursue, then, is not whether the "nation" is disappearing, as proponents of cosmopolitanism would have it. Rather, the question is how the *right form* of national ethical frameworks can be cultivated today, for the betterment of tomorrow.

These developments were not confined to sociology alone; rather, they fed back into the same philosophical conversations that had endorsed cosmopolitanism decades earlier. Martha Nussbaum herself struggled to maintain her stance that nations were dispensable. Responding to criticisms from Charles Taylor that her dichotomy between patriotism and nationalism was too rigid,[65] Nussbaum conceded that "currently, and for the foreseeable future, nations are critical for the promotion of people's well-being and life opportunities."[66] Thus, rather than decry nationalism, Nussbaum now argued that patriotism holds the potential for thinking beyond the limits of one's immediate environment and has the potential to foster cosmopolitanism by aiding in the development of global sensitivities. For example, in a book reflecting on the tradition of "separation of church and state" instituted by Rhode Island's founder, Roger Williams, Nussbaum maintained that recovering America's national traditions could serve universal ends because

> America has always been unusual among the nations of the world. . . . We do not think that we are fundamentally people of a given race, or soil, or religion. We are held together by ethical commitments (to equal respect and the value of liberty) that transcend particular groups. New immigrants can join us without changing religion or ethnicity, coming to revere those values. Such "cosmopolitan" ideas came to be seen as the mark of the enlightened person.[67]

As the years wore on, Nussbaum even protested her own labeling as a "cosmopolitan" philosopher.[68]

The sociologists Daniel Hirschman and Isaac Reed differentiate between two types of explanations in sociology. One focuses on how things in the social world are formed historically, and the other focuses on the changing force competing social effects exhibit.[69] From this view, Nussbaum's initial formation story about nationalism—describing it as a retrogressive movement associated with naïve patriotism—consistently strained against accumulating evidence suggesting that nationalist movements also promote positive humanistic goals (for example, as the basis of distinct civil rights). This was particularly so as Nussbaum's philosophy moved from abstract questions about the nature of the social good toward policy-oriented writing.[70] A quarter of a century on, Nussbaum admitted that "the nation is a unit of both practical and normative importance" in a collection of essays titled *The Cosmopolitan Tradition: A Noble but Flawed Ideal.*[71]

Scholars working on the positive, generative sides of nations and nationalism do not, by and large, deny that nationalism can generate xenophobia. However, they push back against the notion that research on nationalism perpetuates harmful assumptions. By linking nationalism to the Anchored Repertoire—emphasizing tradition, locality, and kinship relations as constitutive moral values—these scholars push back against the allegations that nationalism in itself is pernicious and that the study of nations and nationalism is morally suspect.

The Efficiency Repertoire: Nations and Nationalism as a Social Scientific Problem

A second example of partial reform draws on the *Efficiency Repertoire*, which values scientific expertise and validity as moral goods.[72] In this repertoire, good social science is value-neutral science that produces the most accurate findings for addressing social concerns. Social science can, as Weber believed, better inform the public's value-based decisions, but it cannot make value determinations and should restrict itself to providing the most accurate findings on social reality.[73] In the study of nations and nationalism, scholars used this logic as they retooled existing sociological measures in their research area. While agreeing that the nation-state remains a salient social category, and accepting that a normative controversy exists about it, these scholars emphasized that the social sciences needed to develop new knowledge about nations and nationalism. In what follows, we show how a drive to operationalize questions of nations and nationalism allowed scholars to circumvent normative questions about methodological nationalism altogether.

One use of the Efficiency Repertoire came from scholars who turned attention from *whether* nationalism was a positive or negative phenomenon to *what* nationalism was. For Rogers Brubaker, the study of nationalisms should focus on the discursive, phenomenological side of nationalism that exists in already existing nation-states—the "heterogeneous set of 'nation'-oriented idioms, practices, and possibilities that are continuously available or 'endemic' in modern cultural and political life."[74] In this view, scholars have thus far focused attention on the nationalisms characteristic of nineteenth-century state-building, associated with projects like the unifications of Germany and Italy. This meant that more "banal" forms of nationalism remained misunderstood.[75] Crucially, from the perspective of academic production, neglecting everyday nationalism left sociologists ill equipped as working scholars to understand the challenges late-twentieth-century Europe was facing.[76]

By calling on sociologists to see nationalism as a common and pervasive discourse, Brubaker pushed to expand the sociology of national phenomena beyond state-building projects. However, shifting focus away from the nation-state did not require scholars to denounce the state or to embrace cosmopolitanism. Rather than collecting evidence of the inconsistency of nationalist claims and thus proving their ultimate demise, Brubaker advocated changing the operationalization of nationalism to *avoid* the morally loaded question of whether nationalism is disappearing in the face of a new cosmopolitan world order:

> Nationalism is not a "force" to be measured as resurgent or receding. . . . "Nation" is so central, and protean, a category of modern political and cultural thought, discourse, and practice that it is hard indeed to imagine a world without nationalism. But precisely because nationalism is so protean and polymorphous, it makes little sense to ask how strong nationalism is, or whether it is receding or advancing.[77]

Brubaker maintained that discursive formulation allowed him to capture the experience of the minorities that emerged from the redrawing of political borders throughout the twentieth century across Europe: Hungarians left outside of the contracted post–World War I Hungary, Muslim former Ottoman citizens cut off from the new Republic of Turkey after the Balkans were redivided, ethnic Germans separated from post–World War II Germany by its new borders, and other such populations. Such groups have understood themselves as inextricably linked to a nation without being its legal subjects or residing within its borders. For Brubaker, this justified increased attention to the ways agents construct a sense of national belonging.

Brubaker posited that sociologists reframing nationalism this way would be better able to point to emerging geopolitical dangers. Eerily foreseeing the Ukraine crises of 2014 and 2022, Brubaker highlighted the similarities between Weimar Germany and post-Soviet Russia in the presence of millions of ethnic Germans and Russians in neighboring states, who look toward their perceived homeland to provide solutions for their social and political problems in their new state. "In the long run," claimed Brubaker, "the political disposition of Russians and Russophone minorities in the [post-Soviet] successor states" will be significantly shaped by "the degrees and forms of integration with Russia (and of detachment from successor state contexts) that they generate."[78] As a moral strategy, Brubaker's reframing allowed him (and others) to take a step back from the debates over the inherent moral worth of nationalism per se, and to think about the study of nationalism as plagued by problems in operationalization, parochial bias, and case selection. If cosmopolitans demanded the end of "methodological nationalism," then Brubaker tried to prove that nationalism simply needed a new methodology.

Nor was Brubaker's claim about the research possibilities all hot air. Building on Brubaker's definition, Bonikowski and DiMaggio recast the study of American nationalism as a question of the distribution of different nationalist discourses.[79] Bonikowski and DiMaggio claimed such distributional analyses could reveal the crucial role sociology had to play in making sense of American nationalism, in particular changes in its popular, seemingly mundane forms. Indeed, rather than seeking findings about whether American nationalism is receding or intensifying (and thereby bringing the question of US nationalism into conversation with scholarship on cosmopolitanism and its limitations), Bonikowski and DiMaggio's research demonstrated the mechanism sustaining several different types of US nationalisms. To justify this approach, the authors claimed that such analysis will be of utility to nonacademics:

Understanding how Americans conceive of their nation may provide hints as to the limits political leaders face when they prosecute foreign wars or seek international cooperation, as well as offer insight into public responses to terrorist attacks and into cultural motivations that influence voters' political choices.[80]

Thus, where authors like Gorski and Calhoun had claimed that, despite its historical transmutations, nationalism can have a positive, generative effect on populations' moral imaginaries, Brubaker's redefinition of nationalism allowed scholars to refocus the study of nationalism on the question of how useful the insights were in predicting political behavior.

Scholars have used the Efficiency Repertoire in other ways to advance our understanding of nationalism while avoiding accusations of upholding regressive "methodological nationalist" views. For example, Wimmer and Min sought to isolate the causes of war by examining changes across a fixed geographical grid over 200 years, regardless of eventual political independence or nationalist politics. Selecting territories based on their national independence alone, these scholars found, would have "greatly reinforce[d] the methodological nationalism that plagues so much of the social sciences . . . the tendency . . . to conceive of the social world as an assemblage of nation-state societies without asking how this came about and what the consequences of this particular form of political organization might be."[81] In a different way, recent advances in field analysis rescaled the *field* concept to account for transnational dynamics, in the context of the colonial state and empire[82] and inter-imperial differences,[83] without engaging questions of cosmopolitanism and its contemporary implications head-on or challenging the enduring salience of the nation-state as a sociopolitical category. Like Brubaker's redefinition of nationalism, such methodological and theoretical innovations allowed scholars to circumvent the criticism of methodological nationalism without forcing them to agree or disagree with its normative implications for contemporary world society.

NONMORAL ACADEMIC CHANGE THROUGH PROFESSIONAL TURF WARS

Of course, not *all* objections to the writings of Ulrich Beck and his followers were rooted in morality. Some revolved around what Andrew Abbott called academic "turf wars," where scholars engage in a "remapping of alien turf into one's own terminology"[84]—in other words, taking over another discipline's subject matter in the hopes of accruing prestige, power, and other professional rewards. Much of the debate between the 1990s cosmopolitans and earlier scholars of globalization took this form and invoked classic methodological-cum-organizational antagonisms without delving into moral arguments.

A prominent example was the controversy between "world city" scholars and cosmopolitan sociologists. Well before the rise of cosmopolitan sociology—as early as 1982—sociologists like Saskia Sassen were calling attention to the global changes afoot in cities across the world, underlining how local governance was a powerful part of an interconnected financial "world system" that traversed national boundaries.[85] The close association between Sassen's approach and "cosmopolitan" thinking is not surprising—Sassen too emphasized the decline of the nation-state by showing how city governance structures were strengthening because of the nation's weakening. However, for Sassen and her collaborators, the rapid rise of 1990s cosmopolitan approaches outside the field of globalization studies could also miss the city as a center of social criticism. Cosmopolitans resisted thinking about "container" visions of the social order, but what was the city but a kind of social container? As a result of the relative proximity of research topics, theorists of the global city had to be explicit about how their work was similar but not subservient to the dictates of the new cosmopolitanism.

Sassen urged that changes at the city level were *like* those documented by cosmopolitan theorists, but that scholarly work on the "world city" had long predated the cosmopolitan wave of scholarship, and in turn scholars needed to retain both distinct perspectives because

> these "domestic" settings are transformed into microenvironments located on global circuits. *They do not have to become cosmopolitan in the process*; they may well remain domestic and particularistic in their orientation and remain engaged with their households and local community struggles. And yet they are participating in emergent global politics.[86]

The point for Sassen was that the rise of the "global city" represented a change in the shape of the nation—a denationalization that produced more powerful effects within the city. However, Sassen conceived of this denationalization process as working through more localized mechanisms than those Beck and others had theorized. In this, Sassen insisted that her ongoing research at the intersection of city governance and global economic finance was valuable because it provided "another set of reasons for supporting the critique of methodological nationalism."[87] Sassen was not alone in arguing that her existing research was a similar but distinct way to understand the concerns cosmopolitan thinkers raised, and was joined by Ronald Robertson,[88] Andreas Wimmer,[89] and others. For them, there was an explicit (and nonmoral) professional value in retaining existing research projects without subsuming them under the notion of cosmopolitanism.

CONCLUSION: TRUMPISM REVISITED

If you checked in on the cultural scene just a few months before Trump's election, in spring 2016, you would likely have thought that cosmopolitan prophets had been right: nationalism seemed nearly dead. At that moment, on both sides of the Atlantic, the threats of resurgent nationalism seemed almost laughable. Yet, as spring turned to summer, the mood started to change. A surprise victory for British exit from the EU (a "Brexit"), and the increasing strength of Donald Trump, alarmed critics. However wounded, cosmopolitan elites did not let the events in the European scene dissuade them. Despite warnings that Clinton's lead was small enough to just be "a normal polling error,"[90] major news outlets like the *New York Times* pointed to Clinton's lead in early voting and to the demographic growth of Latinx voters as sure signs that Trump's nationalist message would be repudiated.[91] Of course, Trump's message was not defeated that fateful November day, and with that shock, sociologists also took notice.

With Trump's unexpected election, the intellectual climate finally turned: now it was cosmopolitanism, rather than nationalism, that seemed passé. Certainly, the reality of nationalism had been apparent to scholars on the ground; but suddenly, their defense of nationalism as a research object seemed substantially more important. Scrambling to make sense of the moment, editors published lists of books from academics and nonacademics to help the public grapple with Trumpism.[92] Arlie Hochschild's *Strangers in Their Own Land*, J. D. Vance's *Hillbilly Elegy*, and Nancy Isenberg's *White Trash* all started hurrying up the best seller lists. Scholars of nationalism, who earlier had seemed concerned with a dying parochial culture, were suddenly vindicated. The sociologist Philip Gorski found himself discussing religious nationalism on television talk shows.[93] Hochschild, Vance, and Isenberg were also making the rounds. Even the domain of cultural fiction seemed to have turned the cosmopolitan corner in the wake of Trump's ascent. By the time of our writing, the story of Chernobyl—that central moment in the narrative of cosmopolitan awakening—had been turned around into a depressing HBO miniseries documenting the role of Soviet leadership in hiding the disaster from the public view. Rather than a "globalized risk" that demanded a new cosmopolitan outlook, in this reading the event demonstrated how dysfunctional nationalist cliques would doom us all.

While this new work on the resurgence of nationalism ran counter to cosmopolitan thinking, the dynamics behind the profound public resonance of Hochschild's *Strangers in Their Own Land* and Beck's *Risk Society* are parallel. Hochschild began her research in rural Louisiana years before a changing of the guard in the White House was conceivable. However, upon publication, her work touched the center of a cultural tectonic shift. "I have lived most of my life in the progressive camp," she writes in her preface, "but in recent years I began to want to better understand those on the right. How did they come to hold their views? Could we make common cause on some issues?"[94] As the Tea Party was gaining popularity in the rural South, Hochschild embarked on an ethnographic study to understand why right-wing voters appeared to be voting against their own interest. When Trump was elected, her study of American nationalism became one of the timeliest books in the stores. As publisher The New Press put it, "When Donald Trump won the 2016 presidential election, a bewildered nation turned to *Strangers in Their Own Land* to understand what Trump voters were thinking when they cast their ballots."[95] Like *Risk Society*, Hochschild's book addressed a key historical conjuncture—in this case, between the cresting rural resentment of the Democrats' politics and American progressives' (now shattered) self-assuredness—and helped guide readers in making sense of them.

Moreover, like Beck's work, *Strangers in Their Own Land* takes a normative epistemological stance. The book brought into public debate a question about how American liberals ought to engage morally with conservative citizens, as a review in *Newsday* put it: "Why do these smart and compassionate people—and many of the people Hochschild interviews are clearly both—support Trump? If that's a question you've asked, Hochschild's book is the perfect place to start."[96] Lauded for its author's sympathetic eye and nearly prophetic foresight, Hochschild's book skyrocketed up the best seller lists, and some sociologists called her work "[a] model of public sociology . . . beautifully written."[97] Indeed, rather than performing an "epistemological break" with the commonsense assumptions of her interviewee (a maneuver Pierre Bourdieu advocated as key to social scientific understanding[98]), Hochschild utilizes the Anchored Repertoire to tell the story through the lens of conservative Americans and gives voice to their observations about the demographic, economic, and social change underway in the country. According to their story, the liberal establishment has invited immigrants, people of color, and the urban poor to cut in line toward the American Dream, while the rural white working class has been left behind despite having worked earnestly toward the same goal. Rather than focusing on the flaws in conservative Americans' story of American change, Hochschild claimed that the story shapes the political preferences of rural whites and sways them toward the conservative side that objectively hurts their economic interests and gives their employers—often large manufacturers—a free hand to employ them in appalling conditions.[99]

Hochschild's move was not without its detractors, though. In a review titled "Who Cares What They Think? Going about the Right the Wrong Way," the sociologist Harel Shapira compares Hochschild's approach to asking someone who shot a person to death to tell us how we should understand what they did. And, based on the story offered (e.g., "I thought they were going to break into my house!"), we should absolve them of their responsibility for the murder they committed. Relying merely on empathy, Shapira warned, impedes our understanding of our research subjects because it obscures the structural reasons why they feel the way they feel. But more importantly, this epistemological position leaves the sociologist ill equipped to criticize the social ills they analyze, or, to take Shapira's example, to call murder by its name.[100] The sociologist Rory McVeigh similarly criticized Hochschild's choice to study extreme conservatives on their own terms as they grapple with their personal and community problems. For McVeigh, a full picture would need to also examine conservatives at their most xenophobic and violent moments as they engage with out-group members.[101] Here again, a question of sociological methods became a question of how morally to conduct research on nationalists. By not challenging her interviewees' view of the situation, Hochschild was making a methodological claim (that sociologists need to employ empathy to understand politically distant communities) and a normative claim (that employing this method would help sociologists in a broader mission of healing American divides).

———

Few scholars today still debate whether cosmopolitanism is indeed taking hold or whether the nation-state system is persisting. Fewer still advocate for sociologists to remake the field entirely in the name of either (as Ulrich Beck and his contemporaries did). Nevertheless, the impact of these normative historical debates on the discipline has been profound. Reformed research trajectories have emerged in response to the moral demands of the cosmopolitan movement in sociology. As this chapter has shown, sociologists' struggles with whether nations and nationalism should be studied, how their study should be framed, and how controversy about them can be addressed or evaded have shaped research directions on numerous topics, including migration, politics, cities, and populism.

Beyond the study of nations and nationalism, the ways scholars engage with moral contention are intertwined with their scholarly creativity. While not all research controversies are vested with moral meanings, morality is a key factor motivating and directing academic conversations. As a result, the maneuvers scholars devise in order to circumvent moral controversy—while rarely discussed—are generative in themselves and operate as a shadow history of the discipline.

CHAPTER FOUR

Chartered Trips

*Remapping Controversy and the Renewal
of Research on the Family*

Many scholarly conversations seem to reach a dead end. Perhaps a debate between two opposing factions comes to a deadlock, with each side digging in its heels and hindering any further research progress. Or perhaps scholars discover that their existing theories cannot explain a fundamental empirical problem in their field. Either way, a scientific field facing a dead end risks stagnation and the loss of academic relevance. However, the philosopher of science Thomas Kuhn famously argued that scientific crises are also the most generative points for scientific progress. For Kuhn, scholarly crises provoke scientists to conduct "extraordinary research"[1]— research that challenges existing conventions about scientific inquiry in their fields—in search of a new way forward. While a crisis may resolve using preexisting scientific theories applied in a new way, it may also lead to paradigm shift: a fundamental change in scientific approach to a research area, transforming research assumptions, methods, and aims.[2]

While Kuhn focused on crises emerging from scientists' struggle to explain puzzling empirical phenomena, crises also occur when scholars disagree over the *moral* justification for their research. Indeed, in this chapter, we focus on one strategy scholars employ to continue research in the face of seemingly irresolvable moral struggles in their field. We call this maneuver *reconstitution*. Reconstitution is a way for a scholar to redirect controversy: scholars move from a controversial terrain to a noncontroversial one by framing a field's research trajectory in a way that does not bear on the stakes of the original dispute. Rather than delving into the original dispute and facing potential criticism from the warring parties, such scholars argue for the value of research on alternative grounds. As Boltanski and Chiapello put it, "Faced with new arrangements whose emergence was not anticipated . . . critique finds itself disarmed for a time."[3] In taking this route, scholars devise a way to continue research in a controversial terrain without getting stuck in existing disputes.

Sidestepping moral conflict may sound like taking the easy way out of the debate. But if we have demonstrated anything so far, it is that efforts to avoid moral denouncement can be as productive as active debate about moral conduct. Chapter 2 centered on how sociologists debate whether lines of research contravene commonly held ethical standards and dehumanize entire populations, and highlighted how those debates shape what research emerges in response. Chapter 3 showed how sociologists respond to criticism of their research field by negotiating the social meanings of their work and reframing it as a morally justifiable compromise between two positions. These chapters have shown that sociologists employ conflicting logics of moral reasoning as they wage debates, often utilizing claims about the situation of debate or the possible reconciliation of differing moral perspectives to overcome existing moral prohibitions on research. However, what happens when two moral perspectives seem deadlocked in debate? How do scholars move forward? How do they reframe the context of debate so as not to collapse into infighting?

The background to a reconstitution effort is a fierce scholarly debate between two or more factions, with each faction mobilizing competing moral repertoires justifying their respective positions and criticizing others. As the debate escalates, new scholars entering the field are required to engage in the controversy: they must either take a side, or reform their practices by acknowledging the ongoing conflict. But then a new line of research emerges: a scholar takes a step back from the debate itself and makes an argument that reframes the discussion in a new way. This reframing highlights a third value which can help transcend the conflict. For instance:

- A debate over whether religious participation is declining can be reframed as a means to demonstrate the value of a different methodological approach, and can fuel a new discussion about how best to investigate religious experience.
- A dispute over whether workplace discrimination is primarily race- or class-motivated can be used as justification for new workplace ethnographies that amplify the voices of non-white, lower SES employees without addressing the question of race vs. class.
- A controversy over whether sociologists should examine the experience of white nationalists may be used as a jumping-off point for research on how narratives are mobilized in political discourse.

In all such cases, rather than embroiling oneself in an existing controversy by taking a side, scholars highlight an alternative value that allows them to reformulate the criticisms involved in the original debate to direct it toward new ends. In doing so, scholars open the way for newcomers to the field to conduct research that is not subject to the now outworn debates that preceded them.

To understand reconstitution, we focus on two controversies in the research on gender, fertility, and work. In the first case, scholars became deadlocked over claims about whether intended fertility statements ("I plan to have X children over the course of my lifetime") are a useful predictor of actual (or "achieved") fertility. Critiquing this debate for defining accurate prediction as the measure of high-quality scientific research, a third group of scholars argued that stated fertility intentions should be understood as a way to capture variations in cultural expectations about fertility. In the second case, scholars reached a stalemate about research on the effects of breastfeeding, with one side pointing to evidence that it was beneficial for the health of children and people who get pregnant, and the other side arguing that promoting breastfeeding was a neoliberal stopgap to address health care inequalities. Soon, a third group of scholars emerged who worked to transcend this debate by emphasizing that breastfeeding was one of a long list of time-intensive practices foisted upon parents in the name of children's well-being and to their detriment in the workplace. Rather than delving into the debate over the comparative health benefits of breastfeeding and its effects on structural inequalities, here scholars reconfigured the topic so as to advance questions of gender equality without immersing themselves in the preexisting debate. In both examples, rather than taking a side or appeal to a middle position in a heated debate about what qualifies as good research, scholars found ways to redirect thinking toward a third conception of the moral goods research can promote.

Recent studies of scientific creativity and progress have noted that scholars advance their fields by combining existing pieces of research in new ways, for example by bridging fields that are not normally in dialogue.[4] While the scholarship on sociological knowledge production has focused on the pragmatic demands of academic sense making[5] and social policy making[6] as drivers of academic research, this chapter shows that such domain-crossing in sociology often entails addressing the moral dilemmas that arise from ongoing academic debate. In this, we suggest that the drive to give academia a moral justification for its activities is a salient motivator for field transformations. Put differently, retracing the steps in sociological reconstitution efforts allows us to rethink how moral justification shapes the social sciences by opening new avenues of debate that expands sociology's list of morally worthy research topics.

The use of binary terms to define gender is increasingly challenged in the literature on gender and sexuality.[7] However, the demographic literature we analyze here describes sex in binary terms, for example by referring to *mothers'* fertility or wages. While terms like "people who can give birth" and "people who can breastfeed" may capture the population demographers study more accurately (especially since demographers typically drop infertile people from datasets on fertility expectations), we remain within demographers' binary terminology for two reasons. First, as in previous chapters, we analyze researchers' explicit discourse and thus rely on their direct quotation. Second, in some cases changing terminology would run counter to researchers' stated aims—namely, highlighting the effects of unequal social arrangements on women specifically. Thus, our use of binary terminology in this chapter is intended to render our analysis continuous with *how the actors in question* were talking about their research subjects.

FERTILITY INTENTIONS: FROM COMPARING INTENTIONS AND OUTCOMES TO INVESTIGATING HOW INTENTIONS ARE FORMED

The Scripps Institute of Population Problems, founded in 1922, was born out of the competing concerns of Ellen Browning ("EB") Scripps and her brother Edward Wyllis ("EW") Scripps. EB, an activist for women's rights, was deeply concerned with women's control over reproduction, likely including concerns about women's access to birth control.[8] EW, having read about the demographic transition (the reduction in childbirth through modernization) and global overpopulation, became interested in the ways science could accurately predict future population rates.[9] Thanks to the largesse of the Scripps family, the Scripps Institute demographers would come to pioneer demographic research on reproduction.[10] Both EB and EW died before their philanthropic endeavors could produce results, and neither oversaw the demographic projects that shot the Scripps Institute to fame. However, the Institute funded a project that would have made a feminist like EB proud: the 1941 Social and Psychological Factors Affecting Fertility Study (also called "the Indianapolis Study"), which included a battery of questions relating to fertility intentions, degree of child wantedness, and the use of contraception.[11] This study focused on a matter of grave concern to birth control advocates, which entailed questions of a woman's independence and access to birth control: can women's statements of how many children they *plan* to have predict the number of children they will *actually* have throughout their lifetime? Particularly in the wake of the Great Depression's immense impact on demographic outcomes, the projections these studies produced were initially lauded in both academic and public outlets as a massive scientific advance.[12]

Where women's rights activists like EB Scripps saw the gap between stated fertility intentions and lifetime achieved fertility as evidence of women's lack of control over their reproduction, many demographers saw it as a pernicious form of measurement error.[13] Indeed, since the Scripps Institute researchers justified adopting fertility intention measures as a way to advance scientific prediction, they viewed the gap between fertility intentions and outcomes as an anomaly that scientists must resolve, and not as a site for social debate. Indeed, rather than address the questions EB Scripps would have posed (namely, how can this gap inform gender equality activism), many demographers instead focused on measures of fertility intentions and outcomes as means of ensuring national population control and preventing overpopulation globally, which must be perfected scientifically.[14]

Throughout the second half of the twentieth century, demographers fundamentally disagreed about how their field ought to treat the gap between fertility intentions and outcomes. Is the existence of the gap a scientific question, framed by the *Efficiency Repertoire*? or does it indicate a social problem, framed by the *Civic Repertoire*? But as this dispute became increasingly complicated by studies suggesting that both sides were incorrect,[15] a third group of scholars insisted that the very problem that had defined fertility intentions as an unworthy measure (their lack of predictive power) could be reconstituted as the basis for a new form of worthy research. Mobilizing the *Anchored Repertoire*, this group reimagined the analysis of unmet expectations as evidence of the gendered sources of reproductive (and thus social) inequality. Rather than focusing on the gap between intentions and outcomes as evidence of either a scientific failure or a social problem, demographers now saw this gap as evidence of the patterns in women's agency in different contexts. Quickly growing into a robust research stream, this work rearranged the scholarship around the analysis of fertility intentions. Now, scholars could still engage in the general question of the significance of fertility intentions while avoiding the old debate over the meaning of the gap between intentions and outcomes.

Rather than as one of simple empirical disagreement and its resolution, we see this historical trajectory as an ongoing struggle between demographers about what the ultimate measure of worth for their research should be: Is it solely scientific accuracy? Is it, conversely, developing large-scale policy interventions? Or is it understanding the lived experience of the populations demographic research represents? Indeed, after years of debating the significance of the gap between fertility intentions and outcomes, scholars were now thinking about this gap as a way to open up discussions about how personal and historical events shape and inform birth decisions.

The Debate: The Gap Between Fertility Intentions and Outcomes, Between a Scientific Problem and a Social Problem

THE GAP BETWEEN FERTILITY INTENTIONS AND

OUTCOMES AS A PROBLEM OF MEASUREMENT

Members of the Scripps Institute began developing their survey for the Indianapolis Study in 1938 after acquiring additional funding from the Carnegie Corporation. As one of the leading designers of the study later recalled, "from the outset the Committee [behind the study] realized that its problem lay in a new field in which the instruments of research themselves would have to be evolved."[16] Recognizing that "little exact information was available regarding the extent or effectiveness of contraceptive practices among married couples in the United States as a whole," researchers saw the study as a way to update, improve, and refine demographic science.[17] For this reason, they took particular interest in questions pertaining to contraception use, incomplete fertility, and family size preferences. Nevertheless, the sample was confined to Protestant white women because restricting the expensive interviews to "a group sufficiently homogenous that in the final analyses" would relieve the researchers of the need to "subdivide the couples by such factors as color, nativity, religion, type of community of residence since marriage, duration of marriage, and age," and would thus allow them to produce valid results more easily.[18] In this sense, the Institute did not at first seek universal replicability across the population; rather, it was interested in means of establishing the utility of measures through rigorous statistical analysis.[19] Indeed, wherever possible, increases in and consistency of response rates were prized over sample generalizability. When pilot studies showed high rates of refusal, the sampling method was redesigned from marriage registries to (the more limited format of) door-to-door interviews. The study upped what it paid respondents to $1 because "paper money—instead of change—might lower the refusal rate somewhat."[20]

Researchers in the 1950s turned this project into one of statistical analysis, valuing the method for its clarity, efficiency, and lack of bias. When Borgatta and Westoff used the then novel techniques of regression and factor analysis to analyze the data, they did so because "one of the characteristic features of the progress of the Indianapolis Study has been the practice of self-examination and self-criticism that its contributors have adopted. Criticisms have revolved around such matters as the lack of theoretical organization of hypotheses, the ex-post facto nature of the Study design, the restrictive homogeneity of the sample, the failure of the study to indicate the 'baby boom' of the 1940's, etc."[21] Rigorous statistical analysis was merely one dimension of a larger project of modernizing demographic data collection and analysis.

While during the first decade of research scholars had noted durable patterns by socioeconomic standing, the introduction of statistical techniques for parsing data allowed scholars to suggest that fertility intentions were a particularly crucial measure for further investigation. Westoff and Kiser focused on cross-correlation analysis and concluded that size of planned family was the strongest predictor of total fertility over the lifetime and that it operated "largely independent of SES."[22] In a follow-up study, Borgatta and Westoff used factor analysis to address the role of fertility intentions, and concluded that the predictive power of fertility preferences was understood as proof of a "successful-rational-modern family," where achieved control of birth (i.e., having as many children as desired) could be shown. Again, in keeping with the scientific orientation of the project, Borgatta and Westoff avoided the political implications of this finding, and instead underlined its significance as part of an ongoing set of experiments to improve demographic science.[23] Rather than point to changes in contraception, women's rights, or the household division of labor as trends worthy of wider attention in the literature, Borgatta and Westoff linked contraceptive control to a cultural shift around marriage and mating ("the small family type emerging in an urban, mobility oriented culture which stressed modern, rational companionate marriage"). The core of the project, for Borgatta and Westoff, was increasing attention to culture in demographic analysis in order to make more accurate predictions, rather than to analyze gender relations.

The Scripps Institute avoidance of the political implications of its own research in the name of scientific objectivity shaped demographic conversations in the years that followed. In a critical 1973 editorial in *Demography*, the demographer Norman Ryder—responding to the growing popularity of fertility intention measures in policy planning—outlined the core principles of quality survey design, and concluded with the "overall charge . . . that our studies [of fertility intentions] have been flawed with respect to every one of these [methodological] components."[24] In this, Ryder proposed "to cast a jaundiced eye on each [methodological choice] in turn." Ryder went as far as to berate his colleagues for not being critical enough of their peers' methodological shortcomings: "Perhaps that is because we of the demographic profession are closely knit, like a kind of extended family, and tend to be gentle in our comments about each other's work, at least in print. . . . Whatever the reason, we have been let off lightly so far."[25] This call for self-critique resurfaced in 1975, when the US Census Bureau projections of population growth began taking fertility intentions data into consideration.[26] Ryder (now joined by the leading Scripps researcher Charles Westoff) penned an editorial warning once again that they believed the measures the Bureau adopted were flawed and that they should not be used for policy decisions.[27]

Reducing bias in fertility intentions data remained an enduring concern among demographers over the following decades. Some scholars drew on psychological studies to help refine fertility intentions data collection,[28] whereas others retained the measures while acknowledging their imperfection (admitting that "nothing seems to work any better"[29]). But across the board, this dominant faction of demographers identified the fertility intentions gap as a *measurement* problem, rather than as representing an actionable social problem among the surveyed populations.

THE GAP BETWEEN FERTILITY INTENTIONS
AND OUTCOMES AS A SOCIAL PROBLEM

The Scrippses and Carnegies were not the only backers of the new science of demography. In 1948, one of the Rockefeller family's research teams returned from the Chungking region of China with evidence of immense demand for modern forms of contraception, particularly among mothers with already "large" families (defined by locals as over four children). As the economist and demographer Paul Demeny recounted, the Rockefellers centered their philanthropy around this finding, contributing to a widespread view that modern contraception technology could and should be distributed to prevent overpopulation. The idea blossomed into an entire advocacy field centered on population control.[30] While demographers in the 1950s worked to develop a hard "scientific" demography, in the late 1970s they found themselves sharing space with policy-oriented and civic-minded demographers who viewed the gap between fertility intentions and outcomes as signifying an unmet need for contraception.

At the center of this transformation was a new public policy viewpoint that saw population control as the key to unlocking successful social development. By the mid-1960s this demographic policy industry had made massive political inroads. In 1965, US President Lyndon Johnson addressed the United Nations and referred to such demographic research to suggest that "less than five dollars invested in population control is worth a hundred dollars invested in economic growth."[31] Within a few years, both the UN and the World Bank would start funding population research. And certainly, researchers noticed. In 1968, the journal *Demography* ran a special issue on "Progress and Problems of Fertility Control around the World," featuring on the cover a red triangle—an iconic symbol of reproductive rights—and the slogan "Two or Three Children—That's Enough!"[32] If the Scripps demographers in the 1950s had framed the gap between fertility intentions and outcomes as a measurement problem, a new generation of demographers starting in the mid-1970s viewed it as a means to discuss birth control as social policy.

One way to revitalize these measures was to accept them as imperfect tools for estimating contraception demand. Rather than trying to reduce the gap between intentions and outcomes by using improved tools of measurement, as the Scripps demographers had done, the gap between intentions and outcomes was now broken up into two parts. One was composed of variations in how people acted upon their intentions, and the other was composed of variation in whether and how societies provided modern contraception. Moreover, these researchers insisted that variations in contraceptive use—and particularly instances in which contraceptive devices failed—meant that there will always be mothers with more children than originally intended.[33] However, since maternal mortality rates were high in developing regions that lacked contraception, demographers maintained that advocacy remained a vital lifesaving measure. In stark opposition to previous generations of demographers who insisted on scientific accuracy and resisted policy interpretations of fertility intentions, this new wave of demographers was willing to admit that their measure produced biased accounts of contraception demand, but that this skewed measure should still carry weight in policy circles.[34]

Unsurprisingly, many of the same scholars of fertility intentions associated with the Scripps Institute reframed their work in the late 1970s to address demography's broader concerns with contraception policy. Notably, this approach was promoted by Charles Westoff, who refashioned his earlier analysis of fertility intentions as a means of measuring "unmet need for contraception."[35] In this influential research, Westoff used the gap between reported fertility intentions and outcomes as a proxy for contraception demand. Limiting his definition to "only to women who intend no more births and are not using contraception," Westoff used data from Asian countries to demonstrate "an almost perfect rank-order negative association between intentions and use across the five countries: Countries with lowest percentages wanting no more children have the highest percentages not using contraception."[36] Confirming the earlier ethnographic findings of the Rockefeller report using cross-comparative statistical methods, Westoff concluded that there was "a considerable unmet need for family planning services."[37] Westoff's finding justified more research, which indeed appeared in the pages of policy reports and demography journals in the ensuing years.[38]

This renewed interest in unmet need for contraceptives did not particularly focus on a transformation of the gender order on the one hand or on the improvement of demographic measures on the other. In an article geared to an emerging class of contraception professionals, Freedman recalled his participation in contraception advocacy efforts in Taiwan, which he described as a "traditional, pronatalist, and patriarchal society."[39] Summarizing the literature, he noted that "the great majority of scholars and leaders in the population field agree that family planning programs are desirable for health and welfare reasons" and advocated that demographers learn about local cultural norms about family size, and then "use the cultural knowledge about specific son and family size preferences . . . to approach subgroups for whom contraception is personally and culturally acceptable."[40] Rather than challenging cultural norms in the name of gender equality, here the demographer took the role of a social engineer working to assist in population control while taking care *not* to upset the gender order. A new kind of demographic common sense thus emerged.[41] Prognosticating upon the eve of the new millennium, the International Relations and Grand Strategy expert Paul Kennedy referred to this literature to suggest that "a detailed proposal for dealing with the demographic explosion in developing countries would simply repeat what numerous studies by international agencies have pointed out: that the only practical way to ensure a decrease in fertility rates, and thus in population growth, is to introduce cheap and reliable forms of birth control."[42] This claim certainly took on a political hue, but it was not a politics of gender equality. Contraception advocates like Freedman saw challenging patriarchal norms (e.g., son preference) as beyond their mission of managing an overpopulating planet.

CRISIS: NEW FINDINGS CONTRADICT
ASSUMPTIONS ABOUT SOCIAL CHANGE

While the study of unmet contraceptive need helped to reinvigorate scholarship on fertility intentions, newer studies revealed that increased access to contraception did not reliably change demographic outcomes. This finding raised a question mark on these demographers' view of their work as promoting population growth change. Early on, critics like Cleland recognized that "constraints of time, money, and expertise often prohibit the development of appropriate forms of attitude measurement,"[43] and urged researchers to "concentrate on measurement of overt behavior and knowledge of an opinion on specific and preferably tangible topics which raise fewer conceptual and methodological problems."[44] While he recognized that "the use of findings [from demographic studies] to convince the apathetic and disarm the opposition has undoubtedly been a most important contribution to date,"[45] he simultaneously warned that the growing divergence between advocacy organization and scholarship meant that "in the future a distinction will have to be made between surveys whose primary objective is the provision of demographic data and those focused on operational aspects of programs."[46] When Freedman, himself a Scripps researcher, proposed and outlined an alternative strain of contraceptive "operations research" for reproductive advocates,[47] critics balked. Analyzing the gap between intentions and outcomes in conjunction with contraceptive access, Pritchett showed that "the magnitude of the impact of contraceptive prevalence, although statistically significant, is very small." According to Pritchett, "this small estimated impact is in sharp contrast to the literature."[48] Similarly, a host of critics emphasized that the use of natural fertility control—notably, the use of extended breastfeeding to postpone the postpartum resumption of menses—had long served as a natural means of population control, and thus modern contraception availability had negligible effects on overall birth outcomes.[49] Rather than holding up existing fertility and contraception studies as a massive success in extending the tools of scientific prediction and contraception to new domains, this literature critiqued existing scholarship as a politically naive tool to promote contraception globally.

This criticism became particularly strong after the Contraceptive Distribution Project of 1975, in which villages in the Matlab region of Bangladesh were randomly selected to receive contraception education and supplies free of charge. Ironically, this study found that overall fertility rates were 1.8 percent higher where contraception was widely available despite similarities in "unmet need."[50] This small difference in outcomes suggested that even extensive social spending on contraception would do little to shift individual birth patterns or stall overpopulation as projected by the policy literature. While to many the political uses of demographic research provided an opportunity, to others it threatened the very objectivity of demographic science.

Nor did the intentions framework provide a stable or durable response to its critics. Indeed, from the outset these researchers had admitted that the gap between outcomes and intentions was an imperfect means of measuring contraception demand but was justifiable on political grounds. Thus, while advocates of demographic studies like Ronald Freedman tried to downplay the seriousness of the findings of the Matlab study, they were also forced to admit that "there is a plausible case for similar tests of the reality of potential demand in other countries where there is a KAP-gap [knowledge-and-practice gap] between verbal responses in surveys and actual acceptance of family planning. . . . The measurement of [contraception] demand is clearly imperfect and examples cited cannot be interpreted unambiguously." Not surprisingly, scholars quickly attached to this empirical failing as a means to criticize the entire subfield. Writing about intentions analysis, the public policy expert Simon Szreter noted,

> The problem for the field of population studies is the intellectual and methodological conservatism that results from the influence of this understandable continuing adherence by policymaking institutions and their officials to a narrow definition of "science" . . . precisely because changes in those radically indeterminate phenomena and relationships that are beyond [policy science's] proper scope to analyze—purposes, values, meanings, social roles, motives, and intentions—in all likelihood hold the key to a satisfactory historical understanding of the processes and causes of fertility change in any particular community. . . . This invisible hand of institutional bias has therefore been responsible for maintaining the privileged position in the field of one particular— and rather dated—form of social science and, with it, the idea of demographic transition.[51]

While intentions may have provided the key to unlocking the secrets of demographic analysis, their attachment and intertwining with policy institutions made researchers focus on outdated paradigms.[52] Even triumphant narratives of the success of contraception policy, spurred by evidence of the influence of contraception on the gap between intentions and outcomes, were forced to note that in the late 1980s "the field lacks a sense of direction and a set of agreed-upon goals."[53] The field had entered into a crisis, finding itself unable to live up to its self-described raison d'être— effecting changes in population trends.[54] It was here that a new trend, focused on reconstituting the debate, intervened.

Reconstitution: Fertility Intentions as a Cultural Construct

One prominent critique of contraception research was that it focused on Western forms of contraception and overlooked local fertility control techniques (e.g., socially sanctioned spells of postpartum abstinence). Late 1980s demographers were finding that "the line separating Western contraceptives from more 'traditional' means of regulating fertility is thin indeed, if not wholly artificial."[55] Building on the "anthropological doctrine, assuming that local cultural perceptions play a crucial role in how people interact with the world," this work recentered *culture* as a tool for improving demographic analysis. In the context of contraception, such scholars emphasized the unique cultural meaning of contraception use, "as devices for spacing children, for avoiding risky high-parity pregnancies, or even (in some cases of pill use) for increasing fertility by regularizing a woman's menstrual cycle," which "merit serious attention in their own right."[56] Given the connections between research on contraception use and demographic studies of fertility intentions, these attempts to blend anthropological views into sociological demography quickly spread. As an article in *Sociological Research & Methods* noted, ethnographers "can discover information that might have been missed by a standard survey," and "including such information in causal models can dramatically alter our substantive conclusions."[57]

At its core, this approach took what seemed to earlier generations of demographers a liability—notably, that "reproductive intentions are tailored to conditions at the time of interview and, thus, share the same possibilities of misinterpretation as other period indices"[58]—and inverted it as the basis for a new form of research. This new wave of research understood self-reported fertility intentions as evidence of relevant local *cultural* processes associated with demographic life, making them valuable in themselves without requiring them to align with concrete fertility outcomes later in respondents' lives. Thus, where demographers had been stuck between the view of demography as making large-scale policy impact and growing evidence of their inability to do so, this new wave of research adopted a new moral repertoire—the Anchored Repertoire—that allowed them to escape this dead end by valuing their research for offering deep understanding and representation of local cultural processes relating to reproduction. Thus, a movement of sociologists broke away from the debate over whether fertility intentions are useful predictors of fertility, and instead started examining the underlying contexts that shape respondents' reports of their fertility intentions.

Early on, R. D. Lee advanced a "moving target" model that assumed that fertility intentions changed across the life course and could be used as a proxy for cultural forces significant in their own right. Reconceptualizing them as a cultural barometer, Lee systematically rethought the gap between intentions and outcomes as a tool to help understand how individuals' changing fertility intentions responded to historical events (such as economic downturns) that cause actors to revise their original intentions. Lee maintained that using the gap between intentions and outcomes in this way was "diametrically opposed"[59] to existing approaches because it saw updating of intentions across the life course as a sociohistorical process worthy of investigation, rather than as an "error" in reporting or knowledge. Moreover, Lee demonstrated that his model, when used in conjunction with outcomes data, "reflects the actual patterns of change in the United States over the past several decades more closely."[60] Treated as a variable, fertility intentions—and particularly the gap between intentions reporting and outcomes—could be used to improve analysis.

This cultural model of fertility grew in popularity in light of Michel Foucault's inquiry into the origins of population science.[61] Quick to follow Foucault's lead were comparative sociological discussions of the "demographic transition," the steep declines in overall fertility modernizing societies witness. Utilizing historical evidence from Europe, van de Walle revealed that demographers were the ones who invented the practice of numerating ideal family sizes. Thus, stated fertility intentions were interesting for another reason: they showed how ideas about population control became a natural-seeming feature of Western self- and family formation. Arguing that explicitly stated fertility intentions were the first signs of individuals taking demographic control of their lives, and were thus a precursor to the demographic transition, van de Walle rejected past claims about stated fertility intentions being an imperfect—but still valuable—proxy for people's eventual behavior. Instead, he concluded that fertility intentions data were valuable because they could "facilitate our interpretation of a change in behavior which is one of the most profound in social history."[62] Intending a family of a particular size was not something that helped explain demographic outcomes—it was itself a demographic outcome with social causes.

Similarly, Jennifer Johnson-Hanks's ethnographic analysis of family planning during Cameroon's period of social unrest (known as *la crise*) emphasized the intense role historical conjunctures played in an individual demographic goal. During such periods of social upheaval, Johnson-Hanks found high variability in fertility intention reporting, and numerous forms of extreme non-response—statements like "God decides how many children I'll have." Arguing that researchers should "take seriously the challenge that [respondents] are posing to intentional action as it is commonly understood,"[63] Johnson-Hanks pointed to the ways in which inattention to historical data undermined the project of demography more generally. She said of her results:

[they] might appear the end of the analysis: Cameroonians experience radical uncertainty in their lives, and—*mirabile dictu*—we find a huge amount of variation in the timing and occurrence of demographic events. This way of combining qualitative and quantitative research so that they both "tell the same story" is widespread. But there is an intellectual danger in agreeing too quickly. Sometimes, ethnographic and statistical analyses use the same terms to analyze quite different things. Uncertainty offers one example. Instead of treating quantitative and qualitative data as complementary, I propose instead to focus on the disjunctures and discontinuities between them, looking for the instances in which confronting ethnographic interpretation with statistical patterns produces a new analysis or at least new questions.[64]

Thus, rather than seeing the disjuncture between intended and achieved fertility as a problem in need of resolution, she concluded that demography needed to rethink its relationship to culture more holistically. In this, her research began an alternative project: to reconstruct how demographers have imagined the interrelationship between cultural values associated with fertility and their utility in prediction. Rather than seeing gaps between intentions and outcomes as an error introduced into a pure and stable set of family preferences, Johnson-Hanks argued that now intentions were useful *because* they keyed the research into highly contingent events that linked large historical events and individual behaviors.

Demographers like Lee, van de Walle, and Johnson-Hanks have thus argued that culture changes how the events demographers sought to explain came about, and is thus something demographers themselves need to analyze. Bledsoe and colleagues examined the adoption of Western forms of contraception in Gambia and demonstrated that declines in overall fertility were a result of mothers using Western birth control to fulfill the local cultural norm valorizing a two-year interval between births, rather than an effort to hit a predetermined numerical ideal. The authors concluded that "explanatory frameworks usually fail to ask whether women may have regular birth intervals not because they are adhering to biological instinct or to cultural norms but because they are trying to create such regularities through careful strategies that can vary from one birth to the next."[65] If previous scholars accepted that fertility intentions are an imperfect predictor because of historical variations in expectations, which scholars considered as a distraction more than anything, this new wave of scholarship saw those same historical processes as key to understanding how the surveillance of demographic processes was intertwined with systems of political power. Thus, while fertility intentions used to be criticized because of their historicity, they were now valued as evidence for that very reason.

While it had drawn a connection to Foucault's historical critique of demography, this movement also remained outwardly committed to the possibility of demography as an objective science. In this, a greater interest in culture among these demographers was largely justified by the moral good of accurate demographic science overcoming the problem existing demographic analyses had with cultural data. Johnson-Hanks insisted that the problems with existing research had resulted from a failed theory of action—one she attributed to Hume—that emphasized predictability as a means of checking the validity of one's claim. Instead, returning to phenomenology and cultural sociology, she claimed that the demographers following Hume had conflated statistical and social uncertainty when they complained about intentions' lack of predictive accuracy, and she concluded that "where the consequences of action are at [the same time] grave but largely unknowable and unfold in multiple time-frames—the inadequacies of a model of intentional action become especially apparent."[66] Suddenly, the problem was not fertility intentions *per se*, but the theory of why intentions mattered. So even though fertility intentions may be useful for demographers interested in forecasting populations, Johnson-Hanks asserted that this framework for understanding intentions was inadequate "for ethnography and especially for a social theory of reasoning population averages."[67] As she put it in another study, "causal explanation in the social sciences requires both adequacy at the level of meaning and related patterns of statistical regularity. . . . Without local knowledge, the translation from rate to meaning is impossible." While a vast series of demographic research communities had emerged to address fertility intentions in a particular way, they ignored cross-cultural variation in "repertoires of alternatives, structures of incentives, systems of value, and horizons of possibility" and were thus not ready to address the "new, interstitial, and ambiguous social forms and demographic regimes [that] are emerging."[68] Put differently, intentions may have been good predictors, but their use as predictors also reflected the shaky foundation at the center of demographic science.

This cultural approach quickly gained adherents and found justification through the Anchored Repertoire: attention to local context provided a morally worthy route to improve demographic science. Unsurprisingly, those already interested in fertility intentions quickly shifted gears: now intentions and the patterns in their distribution over time were reinterpreted as significant grounds for rebuilding demography with the understanding that intentions were a measurement of culture.[69] In a coauthored volume on the subject, Johnson-Hanks joined other scholars of fertility intentions to explain the significance of taking local interpretations seriously:

> the ongoing discussion about gay marriage in the United States occurs in a context of the war on terror, rising oil prices, new turmoil in the Middle East, greater sexual freedom, decreasing marriage rates, and aging baby boomers. All of these facts constitute part of the context, but only some of them are part of the conjuncture. . . . Decisions about fertility are notoriously dependent on work, and cross-country moves may hinge on a child finishing high school: "conjuncture" nicely captures the fact that the specific configurations of context in which action occurs are a striking juxtaposition of different life domains. Is work the context for reproduction? Or reproduction the context for work? Thinking instead about "conjunctures" in which work and reproductive trajectories become mutually salient and their futures equally indeterminate renders the question moot.[70]

As the authors noted, such a model of culture made the old debate about fertility intentions moot by reincorporating fertility intentions as valuable indicators of how actors think about their structural position. In an influential analysis of fertility intentions, Hayford summarized this new position succinctly: "to fully understand the relationships between intentions and behavior, we need to analyze changes in intentions as well as correspondence between intentions and behavior at particular points in time."[71] Similarly, in France, calls emerged for a new "French School" in demography with a context-based approach to culture. At the center of these was a question of disciplinary progress: "a broader conception of the individual is needed. The implicit or explicit idea of a simple *Homo demographicus*, like the often-derided *Homo economicus* must be abandoned."[72] In effect, the worry that fertility intentions were a faulty concept had been supplanted by a new normal: intentions had to be measured in *conjunction* with variations in the social structure. Rather than put culture and structure in opposition to one another, the data were reimagined as informing different parts of the same whole.

Since then, a robust literature on fertility intentions has flourished and developed in several directions. Notably, these measures also utilize the logic of anchoring to justify why cultural analyses matter. Returning to Morgan and van de Walle's concerns about diverse forms of nonresponse, Frye and Bachan found that what quantitative demographers called "contextual" and "individual" variables still failed to account for variations in non-numeric response; they concluded that only "qualitative data that enable researchers to investigate the answers people give, rather than simply whether they are words or numbers, would further enhance our understanding of how non-numeric fertility preferences are socially patterned."[73] Undertaking a focused study of fertility underachievement, Nitsche and Hayford find "a bachelor's degree may provide women with the agency to realize their desires for small families more than their desires for large families"; they call for more research on how "the agency (and economic resources) provided by education may be more salient in contexts where infertility treatments are more effective and more widely available."[74] Conducting an independent study of "fertility flexibility," Trinitapoli and Yeatman conclude with a call for "the development of even a few abbreviated measures" to be implemented across demographic contexts, because "the ability to make clear, cross-cultural comparisons will be essential for advancing research on [fertility] flexibility with respect to its role in fertility transitions, but standardized measures cannot retain the contextual and temporal specificity we demanded here."[75] Expanding her concerns about the conflation of different forms of non-response, Johnson-Hanks extended her analysis to a more general question of how such selection process (or situations where "we should expect people to select themselves into and out of denominators in systematic and meaningful ways, because their 'choices' are at once voluntary and prestructured by their experiences"[76]) shaped other population puzzles. Whereas her earlier studies had asked who is included in the group of relevant fertility expectations, she now maintained that "the question 'who is in which group when?' is a fundamental question for population studies, and a surprisingly theoretical one. At all levels of aggregation, from the most micro of interactional setting to the most macro of global politics, populations are made one event at a time."[77] Far from being a concern of sociologists of the family alone, it appeared lessons learned in demography needed to be spread more widely; as Trinitapoli put it, "to the extent that our research can both expose and address the fault lines of inequality that structure contemporary populations, this work may be more moral reckoning than estimation problem."[78]

Demographers have spent decades struggling over the meaning of the gap between stated fertility intentions and concrete outcomes. One set of demographers, evaluating demographic research through the Efficiency Repertoire, used exploration of this gap as an opportunity to improve demographic research methods. Another set of demographers, evaluating demographic research through the Civic Repertoire, maintained that this gap indicated a social problem that their subfield should address; but when scholars utilizing this approach discovered that their research did not lead to societal change, their civic justifications for research collapsed. And a third group of scholars devised a way out of this dead end by drawing on the Anchored Repertoire, which emphasizes the worth of research giving voice to local concerns. Rather than delving into the debate between the Efficiency and the Civic repertoire, this new group of scholars described their move as both producing better predictions and offering more just representations of their research subjects.

Since demography is a predominantly quantitative field, it has been focused on developing research instruments (e.g., surveys) to improve scientific measurement. As such, it should come as no surprise that the competing interpretations of a single measure could be seen as a means to drive progress in the field.[79] However, many subfields in sociology are not centralized around the idea of measurement validity, but begin from outside of the Efficiency Repertoire. The next example will show a different way in which reconstitution turns to alternate moral frameworks to justify new directions for research.

BREASTFEEDING AND WOMEN'S LABOR OUTCOMES

Few areas in the intersection of demography and public health are as contentious as the literature on women's investments in their children, and particularly on breastfeeding. For decades, public health scholars and officials have cast breastfeeding as a morally laudable practice that could be sustained by extended forms of government aid to low-income mothers. However, critical feminist scholars have lamented that this approach ignored the long-term negative association between time-intensive investments like breastfeeding and mothers' labor market outcomes. A fierce debate ensued around whether intensive parenting demands impact mothers' lifelong wages, leading concerted efforts at reconstitution by a third group. These latter scholars pointed to breastfeeding as a practice uniquely situated to theorize and empirically explore the relationship between motherhood and the structures that reproduce gender inequality. This direction allowed scholars to circumvent the debate over breastfeeding recommendations and focus attention on what the persistence of this debate said about gender equality.

When he died in 2013, former US surgeon general Charles Everett Koop had achieved a notoriety uncommon for a public health expert. The *Washington*

Post asserted that Koop, with his iconic no-mustache beard and colorful bow ties, "was the only surgeon general to become a household name." A proponent of media engagement, Koop gained notoriety by appealing directly to the public in advertising campaigns—first against second-hand smoke, and then to inform the public about the emerging HIV-AIDS epidemic—that not only frustrated his boss (Ronald Reagan) but also durably changed American health. A pediatric surgeon for thirty-five years prior to his appointment, Koop also led the effort to re-popularize breastfeeding in America after steep declines in the first half of the twentieth century.[80] Coordinating with the breastfeeding activist organization La Leche League (LLL), Koop gathered researchers at the forefront of children's health and feeding knowledge to the White House. Urging that "research findings have documented the benefits of human milk and lactation for babies and mothers," Koop summarized the main goals of the meeting:

> The last decade has seen a steady increase in breastfeeding, predominantly among middle- and upper-income, educated, white women. We need to identify and reduce the barriers that interfere with breastfeeding, especially in those population groups with low prevalence of breastfeeding among women who are minority, low income, and less educated.[81]

While much about breastfeeding has changed in the forty years since Koop organized his infant feeding meetings, the ways and reasons the state supports breastfeeding have largely stayed the same. For instance, in 2011, the Department of Health and Human Services issued a *Blueprint for Action on Breastfeeding*, emphasizing the specific health benefits of breastfeeding and highlighting the "Socioeconomic Benefits," which it specified as follows:

> Breastfeeding provides economic and social benefits to the family, the health care system, the employer, and the nation. Families can save several hundred dollars over the cost of feeding breast milk substitutes, even after accounting for the costs of breast pump equipment and additional food required by the nursing mother. Breastfed infants typically require fewer sick care visits, prescriptions, and hospitalizations, especially if breastfed exclusively or almost exclusively. Consequently, total medical care expenditures were about 20% lower for fully breastfed infants than for never-breastfed infants. Because of the high occurrence of poverty among African Americans, these families would benefit

substantially from breastfeeding their infants. Employers also benefit when their employees breastfeed. Breastfed infants are sick less often; therefore, maternal absenteeism from work is significantly lower in companies with established lactation programs. In addition, employer medical costs are lower and employee productivity is higher.[82]

In an individualistic formulation that seems typical of American political culture, breastfeeding is valued here because of its ability to reduce costs and to promote health, and thus as a way of supporting "the family, the health care system, the employer, and the nation." In this, Koop's "efforts to promote informed decisions by more women to breastfeed their babies"[83] implied that a good (or worthy) mother actively worked to breastfeed her child. Indeed, even today mothers themselves routinely use the stream of feeding research Koop endorsed to justify long-term exclusive breastfeeding despite consistent challenges.[84]

The Debate: Breastfeeding as an Engine for Inequality

INABILITY TO MEET BREASTFEEDING RECOMMENDATIONS AS A FAILURE OF NEOLIBERALISM

The fact that many mothers did not meet public health breastfeeding recommendations has propelled continued reflection on how such directives put disproportionate strain on mothers. Of course, feminists have long argued that breastfeeding is part of a hegemonic discourse that sustains the patriarchal division of labor at home and in the workplace (see below).[85] However, because the initial policy decisions had focused so heavily on the *public* benefits to breastfeeding, scholars initially relied on civic logics—those that outline the means to achieve equality in the social and political realms—to criticize existing breastfeeding recommendations and research. Some claimed that epidemiologists were to blame, with critics contending that public health authorities have misrepresented the health benefits of breastfeeding to exert paternalistic control over children's health.[86] Others emphasized how breastfeeding logics reinforced class inequalities and compared pairs of children who had been raised by the same mother but were not both breastfed, finding few health benefits for the breastfed child.[87] Exploring the effect of "welfare-to-work" programs on the rate of breastfeeding, Haider and colleagues insisted that "there is political and popular support for policies that encourage welfare recipients to work, and these policies have been applied to mothers whose children are just a few months old. Our results suggest that these policies could impose a significant cost on infants and their mothers by reducing the prevalence of breast-feeding."[88]

Rather than focusing on the overtly gendered dimensions of these inequalities, here scholars focus on the collective whole and how it can be used to rhetorically justify different policy choices.[89] While Haider and associates focused on welfare-to-work programs, others drew attention to the fact that longer leaves from work increased breastfeeding in both duration and frequency and asked if this was the best social policy for a society.[90] Similarly, scholars like Joan B. Wolf have emphasized that breastfeeding recommendations were formed within the confines of "a neoliberal risk culture" that devalues care work to the detriment of women and society as a whole.[91]

In this research, critics argued that breastfeeding policy is itself contradictory—while it presents itself as restoring public confidence in breastfeeding as a healthy behavior, its real interests lie in the reproduction of systems of inequality. Soon these arguments appeared in popular press op-eds that insisted the public obsession with mothers' breastfeeding was clearly an attempt to evade social responsibility for feeding and to displace the excessive time constraints onto mothers.[92]

REFORMING THE STUDY OF BREASTFEEDING AND LABOR OUTCOMES TO RECONCILE THE DEBATE

In hopes of reconciling this debate, many researchers sought to uphold both perspectives—that breastfeeding was good health policy for both mother and child, but that it also created inequalities elsewhere that could be solved through careful policy planning. One prominent stream of research in this vein focused on the amount of time needed to breastfeed, emphasizing that mothers who moved to part-time work could gain enough flexibility to continue exclusive breastfeeding while staying attached to the labor force.[93] Further studies teased out the effects of breastfeeding on work, using complex modeling strategies to understand the interplay between work and breastfeeding outcomes. Using National Longitudinal Survey of Youth data, Chatterji and Frick explored within-family sibling comparisons to examine the effects of breastfeeding on work.[94] They found that working postpartum has negative consequences for breastfeeding outcomes, but that the decision to breastfeed is not consequential for future work outcomes. By contrast, a series of articles by Fine, Mandal, and colleagues utilized local policy interventions to model breastfeeding and work outcomes.[95] They find that breastfeeding competes with work, but also that the decision to breastfeed negatively affects future work outcomes. Taken together, studies in this vein tackle the cardinal importance of the relationship between breastfeeding and work outcomes for women by outlining how policies at work can be manipulated to promote this healthy behavior.

By focusing on the conflict between mothers and employers, such scholars were able to avoid the charge that they were ignorant of the inequalities associated with breastfeeding, while also refusing to challenge the official view of breastfeeding issued by public health agencies. In this, the emphasis on policies that could reduce conflict between breastfeeding and a mother's own interests reiterated the broad emphasis on market mechanisms that predominated in state reports. For instance, Ryan and coauthors concluded their study of breastfeeding rates and mothers' postpartum work patterns by urging that "increased maternity benefits are potentially costly to employers, but may be offset by the improved infant health and greater employee morale, productivity, and retention when breastfeeding is extended."[96]

Reconstitution: Breastfeeding and Labor Outcomes as a Question of Womanhood

While critics had already emphasized the inequality associated with different feeding practices, they had often failed to address the concerns critical feminists and mothers expressed in the public discourse. For these critics, the public emphasis on the health benefits of breastfeeding largely neglected the deeply gendered scripts surrounding the practice. In the *New York Times*, Alissa Quart criticized the "milk wars" between lactation advocates in online forums, and concluded that "unfortunately, there are few places for women to turn for balanced advice on the matter."[97] As a result, a third wave of scholarship emerged that used the Anchored Repertoire to explicitly center the discussion around understanding mothers and their experiences of breastfeeding.

Leading this charge was Jacqueline Wolf, who maintained that "feminist scrutiny today of societal and medical attitudes toward breastfeeding might prove to be as valuable to women and children as feminist criticism of birthing practices was thirty years ago."[98] In this, Wolf aimed to highlight the explicitly gendered interests at stake in the breastfeeding debates. She returned to the influential La Leche League text, *The Womanly Art of Breastfeeding*, and focused on its presentation of breastfeeding as an important form of care uniquely shared between mother and child.[99] While public efforts at breastfeeding reform had taken LLL insights into consideration, Wolf lamented that physicians had inadequate knowledge of the variety of benefits (both social and health) that derived from the bonds produced by breastfeeding, and that public agencies still placed the burden of breastfeeding on mothers instead of engaging society to promote the practice through new social organizations (i.e., Public Human Milk Banks).[100] Perhaps worse, she also found that many feminists had moved away from breastfeeding as a cause, because of a fear of aligning with a Reagan-appointed surgeon general. Wolf's call to arms explicitly challenged such trends: "Given a host of controversies—LLL's singular influence in the breast-feeding world, the organization's emphasis in its messages to mothers, the American tendency to define women in terms of their bodies, and the propensity to blame mothers for sick children—it would be unsurprising if some feminists recoil from the suggestion that they embrace breast-feeding as a feminist issue. Yet this retreat from a vital women's issue has engendered silence on the part of feminists even when breastfeeding controversies beg for feminist voices." Wolf therefore called upon mothers to act collectively in the name of breastfeeding, noting that by relying on the "growing body of research indicating that the propensity to formula feed causes excess maternal and infant morbidity and mortality in the United States, feminists can urge government and health organizations to estimate and publicize the cost of formula feeding to society. Under the rubric of preventive medicine, feminist organizations can call on Medicaid and private health insurers to reimburse for breast-feeding–related expenses such as breast pumps and lactation consultant services."[101]

Indeed, Wolf called her peers to action by noting, "If not feminists, who will push for the reconciliation of women's busy lives and their infants' need for their milk?"[102] Rather than rejecting the health benefits of breastfeeding or insisting that it could be studied to understand new forms of social inequality, Wolf sought to reconstitute the field of breastfeeding research as explicitly directed to honoring the bonds the practice forms.

As a result, a new stream of the literature has emerged—one where breastfeeding research was situated as a key part of total mothering,[103] an extreme form of gendered parental investment that critics insist undercuts the household more generally. One popular stream of this research has entailed cultural-historical reconstruction of breastfeeding campaigns to understand "how women and mothers are construed and how gender relations are negotiated within breastfeeding discourse," and has advocated for breastfeeding to be viewed "as part of a wider negotiation of gender relations."[104] Others interviewed mothers who felt they had failed to achieve their breastfeeding goals to explore questions such as "For women who want to breastfeed, what do they experience when they then use formula? How does this impact their sense of being a 'good mother?'"[105] A core claim of this research is that for mothers, breastfeeding has become a "moral minefield"[106] where a mother's "experience of formula feeding seems best described as one of moral collapse."[107] Here breastfeeding discourse is a primary object of concern, not because of its possible health effects or what it says about the society's civic institutions, but because it allows researchers to understand how ideas about the home and family are being reworked.

While it did not directly dismiss the health benefits of breastfeeding, work in this vein downgraded its emphasis on childhood health and instead turned to how breastfeeding fit within the larger culture of parenting. Focusing on the low rates of breastfeeding among African American mothers, many argued that the policy emphasis on "education" neglected the larger structural inequalities that made breastfeeding an act only for "exceptional" mothers.[108] For instance, Kukla insisted that "we need to correct the extent we try to protect infant health—not to mention the health of the nation—by trying to fix mothers' characters, at the level of their personality and their choices, rather than working to change the socially embedded status of maternal practices so as to make healthy choices more workable."[109]

These scholars do not reject the idea that breastfeeding is beneficial for children, nor the idea that breastfeeding should be supported by public agencies, but their focus has turned dramatically to how public support of breastfeeding exacerbates inequalities within the household which disproportionately affect mothers. Similarly, Maralani and Stabler maintain, "our results suggest that breastfeeding duration in the United States may serve as a proxy that helps to shed light on a set of otherwise unobservable characteristics encompassed by a subset of higher-SES families and how they engage in parenting and child investment."[110] In all these cases, the same research activity—analyzing breastfeeding rates and their proximate causes—is no longer understood as a question of public health; it is understood as a means to think about how public health pronouncements fit within the ongoing revolution in gendered labor division.

As a result of this reconstitution, the field of breastfeeding research started tackling questions that pertained not only to the incidence of breastfeeding, but also to its effect on mothers more holistically. In these studies, the reconstruction of breastfeeding appears complete—the moral stakes of the old debate have been circumvented in the name of the moral good of promoting cohesive family units. Analyzing breastfeeding rates alongside mothers' labor force participation, Rippeyoung and Noonan claimed:

> Our main goal is not to advocate breastfeeding over formula-feeding or vice versa, but rather to examine whether mothers who work outside the home pre-birth face different income trajectories after birth as a function of type of infant feeding. Results from this study will be useful to policymakers concerned with gender equity in the workplace and those interested in increasing overall rates of breastfeeding. . . .[111]

Others built on the criticisms that breastfeeding campaigns reinforced a neoliberal culture of managed risk that blamed individuals for social neglect,[112] but expanded on these ideas by turning to Levinas's ethical formulation in which "moral obligation and individual autonomy need not be opposed." Here again, the core debate about the benefits or harms of breastfeeding are reconstituted; now they are a means to argue that "the responsibility to ensure that children are fed is not limited only to parents and extends to everyone in society: each of us is obligated to provide assistance . . . for individuals who breastfeed."[113] Similarly, others highlighted how breastfeeding promotion materials constructed women's identities solely "in terms of providing the best possible opportunities for their children and the risks associated with a failure to breastfeed are drastically overstated."[114] In all these efforts attention is redirected to recognize that the family is not the mother's responsibility alone, but rather that "doctors, midwives, nurses, child characteristics, grandparents, partners, employers, and broader socio-historical contexts are also important when it comes to breastfeeding decisions."[115]

In her initial call to arms, Wolf was clear about why an approach that took mothers' perspective seriously mattered: when men were in charge of the discussion, they often perverted language against women's interests. As she put it regarding breastfeeding, "feminists have long known that terms like *family values* and *pro-life* are empty tactical phrases. When an allegedly profamily presidential administration chooses the growth of the formula industry over the health of babies, feminists can use the incident to expose the 'family values' rhetoric for what it is—language designed to mask egregious behavior."[116]

Indeed, feminist scholars had long seen the advice of medical authorities like Koop (despite his standing as "America's doctor") as just this kind of double-dealing. Koop, for instance, was famously pro-life in his personal life, but maintained that his position never affected his politics or policies despite the fact that he was appointed by a "family values" president, Ronald Reagan. Critical feminist commentators widely rejected his claim to neutrality. While Koop and his cohort may have seen the collapse of breastfeeding as a failure of American mothers, as Wolf had it, "in lobbying for societal support of breastfeeding mothers, feminists can simultaneously reopen a national dialogue about an array of currently dormant feminist goals."[117]

————————

The debates over breastfeeding have focused on different views about the social goods science should provide. Claims included the position that social science should help reduce health care costs, that it should reduce social inequality, and that it should honor the ties of familial association. While along the way some people used one framework to denounce another, here we have focused on how those concerned with the moral logics of the home found a way to avoid denunciation and instead promote an alternative stream of research. The history of research on breastfeeding shows how relative moral pluralism about the social world allows researchers to justify new avenues of inquiry where heated debate threatens to stall a field of research.

DISCUSSION

In *The Structure of Scientific Revolutions*, Thomas Kuhn suggests that scientific paradigm shifts transform the narratives scientists hold about their research subjects: "Rather than being an interpreter, the scientist who embraces a new paradigm is like the man wearing inverting lenses. Confronting the same constellation of objects as before and knowing that he does so, he nevertheless finds them transformed through and through in many of their details."[118] Such a shift of perspective, we suggest, pertains not only to explanatory power; it also pertains to the value and the moral standing of the research program in question. For Jennifer Johnson-Hanks and colleagues, value came from a deep understanding of the cultural processes that generated fertility intentions; for Jacqueline Wolf and colleagues, it came from the use of research to amplify women's parenting experience. In all these cases, scholars transcended a preexisting debate and used it as a jumping-off point to identify other worthy research trajectories. Scholarly change, then, does not come only as a response to scholarly ineffectiveness; it can also emerge as a new narrative of morally justifiable research.

Calls for reconstitution constantly provide new moral justification for research in different directions. The intersection between race, gender, and class, for example, has been particularly prominent in this regard, as Black sociologists especially have pointed out the neglect of race as a core category in studies of labor, fertility, and parenting.[119] This neglect has been presented not as a simple scholarly oversight, but as an actively harmful move which has affected the livelihood and health of non-white women. The fact that there was a moral impetus to all of these acts of reconstitution does not detract from their factual basis. Rather, as Boltanski suggested, their factual basis was made salient and pressing by the moral claims sociologists made about them. As we have shown in this chapter, such claims can lead to a large-scale shift in social science research pathways.

On Moral Grounds

We started this book by parroting Eleanor Shellstrop, the protagonist of the NBC show *The Good Place*, as she protested the one-dimensional metric by which human goodness is measured in the afterlife. As the series unfolds, the characters come to appreciate the complexity and multiplicity of the scales by which morality is evaluated, leading to structural changes in the afterlife's point system. But the show also introduces us to Doug Forcett. Having experienced a powerful metaphysical vision in his youth, Doug has accrued unparalleled accurate knowledge of the moral rules of the universe. He now lives "off the grid," in an eco-friendly manner, and supports various progressive political causes. Doug even recycles his urine into drinking water to minimize his environmental impact, and when he accidentally steps on a snail he decides to walk for three weeks across Canada to donate to a snail charity. When urged to relax a bit, he declines:

> Thank you. . . . But no. . . . What if I relax and do something that loses me just enough points to keep me out of the Good Place and I'm tortured for eternity? No, I have to make every moment count. It's the only rational way to live. Now, if you'll excuse me, I'm going to walk to Edmonton to give $85 to a snail charity.

Nevertheless, Doug has only accumulated half the points necessary to make it to the Good Place after he dies. How is this possible?

Doug has failed to recognize the moral diversity of life. Because of this, he wears his morality like a straitjacket. He desperately tries to ensure others' happiness, but he acts without consideration of competing moral goods. Doug prefers a moral decision that ensures he will avoid harming others, rather than one that could risk punishment in the name of something more valuable. Doug's worldly impacts are all positive—the few who meet him do feel better—but he lives without true social connection, unable to contribute to a more just world. In this sense, Doug has missed the forest for the trees. He is *morally myopic*—shortsighted in his application of moral frameworks in the face of competing interpretations.

Moral myopia has many forms in the social sciences, some of which come out of the very intention to make social scientists more mindful of the consequences of their research. During what American cultural anthropologists call "the crisis of representation," anthropologists developed a deep concern about their complicity with systems of domination through their research. In response, they began experimenting with new ways of representation that did not position ethnographic subjects as mere objects of analysis, but rather saw them as conscious subjects who actively participate in the production of anthropological knowledge.[1] These methods prescribed an intensified self-reflexivity about power asymmetries between researchers and their ethnographic sites. This revamped anthropological reflexivity succeeded as a moral project, but it has also been criticized for depriving anthropology of the critical edge needed to address harmful social phenomena. As the anthropologist Richard Edgerton noted, the intensely cautious anthropologists of the 1990s lost their ability to produce claims about a society, let alone evaluate the health of social groups. This, claimed Edgerton, leaves anthropology with no ability "to distinguish what is harmful for human beings from what is beneficial to them" or to identify "sick societies."[2] To address this shortcoming, Edgerton advocated a renewed emphasis on normativity within the field.[3] Cultural anthropology and neighboring disciplines (such as science and technology studies) have developed their own movements that reflect on the contributions of science to the social good, and continue to grapple with their own shortsightedness when it comes to the plurality of moral positions on good social science research.[4]

Throughout this book we have focused on the opposite of being morally myopic: being value-pluralistic. As the philosopher Isaiah Berlin described it, value pluralism is the view that multiple and mutually exclusive ways of defining moral goodness coexist. Adopting this view also means recognizing that life is characterized by valid moral criticisms and justifications that can adequately address those criticisms.[5] In the end, individual scholars must fashion their own intellectual self-identity based on their vision of, and engagement with, ethical debates of just this kind (particularly during the intense period of graduate school education).[6] In this vein, this book has argued that the discipline offers a plurality of repertoires its members can use to justify how sociological work contributes to the common good and what makes sociological work *morally* worthy.

The mere existence of a plurality does not suggest that every sociologist agrees that it should exist. Indeed, the book has shown numerous ways academics try to disqualify some ways of valuing research. Many readers would recognize statements such as "your work is not real sociology—it's just activism!" or "you're not even seeing people—it's just numbers for you" as a way sociologists reject their peers' work as falling below sociological standards and certainly not contributing to the public good. Certainly, few social science departments function solely through what Jürgen Habermas called "communicative action," when a consensus is achieved through rational deliberation and actors coordinate their actions based on their shared understanding of the merits of a collective goal.[7] But this book has shown that academic communities can find ways to communicate about the good of science without all actors embracing plurality, let alone coordinating their actions. Indeed, the existence of multiple repertoires to evaluate moral worth does not rely on every single member of a community accepting all forms of evaluation in the same way. Luc Boltanski demonstrated that societies harbor a "grammar of normalcy," which denotes the array of claims one would deem as logically acceptable *even if one disagrees with them* and even if they are incompatible with one's own position (i.e., as opposed to claims one would perceive as insane).[8] The same is true for academic communities: many factions do not agree with (or even fully understand) their colleagues' stances about research, seeing them as nothing more than a nuisance; but at the same time they understand that in order to remain viable, the discipline has to tolerate some diversity of moral justifications for research and critique.

———

Sociologists often contend that the discipline's diversity of moral motivations stalls its progress.[9] However, this argument begins from the faulty premise that progress should be measured by a discipline's ability to put an end to debate. As the moral philosopher Joseph Raz contended, life in a value-plural society inevitably entails some level of conflict.[10] For Raz, groups can hold multiple moral values that are irreducible to one another and cannot be summed up under umbrella terms such as "happiness," "self-fulfillment," or "freedom." Similar incompatibility applies to the moral repertoires sociologists employ: the methodological rigor of a work, its theoretical originality, and its loyalty to its research subjects' experience are measures based on different metrics of worth, and cannot be subsumed under any other measure. While members of a community may come into conflict, a pluralistic society is one in which members recognize that if they are to maintain the common goods they hold as a community (in the case of an academic discipline: departments, funding agencies, professional associations, etc.), they must coexist with people who hold values incommensurable with their own.[11]

Such coexistence with incompatibility can spark productivity and entrepreneurship. Organizational sociologists like David Stark have shown that certain levels of contention can bolster entrepreneurship and push actors to coordinate their action creatively: "it is through *unshared* typifications, through uncommon attributions, through divergent or misaligned understandings that problematic situations can give way to positive reconstructions."[12] This same potential holds for academic moral diversity, and the debates it spurs. Indeed, rather than think of sociology's diversity of moral justifications as a liability, perhaps it is time sociologists began thinking of it as a *feature* of the discipline that demonstrates academics' capacity to think through morally contentious topics. Rather than asking if moral debate limits sociology as a science, perhaps we should focus on how sociology is *already* openly committed to science. Indeed, a more productive reading is that sociologists have improved their science by producing work that transcends moral narrowness, upsets our normative assumptions, or finds unlikely allies by reconfiguring how we apply moral frameworks.

While certainly not *all* contention is productive (and we certainly do not recommend increasing contention between sociologists), we maintain that sociology's constant questioning of what constitutes the common good is better served by this diversity. At least overtly, the discipline should be a space where a debate about inequality entails questions about not only what is happening in the social world, but also how we understand *equality*. Axel Honneth has argued that the social sciences, and particularly social theory, are "concerned with supporting actors as participants in public debate and, hence, with assisting them to articulate their (often implicit) normative expectations and demands." For Honneth, in democratic societies "the task of justification is always a public task, rather than a theoretical undertaking; and this is why social theory can fulfill its critical mission only in the *public sphere*."[13] If the mission of sociology lies in its relationship to the public, then value-pluralistic social sciences serve the demands of increasingly pluralistic societies.[14] Indeed, researchers like Michèle Lamont and Peter Hall have argued that a good society is a society that offers its members *multiple* ways of defining the good—and thus multiple ways to excel. Lamont and Hall's claims suggest that for social science, too, harboring multiple measures of worth contributes both to academic collective flourishing and to social science's ability to contribute positively to a public discourse that supports plurality. To understand how such debates work, each of the preceding chapters showed how working scholars address moral diversity, and how such diversity enriches the discipline.

––––––––––

Our point has *not* been to make a "final statement" about the debates we have covered herein. Rather, we used them as key examples of how innovative sociological research utilizes different moral maneuvers to address controversy. Many of the debates we covered here will continue not only to intensify in the years to come, but also, hopefully, to produce fruitful ideas about sociological intervention. Moreover, with corporate sponsorship of research on the rise and with laws banning critical race theory coming into fashion, the threat of moral myopia in the social sciences is ever more present. In such a climate, scholars will need to learn to maneuver through increasingly volatile "moral minefields." Chapter 2's discussion of race, genetics, and inequality certainly appears to continue, with new op-eds and scholarly profiles emphasizing the ongoing moral stakes of different research projects. For instance, a recent profile of the behavioral geneticist Kathryn Paige Harden in *The New Yorker* asked, "Can Progressives Be Convinced Genetics Matter?"[15] and reviewed the similar debates in psychology centered on the possibility of using genetic data to foster civic equality. By focusing on how debates on genetics in sociology have employed multiple ideas about the goods sociology ought to provide, we suggested that conversations on deeply controversial sociological topics allow sociologists to better respond to their critics and to push the field to maintain relevance in an ever-changing world.

Remaining responsive to moral diversity in this way can often be difficult, even for sociologists. As we have repeatedly underlined, sociological debates are simultaneously evaluative and empirical, and they require scholars to creatively reimagine their activities in the face of moral and factual uncertainty. One space of particular creativity is the ability to reach compromises, as outlined in chapter 3's debate between the methodological cosmopolitans and their peers in the sociological study of nations and nationalism. Here, scholars of nationalism did not ignore the moral criticism raised by the cosmopolitans, nor did they claim that the particularities of the social situation demanded an exception to the critique. Rather, they emphasized that the existing knowledge associated with nations and nationalist projects could be reformed to address the complaints of the critics, and thus could be put to morally worthy ends. While critics of contemporary sociology have described its commitment to morality as a dogmatic commitment to liberal truths,[16] we showed how actors work to ensure that divergent views of what is morally worthy can coexist in sociology and often be used to enrich one another.

We have also argued that the drive to ensure that sociology is morally defensible can also be viewed as propulsive force in the field. Chapter 4 turned to the ways some of the most fervent debates between researchers can bestow new moral value on novel directions in research. The chapter focused on the debates about the utility of stated fertility intentions for demographic analysis and on the effects of maternal breastfeeding on mothers' labor market outcomes. It tracked two instances where debates about the applicability of moral logics propelled new research on topics scholars thought they had well understood. In both cases, the chapter highlighted how scholars routinely define sociological advancement by a focused rethinking of where the social good lies in research. Rather than merely view moral criticism as limiting or biasing research, here we show how it contributes to disciplinary change. That is, we show how claims of moral justification are used to demand that other scholars include more data in their analysis and refocus their data collection efforts to ensure morally worthy social outcomes.

Crucially, our view of value pluralism does not mean that everything goes, or ought to go, when it comes to justifying research. The fact that multiple repertoires of morality exist should not imply the type of moral relativism that suggests that something is right or wrong based simply on whether a group thinks it is right or wrong.[17] The book has shown how sociologists have policed boundaries of acceptable research, and that actors have rejected certain ways of justifying sociological research—in particular when it came to research that denies the humanity of its research subjects. Pluralism cannot be understood to mean an indefinite number of positions, akin to some of the more radical proposals in the sociology of science. Chantal Mouffe, for example, has recently argued for an "agonistic" system of deliberation, which denies the possibility of consensus formation and instead encourages encounters between adversaries on equal grounds where all differences are respected.[18] As Mouffe's critics have pointed out, this approach is untenable in reality because it requires rejecting all actors who do try to dominate others or who do not respect differences, requiring some yardstick of acceptable behavior which Mouffe has rejected a priori. Monica Prasad has additionally noted that creativity, which Mouffe herself prizes, relies on a certain level of closure or consensus in debates (e.g., agreement on the disputed objects, agreement on unacceptable positions, etc.).[19] Our claim in this book is not about radical openness to diverse claims; rather, it is about there being a finite number of acceptable ways of justifying research that are defined and negotiated historically. Not everything goes, but certainly more than one thing does.

———————

Throughout the book we have highlighted the ways social science has responded to, and in turn helped to engage with, public concerns in the Anglo-American sociological scene. This evidence has demonstrated that maintaining moral pluralism amongst sociologists—together with their neighbors in political science, cultural anthropology, psychology, and other social sciences—ensures that scholars develop new ways of thinking about public morality and help to advance public ethical debates. Indeed, beyond the academic debates we have analyzed, sociologists' moral justifications have also disseminated widely into public discourse.[20]

Perhaps one of the best-known examples of sociologists offering a new justification for behavior has been in efforts to destigmatize recreational marijuana use. American attitudes about the moral legitimacy of marijuana use have shifted considerably over the past century, from morally polluted over the twentieth century to a wide acceptance in recent decades.[21] The struggle to decriminalize marijuana emerged in the 1950s, after a wave of moral panics about drug use led to its prohibition in the 1930s.[22] In an article generations of sociologists-in-training have read as an example of outstanding qualitative research,[23] the sociologist Howard Becker argued that when used to excess the drug may indeed be panic-inducing, but that a novice can learn to control the experience through proper training, making marijuana use enjoyable and enlightening. While the paper was initially a flop, Becker soon became *the* expert on the social effects of marijuana use. Becker later recalled,

I presented the paper at a meeting of the Midwest Sociological Association, no more than a dozen people showed up to hear it and the questions they asked when I was through made clear how much it puzzled them. No one could see the point of doing such an odd thing. . . . Fast forward to the mid-1960s. Several things had changed in the interim. Middle-class youth, especially college students, had begun smoking marijuana, and the grown-ups were worried. I no sooner arrived at Northwestern University as a new professor in 1965 than a bunch of NU students were arrested for possession of marijuana and I was in demand as an "expert" on what had suddenly become a "real problem."[24]

Certainly, Becker did not "invent" the notion of learning to use marijuana recreationally, but he did become one of its leading scholarly representatives because he articulated a new perspective at the conjuncture of changing public preoccupation with marijuana and expert authority.[25] Indeed, he continued to serve on the leadership board of the National Organization for the Reform of Marijuana Laws—NORML—which maintained that marijuana prohibition is the result of misunderstandings about the drug itself. NORML was at the forefront of the legal and public advocacy battle to disentangle marijuana from its negative moral framings, and to popularize a different framing—that smoking marijuana can be harmless fun.[26]

Sociologists have also contributed to public moral discourse by popularizing concepts by which to *denounce* behaviors and attitudes. While the concept of *color-blind racism* was already in use in the late twentieth century, Eduardo Bonilla-Silva's 2003 book *Racism without Racists* popularized this idea as a critical tool that can be mobilized to expose the structural inequalities that permeate American society (and beyond) and to underscore white individuals' by-and-large blindness to and complicity with racist systems of oppression. Indeed, the usefulness of Bonilla-Silva's conceptual framework for waging criticism is evident in articles with titles such as "'I Am Not a Racist But . . .': Mapping White College Students' Racial Ideology in the USA,"[27] "'I Did Not Get that Job Because of a Black Man . . .': The Story Lines and Testimonies of Color-Blind Racism,"[28] and "'It Wasn't Me!': How Will Race and Racism Work in 21st Century America?"[29] By problematizing sites such as college campuses, workplaces, and, indeed, American society as a whole, and by pointing particularly to white indignation at the mere suggestion that systemic racism exists, Bonilla-Silva provided a potent critical tool couched in the *Civic Repertoire*, which evaluates research products according to its contribution to civic equality. For Bonilla-Silva, the debate was not solely about the *policy* issues; it was rather about the pervasiveness of actual racism in society, including (or perhaps particularly) among those who most fervently deny it.[30] Through a series of articles and several books, Bonilla-Silva and his collaborators, along with peers in the neighboring social sciences,[31] brought this critical framework to the fore of the sociology of race in the early 2000s, and received public attention as well.[32] By 2021, *Racism without Racists* was cited more than 10,000 times.[33]

Beyond academic success, the framework of *color-blind racism* succeeded publicly and influenced civil discourse on racism. First, it articulated a problem with which turn-of-the-century scholars and public commentators were grappling—namely, how is it that despite considerable progress in the legal sphere, race-based disparity remained so stark in the US? By positing that good intentions and self-distancing from racism insufficiently counteract systemic racism, Bonilla-Silva provided an explanation that resonated with the more general preexisting sense that racism remains a prevalent social problem. Second, the notion of *color-blind racism* as explicated by Bonilla-Silva circulated in some of the leading progressive venues, and demonstrated its usefulness in capturing the enduring pervasiveness of racism. In a *New York Times* piece called "Straight Talk for White Men," Nicholas Kristof, discussing several sociological studies of racism and misogyny in the labor market, cited Bonilla-Silva's work and examples: "the bigger problem seems to be well-meaning people who believe in equal rights yet make decisions that inadvertently transmit both racism and sexism." The solution? "Acknowledging systematic bias as a step toward correcting it."[34] Third, the notion of *color-blind racism* also came with specific guidance about how to counteract it—namely, through identifying white privilege and providing space for non-white individuals to flourish independently. Bonilla-Silva offered a set of specific identifiers for color-blind racism that can be employed on both positive and negative utterances about racial minorities.[35] This way, he provided guidance about how dominant group members' accounts of race relations should not be taken at face value, but treated critically as potentially masking underlying structural racism. Bonilla-Silva's approach offered tools that allowed the analyst to take what Paul Ricœur called a *hermeneutics of suspicion*—"a tearing off of masks, an interpretation that reduces disguises"[36]—toward all social sites.

In writing this book, our aim was to underscore that there are multiple systematic ways of talking about the good life that are already utilized to guide change in disciplines like sociology, that the critiques and debates that unfold in academic journals in these fields enrich our understanding of these moral viewpoints, and that this enriched understanding helps consumers of sociological knowledge navigate a world of increasing complexity. Throughout this book we have asked the reader to think about moral claims as a set of public repertoires that groups employ to determine the legitimate course of individual and collective action. No individual can ever live up to the demands of any one of these abstract moral systems. Rather, the systems provide groups with means for thinking about what justice would look like in a perfect world, and how sociological research can contribute to that project.

Of course, any decent sociologist will tell you that "talk is cheap,"[37] but we would venture that it is not worthless. Even if the ways academics talk about justice are always constructed (or "made up"), they can also identify and outline what people think the good society should look like and how groups can bring it about. And a more perfect universe will never emerge if we do not at least think about it, talk about it, and try for it. Something you can learn on *The Good Place*, from your local sociologist, or even in your own neighborhood.

Researching the Good in Research Justifications

Numerous readers have noted that the contemporary "sociology of cri-tique" (or the new French pragmatist sociology) is laden with specialized terminology and that a burgeoning secondary literature interpreting this work has emerged. Within the scope of this book, we cannot do justice to the entire breadth and depth of these projects. But in this afterword, we lay out the core framework we employ in the book and link it to pragmatist so-ciological theory on public debates over social arrangements and justice.

Pragmatist sociological theory begins with the assumption that the sociologist does not know more about the actors and what they do than the actors themselves know. Where critical sociology has tended to as-sume that actors' expressed judgments reflect their class history or field position, pragmatists urge us to recognize that individuals regularly act like critical sociologists. Indeed, individuals often use a rhetorical strategy common to critical sociology—that of "unveiling" truth claims by pointing to an author's social position and making claims such as "you're only say-ing this because you are (fill in the blank)" (e.g., a communist explaining to a capitalist that they believe in the system because it benefits them). In this sense, pragmatist sociologists maintain that sociologists cannot assume they know any more than what the actors they study know about a situa-tion.[1] Instead, sociologists should base their accounts on actors' explicit interpretations and criticisms of existing social arrangements.

This stance leads to a host of methodological commitments that obtain when conducting research,[2] as well as to a common misperception about pragmatist sociology: that it invites us to ignore structural inequalities and to assume that actors are free from constraints as they engage in social situations.[3] However, pragmatist sociology disagrees with other sociologi-cal frameworks primarily on *epistemological* grounds: we the sociologists are simply taking the viewpoint that everyone around us can be a critical sociologist as well, and that structural inequalities will reveal themselves through actors' stated claims. Rather than seeking to undermine what actors claim, historically informed pragmatist sociological research grasps structures and the changing strategies actors use to grapple with them *through* an analysis of these claims.

Pragmatist sociologists argue that, during debate, individuals (and scholars) refer to abstract concepts of justice and worthiness. Throughout the book, we have called these principles "moral repertoires" to underline that they are coherent packages of moral preferences and arguments that recur in both interactional disputes and abstract reasoning about the nature of the good society. We claimed that academic discourse is laden with moral meta-communication, which is the conversation scholars have about the moral justification for their research, appearing often in prefaces, discussion sections, newsletter thought pieces, keynote addresses, and other contexts where academics take a step back from the nuts and bolts of the research itself and reflect on its broader trajectory.[4] Here, we argue, is where moral repertoires emerge most prominently in scholarly conversations. In what follows, we outline basic definitions and provide methodologically oriented examples for each of the repertoires we have identified as common in academic debates.[5] We hope these definitions help the reader clarify our analysis (since we often refer to these repertories by name) and apply them to other moral debates as well.

EFFICIENCY REPERTOIRE

Key measures of worth: productivity, efficiency, objectivity, expertise.
Typical claim: "Good sociological work provides scientific tools to accurately measure social phenomena. Inefficient research practices undermine the discipline as a whole."

- Focused on *accurate* descriptions of social experience, this repertoire critiques others for their failure *to objectively describe the world*.
  o Focused also on the *effort* and *diligence* the researcher has put into the scholarship (e.g., the author digitized an entire archive, brought together huge datasets, conducted an unusually large number of in-depth interviews).
- Here a worthy researcher is one who *is systematic and organized*, and follows a research process that emphasizes *validity and precision of predictions*.
- Using this repertoire, a scholar frames their research in an *instru-*

mental manner *by insisting that "data-driven" approaches provide the surest basis to guide the transformation of social arrangements.*

   o Conversely, a scholar uses this repertoire to frame their research in a *reflexive* manner *by insisting that "data-driven" approaches provide the surest basis to critique existing social arrangements.*

- Using this repertoire, scholars judge one another according to whether *their research is methodologically and empirically rigorous,* and thus scholars are celebrated for their ability to *reduce errors in data analysis, collection, and organization.*

   o Conversely, scholars who are judged by others (both research subjects and other scholars) to be *methodologically sloppy or outdated* are criticized.

- From the view of this repertoire, social scientific progress can be measured according to the degree that *it produces dependable methods to determine truth and fact about the social world.*

Examples of Work Employing the Efficiency Repertoire

Charles C. Ragin, *The Comparative Method: Moving Beyond Qualitative and Quantitative Strategies* (Berkeley: University of California Press, 1987).
Stephen L. Morgan and Christopher Winship, *Counterfactuals and Causal Inference: Methods and Principles for Social Research* (Cambridge, UK: Cambridge University Press, 2007).

CIVIC REPERTOIRE

Key measure of worth: collective interest, mutual recognition, equality. Typical claim: "Sociology by definition promotes civil values that make this society a better one. Any research that does not promote civil values (e.g., by helping overcome inequality) is not good research."

- Focused on descriptions of social experience that generate *practical interventions that lead to social change,* this repertoire critiques others for their failure to *transform an unjust society.*
- Here a worthy researcher is one who *studies and fights against pressing social problems,* and thus one who follows a research process that emphasizes *public engagement and political activism.*
- Using this repertoire, a scholar may frame their research in an *occupational* manner by insisting that *their work as an activist improves the quality of their scholarship.*

    o Conversely, a scholar may use this repertoire to frame their re-
search in a *policy* manner by insisting that *their work as an activist
is improved by the critical distance their scholarly training produces.*

- Using this repertoire, scholars judge one another according to
whether *they affect changes toward a more just society*, and thus scholars are celebrated for their ability to *inform policy, influence public
movements for change, and highlight the struggles of excluded persons.*
    o Conversely, scholars whom others (both research subjects and
other scholars) judge to be *apathetic* are devalued and criticized.
- From the view of this repertoire social scientific progress can be
measured according to the degree that *it helps (or has helped) bring
about a more just set of social arrangements.*

Examples of Work Employing the Civic Repertoire

Monica Prasad, *Problem-Solving Sociology: A Guide for Students* (New York: Oxford University Press, 2021).
Tukufu Zuberi and Eduardo Bonilla-Silva, *White Logic, White Methods: Racism
and Methodology* (Lanham, MD: Rowman & Littlefield Publishers, 2008).

ANCHORED REPERTOIRE

Key measures of worth: community, loyalty, tradition.
Typical claim: "Sociologists are morally obliged to deeply understand and
to give voice to local and familial experience, especially when it comes to
underrepresented groups."

- Focused on *immersive* or *thick* descriptions of social experience, this
repertoire critiques others for their failure to *adequately represent the
lived experience of social actors.*
- Here a worthy researcher is one who *gives voice to the concerns of
their research subjects,* and one who follows a research process that
emphasizes *collaboration between scholar and subject.*
- Using this repertoire, a scholar frames their research in a *progressive*
manner by insisting that *they have given voice to underrepresented
experiences.*
    o Conversely, a scholar uses this repertoire to frame their research
in a *conservative* manner by insisting that *they have given voice to
vanishing traditions.*
- Using this repertoire, scholars judge one another according to *the
degree of familiarity a researcher achieves with their subjects,* and thus

scholars are celebrated for their ability to *access revealing and over-looked phenomena.*

     o Conversely, scholars whom others (both research subjects and other scholars) judge to be *disloyal to their research subjects* are criticized.

- From the view of this repertoire, social scientific progress can be measured according to the degree that *research subjects recognize themselves in their scholarly representations.*

Examples of Work Employing the Anchored Repertoire

Annette Lareau, *Listening to People: A Practical Guide to Interviewing, Participant Observation, Data Analysis, and Writing It All Up* (Chicago: University of Chicago Press, 2021).

Linda Tuhiwai Smith, *Decolonizing Methodologies: Research and Indigenous Peoples* (New York: Bloomsbury Publishing, 2021).

CREATIVITY REPERTOIRE

Key measures of worth: originality, nonconformity, innovativeness.
Typical claim: "Developing creative and significant theoretical or methodological advances is the purest form of sociology, which gives meaning to sociological research. Work that is not theoretically or methodologically innovative is insignificant."

- Focused on *non-normal* descriptions of social experience, this repertoire critiques others as *boring, unimaginative, or tired.*
- Here a worthy researcher is one who *generates novel concepts and approaches,* and one who follows a research process that emphasizes *newness, experimentation, and counter-normative thinking.*
- Using this repertoire, a scholar may frame their research in an *instrumental* manner by insisting that *their research expands the field's capacities and is thus a reflection of "the state of the art."*
  - o Conversely, a scholar may use this repertoire to frame their research in a *reflexive* manner by insisting that *their research expands the field's capacities and reflects their own personal experience and idiosyncrasies.*
- Using this repertoire, scholars judge one another *by the degree of heterodoxy of ideas* and thus scholars are celebrated for their ability to *propose new lines of inquiry.*
  - o Conversely, scholars whom others (both research subjects and

other scholars) judge to be *repetitive or derivative* are devalued and criticized.

- From the view of this repertoire, social scientific progress can be measured according to the degree that *it devises novel theoretical or methodological thinking.*

Examples of Work Employing the Creativity Repertoire

John Levi Martin, *Thinking Through Methods: A Social Science Primer* (Chicago: University of Chicago Press, 2017).

Kristen Luker, *Salsa Dancing into the Social Sciences: Research in an Age of Infoglut* (Cambridge, MA: Harvard University Press, 2008).

CHARISMATIC REPERTOIRE

Key measures of worth: reputation, deference to academic stars.
Typical claim: "Scholar A is the most well-known and highly regarded expert in this area. Sociologists who critique scholar A are uninformed and often heinous."

- Focused on descriptions of social experience *propounded by charismatic leaders*, this repertoire critiques others for their failure to *acknowledge the history of ideas and the importance of individual thinkers.*
- Here a worthy researcher is one who *engages with the ideas of canonical thinkers*, and follows a research process that emphasizes *extension or elaboration of a scholarly tradition.*
- Using this repertoire, a scholar may frame their research in an *occupational* manner *by arguing that the ideas of the charismatic can be used to reshape or address contemporary problems in the field.*
    - o Conversely, a scholar may use this repertoire to frame their research in a *policy* manner *by arguing that the ideas of the charismatic can be used to reshape or address contemporary problems in society.*
- Using this repertoire, scholars judge one another according to whether *their work contributes to the tradition inaugurated by the charismatic* and thus scholars are celebrated for their ability to *resemble or "channel" the thinking of the charismatic. In the extreme, this results in the scholar being represented by others as the charismatic's contemporary successor.*
    - o Conversely, scholars whom others (both research subjects and other scholars) judge to be *misrepresenting the charismatic's ideas,*

> *or to be falsely claiming the charismatic's ideas as their own*, are
> devalued and criticized.

- From the view of this repertoire, social scientific progress can be measured according to the degree that *it rediscovers the "deep" insights of charismatic scholars and finds contemporary means to extend and enhance their original theories.*

Examples of Work Employing the Charismatic Repertoire

John Goldthorpe, *Pioneers of Sociological Science: Statistical Foundations and the Theory of Action* (Cambridge, UK: Cambridge University Press, 2021).
Aldon Morris, *The Scholar Denied: W. E. B. Du Bois and the Birth of Modern Sociology* (Oakland: University of California Press, 2015).

MARKETABILITY REPERTOIRE

Key measure of worth: ability to attract funding, public attention, competitiveness.
Typical claim: "Sociologists need to conduct research that draws donors to their university and wins grants, on topics that are in high public demand and appeal to public interest. This would be the best contribution to their institutions and to their fields, and would also make sure sociology remains publicly relevant."

- Focused on descriptions of social experience that generate *public interest*, this repertoire critiques others for their failure to *produce publicly relevant findings.*
- Here a worthy researcher is one who *can sell their ideas to others*, and follows a research process that emphasizes *branding and sales strategies.*
- Using this repertoire, a scholar may frame their research in an *occupational* manner by insisting that *by drawing in resources and attention, they support future generations of scholarship.*
  - o Conversely, a scholar may use this repertoire to frame their research in a *policy* manner by insisting that *by drawing in resources and attention, they provide information for the decision makers of society.*
- Using this repertoire, scholars judge one another according to whether *their research generates opportunities for funding* and thus scholars are celebrated for their ability to *conceptualize studies with wide appeal.*

- o Conversely, scholars whom others (both research subjects and other scholars) judge to be *too niche and publicly irrelevant* are singled out for ridicule and exclusion.
- From the view of this repertoire social scientific progress can be measured according to the degree that *sociological research is responsive to shifts in the market of ideas.*

Examples of Work Employing the Marketability Repertoire

James S. Coleman, "The Rational Reconstruction of Society: 1992 Presidential Address," *American Sociological Review* 58, no. 1 (1993): 1–15.
Jessica Calarco, *A Field Guide to Grad School: Uncovering the Hidden Curriculum* (Princeton, NJ: Princeton University Press, 2020).

NETWORK REPERTOIRE

Key measures of worth: collaboration, interconnectedness, interdisciplinarity, internationality.
Typical claim: "Sociologists need to study the international networks, flows, and interactions that now characterize our world, and to cooperate with international scholars in doing so. Not doing so reinforces an old and pernicious world order." AND/OR "Sociologists need to engage with other disciplines, rather than stay confined to their own methods and assumptions. Interdisciplinary research is where real synergy happens."

- Focused on descriptions of social experience *that emerge from the crossing of social boundaries*, this repertoire critiques others for their failure to *incorporate perspectives from socially and spatially distant others.*
- Here a worthy researcher is one who *engages in research across traditional scholarly and political boundaries*, and follows a research process that emphasizes *network metaphors, transnationalism, and interdisciplinary connections.*
- Using this repertoire, a scholar may frame their research in an *occupational* manner by insisting that *new networks of association are the basis for new disciplinary subfields and specializations.*
    - o Conversely, a scholar may use this repertoire to frame their research in a *policy* manner by insisting that *new networks of association reveal previously ignored shared interests.*
- Using this repertoire, scholars judge one another according to whether *their research addresses problems of global or cross-disciplinary*

interest and thus scholars are celebrated for *being intellectual and cultural omnivores.*

   o   Conversely, scholars whom others (both research subjects and other scholars) judge to be *parochial* are devalued and ignored.
-   From the view of this repertoire social scientific progress can be measured according to the degree that *it connects insights from seemingly disparate perspectives in the name of a global community.*

Examples of Work Employing the Network Repertoire

Kevin J. A. Thomas, *Global Epidemics, Local Implications: African Immigrants and the Ebola Crisis in Dallas* (Baltimore, MD: Johns Hopkins University Press, 2019).

Nicholas A. Christakis, "Let's Shake Up the Social Sciences," *New York Times*, July 19, 2013.

———

In academic meta-communication, scholars draw on moral repertoires to enact different maneuvers in relation to each other's work. In the book, we highlighted three such maneuvers:

-   *Delegitimation*—denouncing former types of research conduct and calling for a complete replacement of existing conceptual tools in a certain field.
-   *Partial reforms*—responding to criticism by changing the moral framing of the conversation in a way that addresses critique without discarding the entire research trajectory.
-   *Reconstitution*—responding to criticism by moving a conversation from a controversial terrain to a noncontroversial one. This is often achieved by framing a field's research trajectory in a way that does not bear on the stakes of the original dispute.

Through ongoing negotiation between different maneuvers, not only the justification for research but also research itself may transform. Where delegitimation may discourage and possibly close off a direction for research, partial reforms and reconstitution may encourage new research trajectories.

While moral repertoires emerge most visibly in scholarly meta-communication, they may also emerge in other types of academic conversation. Specifically, such repertoires may emerge in discussions about the nature of the studied phenomena themselves. Sociologists of religion, for example, may disagree in their meta-communication over the proper ways to conduct their research, but they may also disagree over the moral worth of religion *as an empirical phenomenon*. Does religion provide disadvantaged populations with resources to organize and to push back against discrimination, or does it stifle their grievances by offering emotional reprieve and promises of a better next life (what Marx called "the sigh of the oppressed")? Does religion spread civic norms that support democracy, or does it promote strife and exclusion? Our analytic framework is suitable for studies of disagreements over the moral nature of empirical phenomena, which often dovetail with meta-communicative disagreements such as the ones we analyzed in this book. We hope future studies will further explore the potential in investigating the moral meanings scholars assign to the empirical phenomena they research.

As we outlined in chapter 2, not all disputes between people utilize these repertoires, as not all situations demand that people weigh competing morally worthy interpretations. In chapter 2, we outlined how actors may describe a dispute in differing ways and act according to different definitions of the situation.[6] Some actors may *reject*[7] the notion that the issue is debatable to begin with and thus refuse to weigh alternative moral frameworks as valid. Similarly, other actors may *ignore* a debate because they see it as irrelevant to their particular research. Such responses are also common in the discipline and have long fueled its boundary wars and fashionable trends in theory. However, throughout the text we have focused on situations in which debate allows people to reimagine social arrangements and propel new advances in scientific thinking.

Acknowledgments

Moral Minefields began with a paper submitted to the *Junior Theorists Symposium*, where Ann Mische provided deeply engaged comments and encouraged us to pursue the topic further. We are thankful to the organizers, Clayton Childress and Anna Skarpelis, for inviting us to present, and to the other participants for their deep engagement. This book developed through many conversations with Jeffrey C. Alexander, Philip S. Gorski, Michèle Lamont, and Vida Maralani, and we thank them for their insight and support over the years.

The Center for Cultural Sociology (CCS) at Yale University generously hosted a book manuscript workshop, and we thank the directors, Jeffrey C. Alexander and Philip Smith, for offering us this opportunity. We are indebted to Jennifer Johnson-Hanks, Peggy Levitt, Paul Lichterman, and Alford A. Young Jr. for participating in this workshop and for providing in-depth critiques and suggestions for our book. CCS Fellows provided additional insightful comments and we are grateful to all of them: Tracy Adams, Vanessa Bittner, Frederico Brandmayr, Jessie Dong, Dana Hayward, Jason Mast, Stephen Ostertag, Javier Perez-Jara, Agata Rojowska, Nicholas Rudas, Willa Sachs, Jan Vana, and Jiwon Yun. We are similarly thankful to the CCS Program Coordinator, Nadine Amalfi, who went above and beyond to make the workshop materialize.

We presented portions of the book in conferences and workshops and are indebted to all participants who provided feedback at those venues. In particular, at the American Sociological Association Annual Meeting, we thank Tim Gill for his detailed feedback; at the Culture Workshop at the University of Notre Dame, we thank David Gibson, Terence McDonnell, Lyn Spillman, and workshop members; at the International Association of Critical Realism meeting at the Cardiff Business School, we thank Jonah Stuart Brundage, Douglas Porpora, Timothy Rutzo, and the participants for their critical engagement; at the Bar Ilan University Center for Cultural

Sociology Conference, we thank Danny Kaplan, Michal Pagis, Ori Schwarz, Hizky Shoham, Ilana Silber, and conference attendees; at the Eastern Sociological Society Annual Meeting, we thank the organizer, Stefan Beljean; at the Harvard Culture and Social Analysis Workshop, we thank Laura Adler, Elena Ayala-Hurtado, Nicole Letourneau, Bo Yun Park, Shira Zilberstein, and workshop participants; at Pennsylvania State University's Culture & Politics Workshop, we thank Gary Adler, Dan DellaPosta, Roger Finke, Eric Plutzer, Charles Seguin, and all other participants; at the Colby College Sociology Colloquium, we thank Neil Gross, Annie Hikido, Damon Mayrl, and the wonderful student attendees; at Ron Jacobs's and Eleanor Townsley's culture salon, we thank our hosts and their guests; and at the North Central Sociological Association Annual Meeting, we are thankful to session organizers and participants.

Andy Keefe and Derek Robey helped us develop the arguments presented in chapter 2, and we are thankful for their input on the chapter and on the entire project. In addition, many colleagues have read drafts and offered invaluable input over the years, and we are grateful to all of them for their suggestions: Katelin Albert, Rene Almeling, Matthew A. Andersson, Elisabeth Becker, James Hurlbert, Matthew Lawrence, Thomas Lyttleton, Margarita Mooney, Erik Nylander, Candas Pinar, Celene Reynolds, Neal Tognazzini, and Jocelyn Viterna.

We are grateful for support we received from the Beyond Positivism: Re-Imagining the Social Sciences? project, funded by the John Templeton Foundation.

At the University of Chicago Press, we thank Elizabeth Branch Dyson for taking on this project and for following through with us from start to finish, to Mollie McFee for her help throughout the process, and to four anonymous reviewers who provided incredibly insightful feedback. Early conversations about this project started with Douglas Mitchell, who passed away in 2019. Doug had an uncanny ability to understand a project better than its own authors, and we are grateful for his insight and advice. We are also grateful to Evan Young for the careful copyediting, Lindsy Rice for overseeing the production process, Carrie Olivia Adams for promoting the book, and June Sawyers for creating the index.

Shai thanks his family—Uri, Dalia, Yael, Danny, Maya, Itay, Idan, and Peter—for their relentless support and encouragement. In line with the book's theme of value pluralism, Shai would also like to thank Rabbi Hirschy and Elkie Zarchi and their family for modeling a unique combination of unwavering orthodoxy and toleration of diversity, and Rabbi Menachem and Mussy Altein for many long discussions of the good, the bad, and the medium. Similarly, Sam would like to thank his family—

including the Stablers (Mom, Dad, Ben, Debi, Amellia, Eli, Erselle, Yared, and Leo), the Fallicks (RIP Abe and Esther), and the O'Hanlons (Laurie, Katie, Jaén, Gabby, Jasper)—and friends—Whitney, Cara, Aaron, TerryAnn, Stefan ("Steve"), Win, Mark, Joe, Luke, Babs, Danny & Gemma, Alex, Alan & Lisa, Ken, and Navin—who have taught him more about what a morally worthy life looks like (especially during the strains of book-writing) than they will ever know. He would also like to thank Sasha and Millie for their endless emotional support.

Both Sam and Shai owe special acknowledgment to their partners. Sam is forever indebted to his wife, Robin O'Hanlon, who has served as a sounding board, moral advisor, and essential source of strength both in the writing of this book and throughout their decade and a half of life together. Shai's partner, Blake Scalet, contributed to the book on all levels, from testing out early ideas to talking through difficult writing phases, and most importantly constantly reminding Shai that there is more to life than work. This book would not have been possible without either of them.

Notes

PREFACE

1. Aldon Morris, "Alternative View of Modernity: The Subaltern Speaks," *American Sociological Review* 87, no. 1 (2022).

2. As Marx famously put it, "The philosophers have only interpreted the world, in various ways, the point, however, is to change it." Karl Marx, "Theses on Feuerbach," in *The Marx-Engels Reader*, ed. Robert C. Tucker (New York: W. W. Norton, 1972). See also W. E. B. Du Bois, "Sociology Hesitant," *Boundary 2* 27, no. 3 (2000): 37–44; Ida B. Wells-Barnett, *The Red Record: Tabulated Statistics and Alleged Causes of Lynchings in the United States, 1892-1893-1894* (Chicago: Donohue & Henneberry, 1895).

3. See Gary King, Robert O. Keohane, and Sidney Verba, *Designing Social Inquiry: Scientific Inference in Qualitative Research* (Princeton, NJ: Princeton University Press, 1994), 86, 109–10.

4. See Stanley Lieberson, "Small N's and Big Conclusions: An Examination of the Reasoning in Comparative Studies Based on a Small Number of Cases," *Social Forces* 70, no. 2 (1991).

5. Isaac Ariail Reed, "Cultural Sociology as Research Program: Post-Positivism, Meaning, and Causality," in *The Oxford Handbook of Cultural Sociology*, ed. Jeffrey C. Alexander, Ronald N. Jacobs, and Philip Smith (Oxford and New York: Oxford University Press, 2012).

6. Philip S. Gorski, "The Poverty of Deductivism: A Constructive Realist Model of Sociological Explanation," *Sociological Methodology* 34, no. 1 (2004); George Steinmetz, "Odious Comparisons: Incommensurability, the Case Study, and 'Small N's' in Sociology," *Sociological Theory* 22, no. 3 (2004).

7. Kieran Healy, "Fuck Nuance," *Sociological Theory* 35, no. 2 (2017): 119.

8. Ample books on the history of sociology do exactly this. E.g., José Itzigsohn and Karida L. Brown, *The Sociology of W. E. B. du Bois: Racialized Modernity and the Global Color Line* (New York: New York University Press, 2020); Patricia M. Lengermann and Jill Niebrugge-Brantley, *The Women Founders: Sociology and Social Theory, 1830–1930* (Boston: McGraw-Hill, 1998); Andrew Abbott, "Living One's Theories: Moral Consistency in the Life of Émile Durkheim," *Sociological Theory* 37, no. 1 (2019).

9. Historically, social theorists like Ida B. Wells have used the term "moral"

when discussing what constituted a moral character, or a set of positive traits, exemplified in Wells's thought by "a true, noble, and refining womanhood." Ida B. Wells-Barnett, "Our Women," in *The Light of Truth: Writings of an Anti-Lynching Crusader*, ed. Mia Bay and Henry Louis Gates (New York: Penguin Books, 2014 [1887]), 21. More recent examples include Elliot Turiel, *The Culture of Morality: Social Development, Context, and Conflict* (Cambridge and New York: Cambridge University Press, 2002); R. Andrew Sayer, *Why Things Matter to People: Social Science, Values and Ethical Life* (Cambridge and New York: Cambridge University Press, 2011).

10. Steven Hitlin and Stephen Vaisey, "The New Sociology of Morality," *Annual Review of Sociology* 39, no. 1 (2013): 55.

11. In this, we follow the "ethical turn" in cultural anthropology in examining morality not as formalized systems of rules, but rather as a lived and experienced phenomenon. For more on the "ethical turn" in cultural anthropology see Didier Fassin, "On Resentment and *Ressentiment*: The Politics and Ethics of Moral Emotions," *Current Anthropology* 54, no. 3 (2013); Michael Klenk, "Moral Philosophy and the 'Ethical Turn' in Anthropology," *Zeitschrift für Ethik und Moralphilosophie* 2, no. 2 (2019).

12. This approach also traces back to the earliest social scientists, including pioneers like Harriet Martineau who have focused on morals to understand local ethical standards under the assumption that understanding morals provides "a key to the mysteries of all social weal and woe." Harriet Martineau, *How to Observe Morals and Manners* (London: C. Knight and Co., 1838), 220. For discussion of formalist approaches to morality see Iddo Tavory, "The Question of Moral Action: A Formalist Position," *Sociological Theory* 29, no. 4 (2011).

13. Hitlin and Vaisey, "The New Sociology of Morality," 55. See commentary on this difference in Jeffrey C. Alexander, "A Cultural Sociology of Evil," in *The Meanings of Social Life: A Cultural Sociology* (Oxford and New York: Oxford University Press, 2003), 109.

14. Our approach is morally relativist in the descriptive sense, by pointing to the fact that different parties hold different moral convictions and investigating the implications of those convictions on social research. This epistemological position does not imply a normative moral relativism—the approach according to which something is right or wrong based on whether a person or group thinks it is right or wrong—or metaethical relativism, the approach that "denies that there is always one correct moral evaluation." See further discussion in Gabriel Abend, "Two Main Problems in the Sociology of Morality," *Theory and Society* 37, no. 2 (2008): 92. For more on a pragmatist sociological position on morality see Shai M. Dromi and Eva Illouz, "Recovering Morality: Pragmatic Sociology and Literary Studies," *New Literary History* 41, no. 2 (2010).

15. We agree with Hitlin and Vaisey that numerous studies have used the term "repertoire" to describe strategic uses of moral positions in order to exclude outgroup members or to achieve certain organizational goals, thereby depleting morality of its substantive, value-laden side. Hitlin and Vaisey, "The New Sociology of Morality," 63. However, we follow authors like Lamont and Thévenot who use the term to denote the grammars by which individuals evaluate and express worth, and in this, we see repertoires as meaning-laden structures rather than mere

strategic tools. Michèle Lamont and Laurent Thévenot, "Introduction: Toward a Renewed Comparative Cultural Sociology," in *Rethinking Comparative Cultural Sociology: Repertoires of Evaluation in France and the United States*, ed. Michèle Lamont and Laurent Thévenot (Cambridge, UK, and New York: Cambridge University Press, 2000), 5–6.

16. Throughout the book we will be drawing on the burgeoning literature on cultural repertoires, which evolved over the late twentieth century in American sociology, in social movement theory and in cultural sociology. E.g., Frontiers of Sociology, Symposium, "Repertoires of Contention in America and Britain, 1750–1830," in *The Dynamics of Social Movements: Resource Mobilization, Social Control, and Tactics*, ed. Mayer N. Zald and John D. McCarthy (Cambridge, MA: Winthrop Publishers, 1979); Ann Swidler, "Culture in Action: Symbols and Strategies," *American Sociological Review* 51, no. 2 (1986); Michèle Lamont, *Money, Morals, and Manners: The Culture of the French and the American Upper-Middle Class* (Chicago: University of Chicago Press, 1992); Michèle Lamont and Laurent Thévenot, eds., *Rethinking Comparative Cultural Sociology: Repertoires of Evaluation in France and the United States* (Cambridge, UK, and New York: Cambridge University Press, 2000). It is important to note that the key works in the new French pragmatist sociology we use in the book do not explicitly use the term "repertoire," which evolved in the American context. However, as Silber notes, some French authors have more recently adopted this term as well in later works (likely because of the collaboration with Michèle Lamont). Ilana Friedrich Silber, "Pragmatic Sociology as Cultural Sociology: Beyond Repertoire Theory?" *European Journal of Social Theory* 6, no. 4 (2003): 428.

17. See examples of such deliberation in Jeffrey C. Alexander, "Modern, Anti, Post, and Neo: How Social Theories Have Tried to Understand the 'New World' of 'Our Time,'" in *The Meanings of Social Life: A Cultural Sociology* (New York: Oxford University Press, 2003), 193–228.

18. Charles Thorpe, *Oppenheimer: The Tragic Intellect* (Chicago: University of Chicago Press, 2006).

19. Raewyn Connell, *Southern Theory: The Global Dynamics of Knowledge in Social Science* (Cambridge, UK, and Malden, MA: Polity, 2007), 27–48; Julian Go, "Race, Empire, and Epistemic Exclusion; or, The Structures of Sociological Thought," *Sociological Theory* 38, no. 2 (2020): 87–90.

20. One example of the effect of reviewing existing work is that readers tend to rely on the review rather than cite the reviewed work. See Peter McMahan and Daniel A. McFarland, "Creative Destruction: The Structural Consequences of Scientific Curation," *American Sociological Review* 86, no. 2 (2021): 369.

21. Lamont and Thévenot, "Introduction: Toward a Renewed Comparative Cultural Sociology."

22. Oliver Bateman, "The Young Academic's Twitter Conundrum," *The Atlantic*, May 10, 2017, https://www.theatlantic.com/education/archive/2017/05/the-young-academics-twitter-conundrum/525924/. For a review of "cancel culture" and its effects on academic discourse see Pippa Norris, "Closed Minds? Is a 'Cancel Culture' Stifling Academic Freedom and Intellectual Debate in Political Science?" *SSRN Electronic Journal*, August 2020.

23. Vincent Jeffries, "Altruism, Morality, and Social Solidarity as a Field of Study," in *The Palgrave Handbook of Altruism, Morality, and Social Solidarity: Formulating a Field of Study*, ed. Vincent Jeffries (New York: Palgrave Macmillan US, 2014), 7–11.

INTRODUCTION

1. Jeff Asher and Rob Arthur, "Inside the Algorithm That Tries to Predict Gun Violence in Chicago," *New York Times*, June 13, 2017, https://www.nytimes.com/2017/06/13/upshot/what-an-algorithm-reveals-about-life-on-chicagos-high-risk-list.html?searchResultPosition=2.

2. Crystal Marie Fleming, *How to Be Less Stupid about Race: On Racism, White Supremacy and the Racial Divide* (Boston: Beacon Press, 2018), 23–48.

3. Ilana Redstone Akresh, "Departmental and Disciplinary Divisions in Sociology: Responses from Departmental Executive Officers," *The American Sociologist* 48, no. 3/4 (2017); Barbara Grüning and Marco Santoro, "Is There a Canon in This Class?" *International Review of Sociology* 31, no. 1 (2021).

4. Christian Smith, *The Sacred Project of American Sociology* (New York: Oxford University Press, 2014), 57–72, 101–14. For critiques of this study see Wendy D. Manning, Marshal Neal Fettro, and Esther Lamidi, "Child Well-Being in Same-Sex Parent Families: Review of Research Prepared for American Sociological Association Amicus Brief," *Population Research and Policy Review* 33, no. 4 (2014): 493–98. For examples from other disciplines see Lindsay McKenzie, "Journal's Board Disavows Apology for 'Transracialism' Article, Making Retraction Unlikely," *Chronicle of Higher Education*, May 18, 2017, https://www.chronicle.com/article/journals-board-disavows-apology-for-transracialism-article-making-retraction-unlikely/.

5. Paul F. Campos, "Alice Goffman's Implausible Ethnography," *Chronicle of Higher Education*, August 21, 2015; Marc Parry, "Conflict over Sociologist's Narrative Puts Spotlight on Ethnography," *Chronicle of Higher Education*, June 12, 2015; Randol Contreras, "Transparency and Unmasking Issues in Ethnographic Crime Research: Methodological Considerations," *Sociological Forum* (Randolph, NJ) 34, no. 2 (2019).

6. E.g., Steven Shapin, *The Scientific Life: A Moral History of a Late Modern Vocation* (Chicago: University of Chicago Press, 2008); Steven Shapin and Simon Schaffer, *Leviathan and the Air-Pump: Hobbes, Boyle, and the Experimental Life* (Princeton, NJ: Princeton University Press, 2011), 69–76.

7. E.g., the debate between Émile Durkheim and Gabriel Tarde over the very nature of sociology, or that between W. E. B. Du Bois and the Chicago School. See José Itzigsohn and Karida L. Brown, *The Sociology of W. E. B. du Bois: Racialized Modernity and the Global Color Line* (New York: New York University Press, 2020), 41, 138–39; Raymond Smock, *Booker T. Washington: Black Leadership in the Age of Jim Crow* (Chicago: Ivan R. Dee, 2009), 157–77; Eduardo Viana Vargas et al., "The Debate between Tarde and Durkheim," *Environment and Planning D: Society and Space* 26, no. 5 (2008): 762–63.

8. E.g., Donald Black, "On the Almost Inconceivable Misunderstandings Concerning the Subject of Value-Free Social Science," *The British Journal of Sociology*

64, no. 4 (2013); Duncan J. Watts, "Common Sense and Sociological Explanations," *American Journal of Sociology* 120, no. 2 (2014): 343; Stephen L. Morgan and Jiwon Lee, "Trump Voters and the White Working Class," *Sociological Science* 5 (2018): 241–42.

9. E.g., Ezra W. Zuckerman, "What If We Had Been in Charge? The Sociologist as Builder of Rational Institutions," in *Markets on Trial: The Economic Sociology of the U.S. Financial Crisis*, ed. M. Lounsbury and P. M. Hirsch, Research in the Sociology of Organizations 30, Part B (Bingley, UK: Emerald Publishing Group, 2010).

10. E.g., Monica Lee and John Levi Martin, "Coding, Counting and Cultural Cartography," *American Journal of Cultural Sociology* 3, no. 1 (2014).

11. Max Weber, "Science as a Vocation," in *From Max Weber: Essays in Sociology*, ed. Hans Gerth and C. Wright Mills (Milton Park, Abingdon, Oxon and New York: Routledge, 2009 [1919]), 148.

12. For a different version of this argument see Smith, *The Sacred Project of American Sociology*, 8–9, 72–75, 146–56.

13. E.g., Ben Shapiro, "A Genius Academic Hoax Exposed That Liberal Arts Colleges Don't Care about Truth," *Newsweek*, October 5, 2018, https://www.newsweek.com/ben-shapiro-genius-academic-hoax-exposed-liberal-arts-colleges-dont-care-1155013; *Wall Street Journal*, "Scientific Fraud and Politics: Look Who Is Lecturing Republicans about Scientific Truth," *Wall Street Journal*, June 5, 2015, https://www.wsj.com/articles/scientific-fraud-and-politics-1433544688. On conservative concerns over liberal academia see Neil Gross, *Why Are Professors Liberal and Why Do Conservatives Care?* (Cambridge, MA: Harvard University Press, 2013), 229–37.

14. Thomas S. Kuhn, *The Structure of Scientific Revolutions*, 4th ed. (Chicago: University of Chicago Press, 2012 [1962]); Paul Feyerabend, *Against Method: Outline of an Anarchistic Theory of Knowledge* (London and Atlantic Highlands, NJ: NLB and Humanities Press, 1975).

15. Pierre Bourdieu, *Homo Academicus* (Stanford, CA: Stanford University Press, 1988); Howard S. Becker, "Whose Side Are We On?" *Social Problems* 14, no. 3 (1967); Alvin W. Gouldner, *The Coming Crisis of Western Sociology* (New York: Basic Books, 1970); Alvin W. Gouldner, "Anti-Minotaur: The Myth of a Value-Free Sociology," *Social Problems* 9, no. 3 (1962): 63. However, see Gouldner's later cautionary word against a total rejection of value neutrality in sociology: Alvin W. Gouldner, "The Sociologist as Partisan: Sociology and the Welfare State," *The American Sociologist* 3, no. 2 (1968): 27.

16. Pierre Bourdieu, *Sketch for a Self-Analysis*, trans. Richard Nice (Cambridge: Polity, 2007), 111–12.

17. Dorothy E. Smith, *The Everyday World as Problematic: A Feminist Sociology* (Boston: Northeastern University Press, 1987); Patricia Hill Collins, *Black Feminist Thought: Knowledge, Consciousness, and the Politics of Empowerment*, 2nd ed. (London and New York: Routledge, 2014); Mali Collins and Jennifer C. Nash, "The Language Through Which Black Feminist Theory Speaks: A Conversation with Jennifer C. Nash," in *Black Feminist Sociology: Perspectives and Praxis*, ed. Zakiya Luna and Whitney Pirtle (Milton: Taylor and Francis, 2021), 60–62. See also Tracey Reynolds, "Re-Thinking a Black Feminist Standpoint," *Ethnic and Racial Studies* 25, no. 4 (2002). Others have noted the impossible standards demands for value

neutrality place on sociology. Karen Lumsden, "'You Are What You Research': Researcher Partisanship and the Sociology of the 'Underdog,'" *Qualitative Research* 13, no. 1 (2013): 6–8.

18. Mary Romero, "Sociology Engaged in Social Justice," *American Sociological Review* 85, no. 1 (2020): 4–9. Examples include W. E. B. Du Bois, "The Atlanta Conferences," in *W. E. B. Du Bois on Sociology and the Black Community*, ed. Dan S. Green and Edwin D. Driver (Chicago: University of Chicago Press, 1978); and Ida B. Wells-Barnett, *The Red Record: Tabulated Statistics and Alleged Causes of Lynchings in the United States, 1892-1893-1894* (Chicago: Donohue & Henneberry, 1895).

19. Romero, "Sociology Engaged in Social Justice," 3.

20. Émile Durkheim, *The Rules of Sociological Method*, trans. Sarah A. Solovay and John Henry Mueller, 8th ed., ed. George Edward Gordon Catlin (New York: Free Press, 1966), 98–99, see also 83. Durkheim championed notions of social "health" that suggested that some moral frameworks are better suited for modern society. Gabriel Abend, "Two Main Problems in the Sociology of Morality," *Theory and Society* 37, no. 2 (2008): 101–2.

21. Pierre Bourdieu, *Science of Science and Reflexivity*, ed. Richard Nice (Chicago: University of Chicago Press, 2004), 59.

22. Bourdieu, *Science of Science and Reflexivity*, 86. See also Bourdieu, *Sketch for a Self-Analysis*, 1–3. Bourdieu's stance on reflexivity involves mapping one's entire research field and understanding what one's position is therein. Understanding one's position will shed light on the constrains on one's research practices, on the ways one constructs their research object, their field's relationship to the state and to various "symbolic assets", etcetera.

23. Nevertheless, the new French pragmatist sociology owes much to Bourdieu—see Thomas Bénatouïl, "A Tale of Two Sociologies: The Critical and the Pragmatic Stance in Contemporary French Sociology," *European Journal of Social Theory* 2, no. 3 (1999).

24. Monika Krause, "'Western Hegemony' in the Social Sciences: Fields and Model Systems," *The Sociological Review* 64, no. 2 (2016): 197–98. Notably, cultural anthropologists' notion of reflexivity has similarly been influential across the social sciences. Cultural anthropologists of the 1980s have argued for "the presence in the text of the writer and the exposure of reflections concerning both his [*sic*] fieldwork and the textual strategies of the resulting account"—George E. Marcus and Michael M. J. Fischer, *Anthropology as Cultural Critique: An Experimental Moment in the Human Sciences* (Chicago: University of Chicago Press, 1986), 42.

25. The 2021 ASA Annual Meeting took up this view of sociology as its theme—see Aldon D. Morris, "2021 Annual Meeting Theme," *ASA Annual Meeting Bulletin*, February 12, 2020, https://www.asanet.org/annual-meeting-2021/theme-and-program-committee. See also Aldon D. Morris, "The State of Sociology: The Case for Systemic Change," *Social Problems* 64, no. 2 (2017).

26. This epistemological position is similarly traceable to Émile Durkheim's work. See Luc Boltanski et al., "Sociology of Critique or Critical Theory? Luc Boltanski and Axel Honneth in Conversation with Robin Celikates," in *The Spirit of Luc Boltanski: Essays on the "Pragmatic Sociology of Critique*," ed. Simon Susen and Bryan S. Turner (London: Anthem Press, 2014), 564.

27. Lee and Martin, "Coding, Counting, and Cultural Cartography."

28. E.g., Heather M. Dalmage, "Bringing the Hope Back In: The Sociological Imagination and Dreams of Transformation (The 2020 SSSP Presidential Address)," *Social Problems* 68, no. 4 (2021): 807.

29. Paul Ricœur, *Freud and Philosophy: An Essay on Interpretation* (New Haven, CT: Yale University Press, 1970), 32–36.

30. See Rita Felski, "Remember the Reader," *Chronicle of Higher Education*, December 19, 2008, https://www.chronicle.com/article/remember-the-reader/.

31. E.g., Mathieu Deflem, "The Structural Transformation of Sociology," *Society* 50, no. 2 (2013): 165.

32. Ralph Matthews, "Committing Canadian Sociology: Developing a Canadian Sociology and a Sociology of Canada," *The Canadian Review of Sociology* 51, no. 2 (2014): 125; Donald W. Light, "Contributing to Scholarship and Theory through Public Sociology," *Social Forces* 83, no. 4 (2005).

33. Stephen P. Turner, *Explaining the Normative* (Cambridge, UK, and Malden, MA: Polity, 2010), 186–91; Steven Lukes, *Moral Relativism* (New York: Picador, 2008), 10–11; Christian Smith, *What Is a Person? Rethinking Humanity, Social Life, and the Moral Good from the Person Up* (Chicago: University of Chicago Press, 2011), 317–83.

34. Weber, "Science as a Vocation."

35. Donna Haraway, "Situated Knowledges: The Science Question in Feminism and the Privilege of Partial Perspective," *Feminist Studies* 14, no. 3 (1988): 587; Pierre Bourdieu, *Pascalian Meditations*, trans. Richard Nice (Stanford, CA: Stanford University Press, 2000), 70–71.

36. Along with empirical research into this question. See John H. Evans, "Consensus and Knowledge Production in an Academic Field," *Poetics* 35, no. 1 (2007): 13–14.

37. Randall Collins, "Why the Social Sciences Won't Become High-Consensus, Rapid-Discovery Science," *Sociological Forum* 9, no. 2 (1994): 169–70.

38. Andrew D. Abbott, *Chaos of Disciplines* (Chicago: University of Chicago Press, 2001), 17.

39. See David Stark, *The Sense of Dissonance: Accounts of Worth in Economic Life* (Princeton, NJ: Princeton University Press, 2009), 4–5.

40. See Robert Wuthnow, *Why Religion Is Good for American Democracy* (Princeton, NJ: Princeton University Press, 2021), 8–9.

41. E.g., Emily Erikson, *Trade and Nation: How Companies and Politics Reshaped Economic Thought* (New York: Columbia University Press, 2021), 48–49; Eva Illouz, *Saving the Modern Soul: Therapy, Emotions, and the Culture of Self-Help* (Berkeley: University of California Press, 2008); Marion Fourcade, *Economists and Societies: Discipline and Profession in the United States, Britain, and France, 1890's to 1990's* (Princeton, NJ: Princeton University Press, 2009); G. Abend, *The Moral Background: An Inquiry into the History of Business Ethics* (Princeton, NJ: Princeton University Press, 2014).

42. Rene Almeling, *GUYnecology: The Missing Science of Men's Reproductive Health* (Berkeley: University of California Press, 2020), 46–53.

43. Hilary Putnam, "Beyond the Fact/Value Dichotomy," in *Science and the Quest for Reality*, ed. Alfred I. Tauber (London: Palgrave Macmillan, 1982); Andrew

Sayer, "Who's Afraid of Critical Social Science?" *Current Sociology* 57, no. 6 (2009); Philip S. Gorski, "Beyond the Fact/Value Distinction: Ethical Naturalism and the Social Sciences," *Society* 50, no. 6 (2013).

44. Andrew Abbott, *Processual Sociology* (Chicago: University of Chicago Press, 2016).

45. Sayer, "Who's Afraid of Critical Social Science?" 777.

46. Judith Janker, "Moral Conflicts, Premises and the Social Dimension of Agricultural Sustainability," *Agriculture and Human Values* 37, no. 1 (2020).

47. Mark Horowitz, Anthony Haynor, and Kenneth Kickham, "Sociology's Sacred Victims and the Politics of Knowledge: Moral Foundations Theory and Disciplinary Controversies," *The American Sociologist* 49, no. 4 (2018): 467.

48. Daniel Hirschman, "Stylized Facts in the Social Sciences," *Sociological Science* 3, no. 26 (2016).

49. Joanna Kempner, Jon F. Merz, and Charles L. Bosk, "Forbidden Knowledge: Public Controversy and the Production of Nonknowledge," *Sociological Forum* 26, no. 3 (2011).

50. Michèle Lamont, *How Professors Think: Inside the Curious World of Academic Judgment* (Cambridge, MA: Harvard University Press, 2009).

51. Pierre Bourdieu and Loïc J.D. Wacquant, "Epilogue: On the Possibility of a Field of World Sociology," in *Social Theory for a Changing Society*, ed. Pierre Bourdieu and James S. Coleman (Boulder and New York: Westview Press and Russell Sage Foundation, 1991), 375–76.

52. Abbott, *Chaos of Disciplines*, 6.

53. Michael Burawoy, "Sociology as a Vocation," *Contemporary Sociology* 45, no. 4 (2016); Patricia Hill Collins, *On Intellectual Activism* (Philadelphia, PA: Temple University Press, 2013); Margaret Abraham and Bandana Purkayastha, "Making a Difference: Linking Research and Action in Practice, Pedagogy, and Policy for Social Justice: Introduction," *Current Sociology* 60, no. 2 (2012); Erik Olin Wright, *Envisioning Real Utopias* (London and New York: Verso, 2010), 12–18.

54. Bellah suggested that even Weber himself—the harbinger of value-free research—utilized his theoretical apparatus to proffer profound critiques of science as part of a generalized critique of the process of rationalization. Robert N. Bellah, "The Ethical Aims of Social Inquiry," in *The Robert Bellah Reader* (Durham, NC: Duke University Press, 2006 [1983]), 39.

55. "NCSA Annual Meeting Theme," North Central Sociological Association, 2015, last accessed April 13, 2015, http://www.ncsanet.org/pdfs/2015%20theme .pdf.

56. Wright, *Envisioning Real Utopias*, 10; Eric Olin Wright, "The Real Utopia Theme at the 2012 ASA Annual Meeting," *Footnotes* 40, no. 5 (2012).

57. Peter A. Hall and Michèle Lamont, *Successful Societies: How Institutions and Culture Affect Health* (Cambridge and New York: Cambridge University Press, 2009).

58. Vincent Jeffries, ed., *The Palgrave Handbook of Altruism, Morality, and Social Solidarity: Formulating a Field of Study* (New York: Palgrave Macmillan US, 2014).

59. Shai M. Dromi, "Penny for Your Thoughts: Beggars and the Exercise of Morality in Daily Life," *Sociological Forum* 27, no. 4 (2012); Andrew C. Cohen and

Shai M. Dromi, "Advertising Morality: Maintaining Moral Worth in a Stigmatized Profession," *Theory & Society* 47, no. 2 (2018); Jan E. Stets and Michael J. Carter, "A Theory of the Self for the Sociology of Morality," *American Sociological Review* 77, no. 1 (2012); Jan E. Stets and A. D. Cast, "Resources and Identity Verification from an Identity Theory Perspective," *Sociological Perspectives* 50, no. 4 (2007); Sarah Quinn, "The Transformation of Morals in Markets: Death, Benefits, and the Exchange of Life Insurance Policies," *American Journal of Sociology* 114, no. 3 (2008).

60. Andrew Abbott, "Varieties of Normative Inquiry: Moral Alternatives to Politicization in Sociology," *The American Sociologist* 49, no. 2 (2018): 132–33.

61. For a review see C. Wright Mills, *Sociology and Pragmatism: The Higher Learning in America* (New York: Paine-Whitman Publishers, 1964).

62. Itzigsohn and Brown, *The Sociology of W. E. B. du Bois*, 17–19.

63. George Herbert Mead, Daniel R. Huebner, and Hans Joas, *Mind, Self, and Society*, ed. Charles W. Morris (Chicago: University of Chicago Press, 2015); Gary A. Cook, *George Herbert Mead: The Making of a Social Pragmatist* (Urbana: University of Illinois Press, 1993).

64. Examples of recent sociological studies drawing on pragmatist philosophy include John Levi Martin, *The Explanation of Social Action* (New York: Oxford University Press, 2011); Stefan Timmermans and Iddo Tavory, "Racist Encounters: A Pragmatist Semiotic Analysis of Interaction," *Sociological Theory* 38, no. 4 (2020); Filipe Carreira da Silva, "Following the Book: Towards a Pragmatic Sociology of the Book," *Sociology* 50, no. 6 (2016); Iddo Tavory and Nina Eliasoph, "Coordinating Futures: Toward a Theory of Anticipation," *American Journal of Sociology* 118, no. 4 (2013); Hans Joas, *The Creativity of Action* (Cambridge: Polity Press, 1996); Stefan Bargheer, *Moral Entanglements: Conserving Birds in Britain and Germany* (Chicago: University of Chicago Press, 2018); Illouz, *Saving the Modern Soul*, 20–21; Jeffrey C. Alexander, "Cultural Pragmatics: Social Performance between Ritual and Strategy," *Sociological Theory* 22, no. 4 (2004); Terence E. McDonnell, Christopher A. Bail, and Iddo Tavory, "A Theory of Resonance," *Sociological Theory* 35, no. 1 (2017); Monica Prasad, *Problem-Solving Sociology: A Guide for Students* (New York: Oxford University Press, 2021), 141–67.

65. Neil Gross, "Pragmatism and the Study of Large-Scale Social Phenomena," *Theory and Society* 47, no. 1 (2018): 88.

66. The new French pragmatist sociology has made little direct reference to American pragmatism, and Boltanski has referred to his movement as "the sociology of critique" rather than pragmatist sociology (although it has been commonly known as pragmatist). Tanja Bogusz, "Why (Not) Pragmatism?" in *The Spirit of Luc Boltanski: Essays on the "Pragmatic Sociology of Critique,"* ed. Simon Susen and Bryan S. Turner (London: Anthem Press, 2014). Laurent Thévenot compared the new French pragmatist sociology to Dewey's approach. Laurent Thévenot, "Power and Oppression from the Perspective of the Sociology of Engagements: A Comparison with Bourdieu's and Dewey's Critical Approaches to Practical Activities," *Irish Journal of Sociology* 19, no. 1 (2011).

67. Ilana F. Silber, "The Cultural Worth of 'Economies of Worth': French Pragmatic Sociology from a Cultural Sociological Perspective," in *The Sage Handbook of Cultural Sociology*, ed. David Inglis and Anna-Mari Almila (London: Sage, 2016).

68. John Dewey and James H. Tufts, "Ethics," in *The Middle Works, 1899–1924, Vol. 5*, ed. Jo Ann Boydston (Carbondale: Southern Illinois University Press, 1976), 171–84.

69. Dewey and Tufts, "Ethics," 185–206.

70. Criteria for what counts as a valid solution are often worked out through such deliberation—see John Dewey, "Democracy and Educational Administration," *Planning & Changing* 22, no. 3-4 (1991).

71. Dewey emphasizes relationality in public decision making, which allows for the creation of an ethical community based on moral and spiritual association. See John Dewey, *The Ethics of Democracy* (Ann Arbor, MI: Andrews & Company, 1888); John Dewey, *Democracy and Education by John Dewey*, ed. and with a critical introduction by Patricia H. Hinchey (Gorham, ME: Myers Education Press, 2018).

72. Luc Boltanski and Laurent Thévenot, "The Sociology of Critical Capacity," *European Journal of Social Theory* 2, no. 3 (1999): 364. See also Luc Boltanski and Laurent Thévenot, *On justification: Economies of Worth* (Princeton, NJ: Princeton University Press, 2006). Boltanski elaborates on the bases for individuals' critical capacity and the conditions for critique in Luc Boltanski, *On Critique: A Sociology of Emancipation* (Malden, MA: Polity, 2011), chapter 2. This perspective aligns with recent work on the social dimensions of cognition that shows that actors are responsive to multiple moral codes, which they elaborate through reflection and critical engagement with research—see Charles Camic, Neil Gross, and Michèle Lamont, *Social Knowledge in the Making* (Chicago: University of Chicago Press, 2011); Charles Camic and Neil Gross, "The New Sociology of Ideas," in *Blackwell Companion to Sociology*, ed. J. Blau (Oxford: Blackwell Publishing, 2004).

73. This approach differs from American pragmatism because it emphasizes the broad, preexisting logics of evaluation actors employ to determine the moral stakes for situations. Some have criticized the "pragmatist" label attached to Boltanski and Thévenot's work, e.g., Louis Quéré and Cédric Terzi, "Did You Say 'Pragmatic'? Luc Boltanski's Sociology from a Pragmatist Perspective," in *The Spirit of Luc Boltanski: Essays on the "Pragmatic Sociology of Critique*," ed. Simon Susen and Bryan S. Turner (London: Anthem Press, 2014), 95–99.

74. On this point see Cyril Lemieux, "The Moral Idealism of Ordinary People as a Sociological Challenge: Reflections on the French Reception of Luc Boltanski and Laurent Thévenot's *On Justification*," in *The Spirit of Luc Boltanski: Essays on the "Pragmatic Sociology of Critique*," ed. Simon Susen and Bryan S. Turner (London: Anthem Press, 2014); Cohen and Dromi, "Advertising Morality." However, in his later work, Boltanski also identified the limitation to actors' awareness and critical abilities in specific institutional and political contexts. See Boltanski, *On Critique: A Sociology of Emancipation*, chapters 3–5.

75. Ilana Friedrich Silber, "Pragmatic Sociology as Cultural Sociology: Beyond Repertoire Theory?" *European Journal of Social Theory* 6, no. 4 (2003). For a broad overview of the background, development, and applications of the new French pragmatist sociology see Paul Blokker, "Pragmatic Sociology: Theoretical Evolvement and Empirical Application," *European Journal of Social Theory* 14, no. 3 (2011); Lemieux, "The Moral Idealism of Ordinary People."

76. Boltanski et al., "Sociology of Critique or Critical Theory?" 562.

77. E.g., Bourdieu, *Homo Academicus*.

78. See particularly Luc Boltanski and Laurent Thévenot, "The Reality of Moral Expectations: A Sociology of Situated Judgement," *Philosophical Explorations* 3, no. 3 (2000): 211–13.

79. We distinguish our approach from recent scholarship which has argued that moral justifications function as a distinct form of "moral capital" in the sense in which Bourdieu uses it. Mariana Valverde, "Moral Capital," *Canadian Journal of Law and Society* 9, no. 1 (1994); Gabriel Ignatow, "Culture and Embodied Cognition: Moral Discourses in Internet Support Groups for Overeaters," *Social Forces* 88, no. 2 (2009). Yet, much like the new French pragmatism, such research not only owes a great deal to Bourdieu's theory but also departs from it in significant ways. See Bruce Curtis, "Reworking Moral Regulation: Metaphorical Capital and the Field of Disinterest," *Canadian Journal of Sociology* 22, no. 3 (1997).

80. For example, a current debate revolves around whether the effect of moral values on human behavior can be measured through questionnaires, or whether values are in fact interests that are not adequately captured through surveying methods. See Andrew Miles, "The (Re)Genesis of Values: Examining the Importance of Values for Action," *American Sociological Review* 80, no. 4 (2015); Ann Swidler, "Culture in Action: Symbols and Strategies," *American Sociological Review* 51, no. 2 (1986). Another conversation looks at the difference between declarative and nondeclarative culture in influencing moral decision making: e.g., Omar Lizardo et al., "What Are Dual Process Models? Implications for Cultural Analysis in Sociology," *Sociological Theory* 34, no. 4 (2016).

81. Ann Swidler, "Comment on Stephen Vaisey's 'Socrates, Skinner, and Aristotle: Three Ways of Thinking about Culture in Action,'" *Sociological Forum* 23, no. 3 (2008): 617.

82. Hirschman, "Stylized Facts in the Social Sciences."

83. E.g., Peter Wood, "The Regnerus Affair at UT Austin," *Chronicle of Higher Education*, July 15, 2012, https://www-chronicle-com.ezp-prod1.hul.harvard.edu/blogs/innovations/the-regnerus-affair-at-ut-austin.

84. E.g., Simon Cheng and Brian Powell, "Measurement, Methods, and Divergent Patterns: Reassessing the Effects of Same-Sex Parents," *Social Science Research* 52 (2015).

85. See also Boltanski's discussion of the Aristotelian concept of *topic* in Luc Boltanski, *Distant Suffering: Morality, Media and Politics* (Cambridge and New York: Cambridge University Press, 1999), xv; Shai M. Dromi and Eva Illouz, "Recovering Morality: Pragmatic Sociology and Literary Studies," *New Literary History* 41, no. 2 (2010): 364.

86. See Rodrigo Cordero, *Crisis and Critique: On the Fragile Foundations of Social Life* (New York: Routledge, 2017). This is in contradistinction to field theory's focus on struggles between actors over symbolic capitals, e.g., Julian Go and Monika Krause, "Fielding Transnationalism: An Introduction," *The Sociological Review* 64, no. 2 (Supplement) (2016).

87. Boltanski and Thévenot, *On Justification*, 277–78.

88. A burgeoning auxiliary literature exists on their approach. For a collection of articles providing some sense of this work see Simon Susen and Bryan S.

Turner, eds., *The Spirit of Luc Boltanski: Essays on the "Pragmatic Sociology of Critique"* (London: Anthem Books, 2014).

89. Paul Lichterman and Isaac Ariail Reed, "Theory and Contrastive Explanation in Ethnography," *Sociological Methods & Research* 44, no. 4 (2015): 590–91.

90. See also Lichterman and Reed, "Theory and Contrastive Explanation in Ethnography," 624.

91. E.g., Kempner, Merz, and Bosk, "Forbidden Knowledge."

92. Indeed, meta-communication was originally defined by Gregory Bateson as a message "which either explicitly or implicitly defines a frame" and thus "gives the receiver instruction or aids . . . to understand the messages included within that frame." Gregory Bateson, *Steps to an Ecology of Mind* (Chicago: University of Chicago Press, 2000), 188.

93. Indirect meta-communication turns attention toward the theoretical logic that changes the frame for the conversation at hand and thus provides the logics scholars have used to denounce the way research has been conducted thus far. See also Jorge Fontdevila, M. Pilar Opazo, and Harrison C. White, "Order at the Edge of Chaos: Meanings from Netdom Switchings Across Functional Systems," *Sociological Theory* 29, no. 3 (2011).

94. Stets and Carter, "A Theory of the Self for the Sociology of Morality," 126.

95. William Hamilton Sewell, *Logics of History: Social Theory and Social Transformation* (Chicago: University of Chicago Press, 2005), 209.

96. Sewell, *Logics of History*, 45 and 108–9.

97. Julia Adams, Elisabeth S. Clemens, and Ann Shola Orloff, "Introduction: Social Theory, Modernity, and the Three Waves of Historical Sociology," in *Remaking Modernity: Politics, History, and Sociology*, ed. Julia Adams, Elisabeth S. Clemens, and Ann Shola Orloff (Durham, NC: Duke University Press, 2005).

98. Sewell, *Logics of History*, 143–45.

99. Jason Seawright and John Gerring, "Case Selection Techniques in Case Study Research: A Menu of Qualitative and Quantitative Options," *Political Research Quarterly* 61, no. 2 (2008): 225–26.

100. While some have argued that efforts that emphasize moral conflict in the study of scientific communication risk selecting on the dependent variable in making a generalizable claim about science, this criticism does not apply to our study. Our analysis of cases of moral-cum-sociological conflict does not suggest that sociological conversations are always moral or that we are providing an exhaustive list of all the possible outcomes of sociological debate. Instead, we focus on highlighting common outcomes to moral controversies in sociology to demonstrate sociologists' capacity to mobilize moral repertoires and to debate them. For a critique of selection on the dependent variable in analyses of scientific communication see Dan Kahan, "Don't Select on the Dependent Variable in Studying the Science Communication Problem," The Cultural Cognition Project at Yale Law School, January 17, 2013, http://www.culturalcognition.net/blog/2013/11/19/dont-select-on-the-dependent-variable-in-studying-the-scienc.html.

101. As Luker put it, these cases are "reasonably representative of the larger phenomenon." Kristin Luker, *Salsa Dancing Into the Social Sciences: Research in an Age of Info-Glut* (Cambridge, MA: Harvard University Press, 2008), 103.

102. E.g., Dorothy E. Roberts and Oliver Rollins, "Why Sociology Matters to Race and Biosocial Science," *Annual Review of Sociology* 46, no. 1 (2020).

103. Pierre Bourdieu, *Sociology Is a Martial Art: Political Writings by Pierre Bourdieu*, ed. Gisèle Sapiro et al. (New York: New Press, 2010).

104. Numerous authors have referred to their study fields as moral minefields to emphasize the grave moral implications of the matters at hand in their research fields. Elizabeth Murphy, "'Breast Is Best': Infant Feeding Decisions and Maternal Deviance," *Sociology of Health & Illness* 21, no. 2 (1999): 205; see also Joyce L. Marshall, Mary Godfrey, and Mary J. Renfrew, "Being a 'Good Mother': Managing Breastfeeding and Merging Identities," *Social Science & Medicine* 65, no. 10 (2007): 2148; Troy Duster, "A Post-Genomic Surprise. The Molecular Reinscription of Race in Science, Law and Medicine," *The British Journal of Sociology* 66, no. 1 (2015): 13. We borrow this term to refer to the terrain sociologists navigate as they conduct their research.

105. We agree with Susen that their differences notwithstanding, Bourdieu's critical sociology and Boltanski's pragmatist sociology share themes that present numerous opportunities for productive dialogue. In this spirit, we do not aim to discredit the rich existing critical literature on academia; rather, we show that working academics can grasp and counteract the power dynamics Bourdieu outlined. See Simon Susen, "Towards a Dialogue between Pierre Bourdieu's 'Critical Sociology' and Luc Boltanski's 'Pragmatic Sociology of Critique,'" in *The Spirit of Luc Boltanski: Essays on the "Pragmatic Sociology of Critique*," ed. Simon Susen and Bryan S. Turner (London: Anthem Press, 2014).

106. Quoted in Irving Louis Horowitz, *C. Wright Mills: An American Utopian* (New York and London: Free Press and Collier Macmillan, 1983), 119.

CHAPTER ONE

1. Pierre Bourdieu and Roger Chartier, "The Sociologist's Craft," in *The Sociologist and the Historian* (Cambridge: Polity, 2015), 5.

2. Irving Louis Horowitz, *C. Wright Mills: An American Utopian* (New York: Free Press, 1983), 41; see also James R. Abbott, "Critical Sociologies and *Ressentiment*: The Examples of C. Wright Mills and Howard Becker," *The American Sociologist* 37, no. 3 (2006): 20–21.

3. Edward Shils, "The Great Obsession," *The Spectator*, July 5, 1963, 20.

4. Norman K. Denzin, "Re-Reading *The Sociological Imagination*," *The American Sociologist* 20, no. 3 (1989): 280.

5. Earl Wright II, *The First American School of Sociology: W. E. B. Du Bois and the Atlanta Sociological Laboratory* (Milton Park, UK: Routledge, 2017), 66.

6. Pierre Bourdieu and Loïc J. D. Wacquant, "Epilogue: On the Possibility of a Field of World Sociology," in *Social Theory for a Changing Society*, ed. Pierre Bourdieu and James S. Coleman (Boulder, CO, and New York: Westview Press and Russell Sage Foundation, 1991).

7. Greg Lukianoff and Jonathan Haidt, *The Coddling of the American Mind: How Good Intentions and Bad Ideas Are Setting Up a Generation for Failure* (New York: Penguin Press, 2018).

8. Pierre Bourdieu, *The Sociologist and the Historian*, ed. Roger Chartier and David Fernbach (Cambridge, UK, and Malden, MA: Polity Press, 2015), 5.

9. Charles Camic, Neil Gross, and Michèle Lamont, *Social Knowledge in the Making* (Chicago: University of Chicago Press, 2011).

10. Michèle Lamont, *How Professors Think: Inside the Curious World of Academic Judgment* (Cambridge, MA: Harvard University Press, 2009).

11. Karl Mannheim, *Ideology and Utopia*, trans. Louis Wirth (London: Routledge, 1936), 142–43.

12. Mannheim, *Ideology and Utopia*, 226.

13. Jeffrey C. Alexander, *Theoretical Logic in Sociology, vol. 1: Positivism, Presuppositions, and Current Controversies* (Berkeley and Los Angeles: University of California Press, 1982), 41–43.

14. Erik Olin Wright, *Envisioning Real Utopias* (London and New York: Verso, 2010).

15. Mannheim, *Ideology and Utopia*, 136.

16. C. Wright Mills, "Situated Actions and Vocabularies of Motive," *American Sociological Review* 5, no. 6 (1940).

17. C. Wright Mills, *The Sociological Imagination* (New York: Oxford University Press, 1959), 21.

18. Patricia Hill Collins, *Black Feminist Thought: Knowledge, Consciousness, and the Politics of Empowerment*, 2nd ed. (London and New York: Routledge, 2014), 15.

19. Patricia Hill Collins, *On Intellectual Activism* (Philadelphia, PA: Temple University Press, 2013).

20. The term has also been translated from French as, e.g., polity, world, and regime.

21. Peter Wagner, "A Renewal of Social Theory That Remains Necessary: The Sociology of Critical Capacity Twenty Years After," in *The Spirit of Luc Boltanski: Essays on the "Pragmatic Sociology of Critique*," ed. Simon Susen and Bryan S. Turner (London: Anthem Press, 2014), 239.

22. Laurent Thévenot, Michael Moody, and Claudette Lafaye, "Forms of Valuing Nature: Arguments and Modes of Justification in French and American Environmental Disputes," in *Rethinking Comparative Cultural Sociology: Repertoires of Evaluation in France and the United States*, ed. Laurent Thévenot and Michèle Lamont, Cambridge Cultural Social Studies (Cambridge: Cambridge University Press, 2000).

23. There are several different types of tests that actors use, about which we cannot go into detail here. See Luc Boltanski, *On Critique: A Sociology of Emancipation* (Malden, MA: Polity, 2011). For a more general discussion of testing as a social practice see Noortje Marres and David Stark, "Put to the Test: For a New Sociology of Testing," *The British Journal of Sociology* 71, no. 3 (2020).

24. Ann Swidler, "Culture in Action: Symbols and Strategies," *American Sociological Review* 51, no. 2 (1986): 278–80.

25. Luc Boltanski and Laurent Thévenot, "The Sociology of Critical Capacity," *European Journal of Social Theory* 2, no. 3 (1999): 359–61; Michèle Lamont, "Toward a Comparative Sociology of Valuation and Evaluation," *Annual Review of Sociology* 38, no. 1 (2012).

26. E.g., Nathalie Heinich, *L'Épreuve de la grandeur: Prix littéraires et reconnaissance* (Paris: Découverte, 1999).

27. Luc Boltanski and Ève Chiapello, *The New Spirit of Capitalism* (London and New York: Verso, 2005), 167–202.

28. David M. Halperin, *Saint Foucault: Towards a Gay Hagiography* (New York: Oxford University Press, 1995).

29. Daniel Zamora and Michael C. Behrent, *Foucault and Neoliberalism*, ed. Daniel Zamora (Malden, MA: Polity Press, 2015).

30. Adam Smith, *The Wealth of Nations. Books 1–3* (Lexington, KY: Seven Treasures Publications, 2009 [1776]).

31. Friedrich Engels, *The Origin of the Family, Private Property, and the State*, ed. Lewis Henry Morgan and Friedrich Engels (New York: Pathfinder Press, 1972 [1884]).

32. Max Weber, *Economy and Society: An Outline of Interpretative Sociology*, ed. Guenther Roth and Claus Wittich, vol. 1 (Berkeley, Los Angeles, and London: University of California Press, 1978), 223–26.

33. Frantz Fanon, *Black Skin, White Masks*, ed. Charles Lam Markmann (New York: Grove Press, Inc., 1967), 60–82; Edward W. Said, *Orientalism* (New York: Vintage Books, 1979), 255–83.

34. Audre Lorde, *Sister Outsider: Essays and Speeches* (Trumansburg, NY: Crossing Press, 1984); Sonia Torres, "La Conciencia de la Mestiza / Towards a New Consciousness: Uma Conversação Inter-Americana Com Gloria Anzaldúa," *Estudos Feministas* 13, no. 3 (2005).

35. Luc Boltanski and Laurent Thévenot, *On Justification: Economies of Worth* (Princeton, NJ: Princeton University Press, 2006); Michael Walzer, *Spheres of Justice: A Defense of Pluralism and Equality* (New York: Basic Books, 1983).

36. Michael J. LaCour and Donald P. Green, "When Contact Changes Minds: An Experiment on Transmission of Support for Gay Equality [retracted]," *Science* 346, no. 6215 (2014).

37. Benedict Carey, "Gay Advocates Can Shift Same-Sex Marriage Views," *New York Times*, December 11, 2014, https://www.nytimes.com/2014/12/12/health/gay-marriage-canvassing-study-science.html.

38. Harry McGee, "Personal Route to Reach Public Central to Yes Campaign," *The Irish Times*, May 14, 2015, https://www.irishtimes.com/news/politics/personal-route-to-reach-public-central-to-yes-campaign-1.2211282.

39. David Broockman, Joshua Kalla, and P. M. Aronow, "Irregularities in LaCour (2014)," *MetaArXiv Preprints*, January 7, 2020 [2015], https://doi.org/doi:10.31222/osf.io/qy2se.

40. Tom Bartlett, "The Unraveling of Michael LaCour," *Chronicle of Higher Education*, June 2, 2015, https://www.chronicle.com/article/the-unraveling-of-michael-lacour/.

41. A *Wall Street Journal* editorial made precisely this claim—*Wall Street Journal*, "Scientific Fraud and Politics: Look Who Is Lecturing Republicans about Scientific Truth," *Wall Street Journal*, June 5, 2015, https://www.wsj.com/articles/scientific-fraud-and-politics-1433544688.

42. Elijah Anderson, *A Place on the Corner* (Chicago: University of Chicago Press, 1978).

43. Michèle Lamont et al., *Getting Respect: Responding to Stigma and Discrimination in the United States, Brazil, and Israel* (Princeton, NJ: Princeton University Press, 2016).

44. We discussed meta-communication in detail in the Introduction. See Paul Lichterman and Isaac Ariail Reed, "Theory and Contrastive Explanation in Ethnography," *Sociological Methods & Research* 44, no. 4 (2015).

45. In a previous article about the debates over the secularization thesis, we analyzed the repertoires scholars invoked as they discussed the phenomenon of secularization and how they should relate to it directly. Here, we focus exclusively on the meta-communication scholars offered about the research—and *not* about the phenomenon of secularization itself—to demonstrate the type of analysis we will be applying in subsequent chapters. For comparison see Shai M. Dromi and Samuel D. Stabler, "Good on Paper: Sociological Critique, Pragmatism, and Secularization Theory," *Theory and Society* 48, no. 2 (2019).

46. Courtney Bender, "Pluralism and Secularism," in *Religion on the Edge: De-Centering and Re-Centering the Sociology of Religion*, ed. Courtney Bender et al. (New York: Oxford University Press, 2013); Philip S. Gorski, "The Return of the Repressed: Religion and the Political Unconscious of Historical Sociology," in *Remaking Modernity: Politics, History, and Sociology* (Durham, NC: Duke University Press, 2005), https://doi.org/10.1215/9780822385882-007.

47. Craig Jackson Calhoun, "The Radicalism of Tradition: Community Strength or Venerable Disguise and Borrowed Language?" *American Journal of Sociology* 88, no. 5 (1983); Philip S. Gorski, *The Disciplinary Revolution: Calvinism and the Rise of the State in Early Modern Europe* (Chicago: University of Chicago Press, 2003).

48. Robert N. Bellah, "New Religious Consciousness and the Crisis in Modernity," in *The New Religious Consciousness*, ed. Charles Y. Glock, Robert Neelly Bellah, and Randall H. Alfred (Berkeley: University of California Press, 1976); Rodney Stark and William Sims Bainbridge, "Of Churches, Sects, and Cults: Preliminary Concepts for a Theory of Religious Movements," *Journal for the Scientific Study of Religion* 18, no. 2 (1979).

49. Bender, "Pluralism and Secularism"; Philip S. Gorski and Ateş Altinordu, "After Secularization?" *Annual Review of Sociology* 34 (2008).

50. José Casanova, "Rethinking Secularization: A Global Comparative Perspective," *The Hedgehog Review* 8, no. 1-2 (2006); Michael Warner, Jonathan VanAntwerpen, and Craig J. Calhoun, *Varieties of Secularism in a Secular Age* (Cambridge, MA: Harvard University Press, 2010).

51. Calhoun, "The Radicalism of Tradition"; José Casanova, *Public Religions in the Modern World* (Chicago: University of Chicago Press, 1994). For similar arguments in recent literature see Peter Stamatov, *The Origins of Global Humanitarianism: Religion, Empires, and Advocacy* (Cambridge: Cambridge University Press, 2013).

52. Rodney Stark and William Sims Bainbridge, "Networks of Faith: Interpersonal Bonds and Recruitment to Cults and Sects," *American Journal of Sociology* 85, no. 6 (1980).

53. Stark and Bainbridge, "Of Churches, Sects, and Cults"; Rodney Stark, *A Theory of Religion*, ed. William Sims Bainbridge (New York: P. Lang, 1987).

54. Rodney Stark, "Secularization, R.I.P.," *Sociology of Religion* 60, no. 3 (1999): 270.

55. We do not mean that sociologists of religion have engaged in moral justi-fication and critique *only* through the topic of secularization. Samuel Perry and Andrew Whitehead, for example, have justified a series of studies of US white Christian nationalism as providing information germane to American democracy. Andrew L. Whitehead, *Taking America Back for God: Christian Nationalism in the United States*, ed. Samuel L. Perry (New York: Oxford University Press, 2020). Other scholars have recently posited that research should push back against racist struc-tures and have examined how racism has affected Black church and American religiosity dynamics—e.g., Anthea D. Butler, *White Evangelical Racism: The Politics of Morality in America* (Chapel Hill: University of North Carolina Press, 2021).

56. Roger Finke and Rodney Stark, *The Churching of America, 1776–1990: Win-ners and Losers in Our Religious Economy* (New Brunswick, NJ: Rutgers University Press, 1992); Rodney Stark and Roger Finke, *Acts of Faith: Explaining the Human Side of Religion* (Berkeley: University of California Press, 2000).

57. Paul Froese, *The Plot to Kill God: Findings from the Soviet Experiment in Secularization* (Berkeley: University of California Press, 2008); Fenggang Yang, "Oligopoly Dynamics: Consequences of Religious Regulation," *Social Compass* 57, no. 2 (2010).

58. Finke and Stark, *The Churching of America, 1776–1990*; Laurence R. Iannac-cone, "Why Strict Churches Are Strong," *American Journal of Sociology* 99, no. 5 (1994).

59. See the strong pronouncements Coleman proffered in his presidential ad-dress to the American Sociological Association—James S. Coleman, "The Ratio-nal Reconstruction of Society: 1992 Presidential Address," *American Sociological Review* 58, no. 1 (1993): 14.

60. Laurence R. Iannaccone, Roger Finke, and Rodney Stark, "Deregulating Religion: The Economics of Church and State," *Economic Inquiry* 35, no. 2 (1997); Stark and Finke, *Acts of Faith*.

61. Brian J. Grim and Roger Finke, *The Price of Freedom Denied: Religious Per-secution and Conflict in the Twenty-first Century* (New York: Cambridge University Press, 2011), 202.

62. Grim and Finke, *The Price of Freedom Denied*, 205.

63. Anthony James Gill, *The Political Origins of Religious Liberty* (Cambridge and New York: Cambridge University Press, 2008), 229.

64. Roger Finke, "Presidential Address: Origins and Consequences of Religious Freedoms: A Global Overview," *Sociology of Religion* 74, no. 3 (2013): 305.

65. Finke, "Presidential Address," 309–10.

66. R. Stephen Warner, *A Church of Our Own: Disestablishment and Diversity in American Religion* (New Brunswick, NJ: Rutgers University Press, 2005), 48.

67. Warner, *A Church of Our Own*, 49.

68. Steve Bruce, *Secularization: In Defence of an Unfashionable Theory* (Oxford: Oxford University Press, 2011); Philip S. Gorski, "Historicizing the Secularization Debate: Church, State, and Society in Late Medieval and Early Modern Europe, ca. 1300 to 1700," *American Sociological Review* 65, no. 1 (2000); Gorski and Altinordu, "After Secularization?"; Mark Chaves and Philip S. Gorski, "Religious Pluralism and Religious Participation," *Annual Review of Sociology* 27 (2001).

69. Philip S. Gorski and Gülay Türkmen-Dervişoğlu, "Religion, Nationalism, and Violence: An Integrated Approach," *Annual Review of Sociology* 39, no. 1 (2013): 197.

70. Casanova, *Public Religions in the Modern World*, 224–25. This book was written before the post-USSR resurgence of Russian religiosity.

71. Gorski, "The Return of the Repressed," 176–77.

72. See especially Froese, *The Plot to Kill God*.

73. Talal Asad, *Formations of the Secular: Christianity, Islam, Modernity* (Stanford, CA: Stanford University Press, 2003).

74. Christian Smith, *The Secular Revolution: Power, Interests, and Conflict in the Secularization of American Public Life* (Berkeley: University of California Press, 2003).

75. Casanova, *Public Religions in the Modern World*, 234.

76. Ahmet T. Kuru, *Secularism and State Policies toward Religion: The United States, France, and Turkey* (Cambridge and New York: Cambridge University Press, 2009).

77. Charles Taylor, "Why We Need a Radical Redefinition of Secularism," in *The Power of Religion in the Public Sphere*, ed. Eduardo Mandieta and Jonathan VanAntwerpen (New York: Columbia University Press, 2011), 36.

78. Christian Smith et al., "Roundtable on the Sociology of Religion: Twenty-Three Theses on the Status of Religion in American Sociology—A Mellon Working-Group Reflection," *Journal of the American Academy of Religion* 81, no. 4 (2013).

79. David Smilde and Matthew May, "Causality, Normativity, and Diversity in 40 Years of U.S. Sociology of Religion: Contributions to Paradigmatic Reflection," *Sociology of Religion* 76, no. 4 (2015): 285.

80. Penny Edgell, "A Cultural Sociology of Religion: New Directions," *Annual Review of Sociology* 38, no. 1 (2012); Peggy Levitt, "Religion on the Move: Mapping Global Cultural Production and Consumption," in *Religion on the Edge: De-Centering and Re-Centering the Sociology of Religion*, ed. Courtney Bender et al. (New York: Oxford University Press, 2013).

81. Nancy Tatom Ammerman, *Sacred Stories, Spiritual Tribes: Finding Religion in Everyday Life* (Oxford: Oxford University Press, 2013); Paul Lichterman, "Religion in Public Action: From Actors to Settings," *Sociological Theory* 30, no. 1 (2012).

82. See especially Edgell, "A Cultural Sociology of Religion," 258.

83. Robert Wuthnow, "General Concepts and Domain-Specific Concepts: An Argument about the Study of Religion in Sociology," *Sociology of Religion* 75, no. 4 (2014).

84. Joseph O'Brian Baker and Buster Smith, "None Too Simple: Examining Issues of Religious Nonbelief and Nonbelonging in the United States," *Journal for the Scientific Study of Religion* 48, no. 4 (2009): 732.

85. Chaeyoon Lim, Carol Ann MacGregor, and Robert D. Putnam, "Secular and Liminal: Discovering Heterogeneity among Religious Nones," *Journal for the Scientific Study of Religion* 49, no. 4 (2010).

86. Christopher H. Seto, "Understanding Delinquency among the Spiritual but Not Religious," *Sociology of Religion* 82, no. 2 (2020).

87. Carolyn Chen, *Work Pray Code: When Work Becomes Religion in Silicon Valley* (Princeton, NJ: Princeton University Press, 2022).

88. Wes Markofski, "The Public Sociology of Religion," *Sociology of Religion* 76, no. 4 (2015).

89. Fenggang Yang, "Exceptionalism or Chinamerica: Measuring Religious Change in the Globalizing World Today," *Journal for the Scientific Study of Religion* 55, no. 1 (2016).

90. Yang, "Exceptionalism or Chinamerica," 8.

91. While not overtly responding to the debate over secularization, itself largely supplanted by a "post-secular discourse," this passage helps capture the sentiments of leading sociologists of religion in the 2020s. Samuel Perry, "Excited to Announce My New Book Project Now Under Contract," Twitter post, updated November 19, 2021, last accessed January 24, 2022, https://twitter.com/socofthe-sacred/status/1461693449040797706.

92. Boltanski and Chiapello originally used the term "mystification" to highlight the evasive features of this response. By contrast, we adopt the term "reconstitution" from Clayman's discussion of Garfinkel to point to the generative sides of this type of discourse. Steven E. Clayman, "Review Article: The Dialectic of Ethnomethodology," *Semiotica* 107, no. 1-2 (1995): 107.

93. Although the three types of responses can occur simultaneously, reconstitution will usually begin at a later stage than the other responses.

94. While a fourth option—ignoring the critique—exists, we confine our discussion here to ways of actively engaging with critiques.

95. To model the three most common types of responses, we draw on Boltanski and Chiapello's model of critiques of capitalism, as developed in their book, *The New Spirit of Capitalism*. We adapt this model to track scholarly debates as well. This model is partially derived from Garfinkel's more generalized model of the responses to perceived injustice—Harold Garfinkel, *Studies in Ethnomethodology* (Cambridge, UK: Polity Press, 1984).

96. While Sullivan is trained as a historian, much of her career was in sociology-adjacent positions with research and publications conversing directly with the sociology of religion.

97. Winnifred Fallers Sullivan, *The Impossibility of Religious Freedom* (Princeton, NJ: Princeton University Press, 2005).

98. Winnifred Fallers Sullivan et al., *After Secular Law* (Stanford, CA: Stanford Law Books, 2011).

99. Winnifred Fallers Sullivan and Lori G. Beaman, *Varieties of Religious Establishment* (London and New York: Routledge, 2016).

100. Sullivan and Beaman, *Varieties of Religious Establishment*, 7.

101. For a compelling example of such discussion see Tukufu Zuberi, *Thicker Than Blood: How Racial Statistics Lie* (Minneapolis: University of Minnesota Press, 2001).

CHAPTER TWO

1. Richard J. Herrnstein and Charles A. Murray, *The Bell Curve: Intelligence and Class Structure in American Life* (New York: Free Press, 1994), 269–316. Coauthor Richard Herrnstein passed away in 1994.

2. For critiques of the book see Clayton P. Alderfer, "The Science and Non-science of Psychologists' Responses to *The Bell Curve*," *Professional Psychology: Research and Practice* 34, no. 3 (2003).

3. Tim Hallett, Orla Stapleton, and Michael Sauder, "Public Ideas: Their Varieties and Careers," *American Sociological Review* 84, no. 3 (2019).

4. Stephanie Saul, "Dozens of Middlebury Students Are Disciplined for Charles Murray Protest," *New York Times*, May 24, 2017, https://www.nytimes.com/2017/05/24/us/middlebury-college-charles-murray-bell-curve.html.

5. Ezra Klein, "The Sam Harris Debate," *Vox*, January 30, 2018, https://www.vox.com/2018/4/9/17210248/sam-harris-ezra-klein-charles-murray-transcript-podcast.

6. E.g., Matthew Yglesias, "The Great Awokening," *Vox*, April 1, 2019, https://www.vox.com/2019/3/22/18259865/great-awokening-white-liberals-race-polling-trump-2020.

7. Christian Smith, *The Sacred Project of American Sociology* (New York: Oxford University Press, 2014); Greg Lukianoff and Jonathan Haidt, *The Coddling of the American Mind: How Good Intentions and Bad Ideas Are Setting Up a Generation for Failure* (New York: Penguin Press, 2018).

8. Melinda C. Mills and Felix C. Tropf, "Sociology, Genetics, and the Coming of Age of Sociogenomics," *Annual Review of Sociology* 46, no. 1 (2020); Dorothy E. Roberts and Oliver Rollins, "Why Sociology Matters to Race and Biosocial Science," *Annual Review of Sociology* 46, no. 1 (2020).

9. Rogers Brubaker, *Trans: Gender and Race in an Age of Unsettled Identities* (Princeton, NJ: Princeton University Press, 2016), 4.

10. Of course, taking such controversial positions may also be professionally beneficial to sociologists. However, in taking a controversial position, scholars also take on a claim of moral responsibility for their activities, and in turn must find ways to publicly justify their stance. We focus on those justifications and their conditions of acceptability, and not on the professional dynamics that may have influenced the debates behind the scenes.

11. "Progress" in academic debate should not be equated with "progress" in social life. For a compelling critique of "progress discourse" see Louise Seamster and Victor Ray, "Against Teleology in the Study of Race: Toward the Abolition of the Progress Paradigm," *Sociological Theory* 36, no. 4 (2018).

12. Hannah Landecker and Aaron Panofsky, "From Social Structure to Gene Regulation, and Back: A Critical Introduction to Environmental Epigenetics for Sociology," *Annual Review of Sociology* 39, no. 1 (2013): 352–53.

13. Aldon D. Morris, *The Scholar Denied: W. E. B. Du Bois and the Birth of Modern Sociology* (Oakland: University of California Press, 2015); Thomas C. Leonard, *Illiberal Reformers: Race, Eugenics, and American Economics in the Progressive Era* (Princeton, NJ: Princeton University Press, 2016); Derek J. Robey, Jocelyn Viterna, and Hannah Katz, "Social Evolutionary Thought in Sociological Theory" (unpublished manuscript, October 8, 2020), PDF file.

14. Bruno Latour, *Science in Action: How to Follow Scientists and Engineers through Society* (Cambridge, MA: Harvard University Press, 1987). (Although Latour would object to the idea that an explanation to a controversy or of its resolu-

tion can be offered, both on practical and meta-theoretical terms. See *Science in Action*, 13, 258.)

15. See for example Gil Eyal, *The Crisis of Expertise* (Cambridge, UK, and Medford, MA: Polity Press, 2019).

16. E.g., Hallett, Stapleton, and Sauder, "Public Ideas," 559–60.

17. E.g., Elijah Anderson, *Code of the Street: Decency, Violence, and the Moral Life of the Inner City*. (New York: W. W. Norton, 1999).

18. William Julius Wilson, "The Moynihan Report and Research on the Black Community," *The ANNALS of the American Academy of Political and Social Science* 621, no. 1 (2009): 34–35.

19. Luc Boltanski, *Love and Justice as Competences: Three Essays on the Sociology of Action*, ed. Catherine Porter (Cambridge and Malden, MA: Polity, 2012). While we use the term "engagement" in this chapter, we differentiate the framework we use from Thévenot's notion of "regimes of engagement," which pertains primarily to coordination between actors over questions of the public good. See for comparison Laurent Thévenot, *L'Action au pluriel: Sociologie des régimes d'engagement* (Paris: Découverte, 2006); Laurent Thévenot, "Organisation and Power: Critical Plurality of Engagement Regimes," *Sociologia del lavoro* 104 (2006).

20. Boltanski calls each cell in the implied two-by-two table a *regime of action* (Boltanski, *Love and Justice as Competences*, 68–78), which is a typical form by which actors characterize a social situation and conceive of appropriate action therein.

21. While the ideal typical form of this regime (called "agape") is unconditional parental love, it may also refer to other peaceful relationships where actors do not seek to establish equivalences and do not find using *cités* to debate justice relevant or important (Boltanski, *Love and Justice as Competences*, 104–28); and see Ilana F. Silber, "Luc Boltanski and the Gift: Beyond Love, Beyond Suspicion . . . ?," in *The Spirit of Luc Boltanski: Essays on the "Pragmatic Sociology of Critique*," ed. Simon Susen and Bryan S. Turner (London: Anthem Press, 2014).

22. Ignoring is distinct in that it sees no cause to offer justification despite known diversity of views on a subject. Once accused, one may claim ignorance or deflect charges of a moral transgression through what sociologists call "techniques of neutralization"—ways of claiming exception to the normal rule (e.g., by condemning the condemners or appealing to higher loyalties). Gresham M. Sykes and David Matza, "Techniques of Neutralization: A Theory of Delinquency," *American Sociological Review* 22, no. 2 (1957): 667–69.

23. Francis Galton, "Eugenics: Its Definition, Scope, and Aims," *American Journal of Sociology* 10, no. 1 (1904): 2.

24. Galton, "Eugenics," 1.

25. Karl Pearson, "Discussion," *American Journal of Sociology* 10, no. 1 (1904): 7.

26. Bernard Shaw, "Discussion," *American Journal of Sociology* 10, no. 1 (1904): 21.

27. G. A. Archdall Reid, "Discussion," *American Journal of Sociology* 10, no. 1 (1904): 16.

28. Called at the time "American Sociological Society."

29. Daniel Breslau, "The American Spencerians: Theorizing a New Science," in *Sociology in America: A History*, ed. Craig J. Calhoun, Chicago Scholarship Online (Chicago: University of Chicago Press, 2007).

30. Francis Galton, "The History of Twins, as a Criterion of the Relative Powers of Nature and Nurture (1, 2)," *International Journal of Epidemiology* 41, no. 4 (2012 [1875]). See also Nicholas W. Gillham, "Sir Francis Galton and the Birth of Eugenics," *Annual Review of Genetics* 35, no. 1 (2001).

31. Herbert Spencer, *The Study of Sociology* (New York: Appleton, 1901), 94; see also Breslau, "The American Spencerians"; Tukufu Zuberi, *Thicker Than Blood: How Racial Statistics Lie* (Minneapolis: University of Minnesota Press, 2003), 23–24.

32. While Spencer's own thought on laissez-faire economy focused on trade rather than social governance, his ideas lent themselves well to anti-socialist thinking in the 1880s and 1890s and were read as supporting laissez-faire policies on government welfare as well—see Mark Francis, "Herbert Spencer and the Myth of Laissez-Faire," *Journal of the History of Ideas* 39, no. 2 (1978).

33. William I. Thomas, "The Mind of Woman and the Lower Races," *American Journal of Sociology* 12, no. 4 (1907).

34. Earl Wright II, *The First American School of Sociology: W. E. B. Du Bois and the Atlanta Sociological Laboratory* (Milton Park, UK: Routledge, 2017); Morris, *The Scholar Denied*.

35. Talcott Parsons, *The Structure of Social Action: A Study in Social Theory with Special Reference to a Group of Recent European Writers* (New York: McGraw-Hill Book Company, Inc., 1937), 3.

36. see David L. Brunsma and Jennifer Padilla Wyse, "The Possessive Investment in White Sociology," *Sociology of Race and Ethnicity* 5, no. 1 (2018): 2–4.

37. Talcott Parsons, *The Social System* (Glencoe, IL: Free Press, 1951), 281; see also Talcott Parsons, *The Evolution of Societies*, ed. Jackson Toby and Talcott Parsons (Englewood Cliffs, NJ: Prentice-Hall, 1977), 208–9.

38. Elsewhere, Parsons contended that the United States' loose federal structure created a tendency for particularism undercutting the universalism promised in the Constitution, allowing for the treatment of Black Americans as second-class citizens. Talcott Parsons, "Full Citizenship for the Negro American? A Sociological Problem," *Daedalus* 94, no. 4 (1965): 1012–13.

39. Ruha Benjamin, "Cultura Obscura: Race, Power, and 'Culture Talk' in the Health Sciences," *American Journal of Law & Medicine* 43, no. 2-3 (2017): 237.

40. Benjamin, "Cultura Obscura."

41. Alondra Nelson, *The Social Life of DNA: Race, Reparations, and Reconciliation after the Genome* (Boston: Beacon Press, 2016).

42. Alondra Nelson, "Reconciliation Projects: From Kinship to Justice," in *Genetics and the Unsettled Past: The Collision of DNA, Race, and History*, ed. Keith Wailoo, Alondra Nelson, and Catherine Lee (New Brunswick, NJ: Rutgers University Press, 2012), 22.

43. Initially in Marion J. Levy, "Some Sources of the Vulnerability of the Structures of Relatively Non-Industrialized Societies to Those of Highly Industrialized Societies," in *The Progress of Underdeveloped Areas*, ed. Bert F. Hoselitz (Chicago: University of Chicago Press, 1952).

44. E.g., Daniel Lerner, *The Passing of Traditional Society: Modernizing the Middle East* (Glencoe, IL: Free Press, 1958).

45. Modernization Theory is not a formalized theory, but rather a set of as-

sumptions common among scholars of international development in the 1950s and 1960s.

46. United States Department of Labor, *The Negro Family: The Case for National Action*, ed. Daniel P. Moynihan (Washington, DC: US Government Printing Office, 1965).

47. For a full account see Lee Rainwater and William L. Yancey, *The Moynihan Report and the Politics of Controversy: A Trans-Action Social Science and Public Policy Report* (Cambridge, MA: MIT Press, 1967).

48. Theda Skocpol, "Wallerstein's World Capitalist System: A Theoretical and Historical Critique," *American Journal of Sociology* 82, no. 6 (1977).

49. Jeffrey C. Alexander, *Fin de Siècle Social Theory: Relativism, Reduction, and the Problem of Reason* (London and New York: Verso, 1995), 19.

50. William Julius Wilson, "The Moynihan Report and Research on the Black Community," 39–40.

51. Oscar Lewis, *Five Families: Mexican Case Studies in the Culture of Poverty*, ed. Oliver La Farge (New York: Basic Books, 1959). Briggs puts the controversy over Lewis's and Moynihan's respective work into the broader sociopolitical context of its time—Laura Briggs, *Reproducing Empire: Race, Sex, Science, and U.S. Imperialism in Puerto Rico* (Berkeley: University of California Press, 2002), 180–88.

52. William Ryan, "Savage Discovery: The Moynihan Report," *The Nation* 201 (1965): 380.

53. Daniel Geary, *Beyond Civil Rights: The Moynihan Report and Its Legacy* (Philadelphia: University of Pennsylvania Press, 2015), 139–71.

54. See account in Wilson, "The Moynihan Report and Research on the Black Community," 35.

55. Douglas S. Massey and Robert J. Sampson, "Moynihan Redux: Legacies and Lessons," *The ANNALS of the American Academy of Political and Social Science* 621, no. 1 (2009): 11–12.

56. Orlando Patterson, "Taking Culture Seriously: A Framework and an Afro-American Illustration," in *Culture Matters: How Values Shape Human Progress*, ed. Samuel P. Huntington and Lawrence E. Harrison (New York: Basic Books, 2000), 204; Wilson, "The Moynihan Report and Research on the Black Community."

57. "Many people stepped forward and endorsed the release of the report or the reading of the report, and that included Roy Wilkins, Whitney Young, and the Reverend Martin Luther King Jr. But soon the left in American politics was seized with an anti–Pat Moynihan passion"—James Q. Wilson, "Pat Moynihan Thinks about Families," *The ANNALS of the American Academy of Political and Social Science* 621, no. 1 (2009): 29.

58. Wilson, "The Moynihan Report and Research on the Black Community," 34–35.

59. Wilson, 37.

60. Jenée Desmond-Harris, "The Real Reason Research Blaming Black Poverty on Black Culture Has Fallen Out of Favor," *Vox*, March 26, 2015, https://www.vox.com/2015/3/26/8253495/moynihan-report-liberal-backlash.

61. William J. Wilson, *The Truly Disadvantaged: The Inner City, the Underclass, and Public Policy*, 2nd ed. (Chicago: University of Chicago Press, 2012 [1987]), 137.

62. Wilson, *The Truly Disadvantaged*, 138.

63. Wilson, 173.

64. E.g., Michèle Lamont, *Money, Morals, and Manners: The Culture of the French and the American Upper-Middle Class* (Chicago: University of Chicago Press, 1992). Examples of cultural studies of poverty include Alford A. Young, *The Minds of Marginalized Black Men: Making Sense of Mobility, Opportunity, and Future Life Chances* (Princeton, NJ: Princeton University Press, 2004).

65. Orlando Patterson, "A Poverty of the Mind," *New York Times*, March 26, 2006, https://www.nytimes.com/2006/03/26/opinion/a-poverty-of-the-mind.html.

66. Patterson, "Taking Culture Seriously," 204.

67. Patterson, 208–17.

68. Mario Luis Small, David J. Harding, and Michèle Lamont, "Introduction: Reconsidering Culture and Poverty," *The Annals of the American Academy of Political and Social Science* 629 (2010): 8.

69. Small, Harding, and Lamont, "Introduction: Reconsidering Culture and Poverty."

70. Anderson, *Code of the Street*, 34.

71. Michael Rodríguez-Muñiz, "Intellectual Inheritances: Cultural Diagnostics and the State of Poverty Knowledge," *American Journal of Cultural Sociology* 3, no. 1 (2015): 91.

72. Eduardo Bonilla-Silva and Gianpaolo Baiocchi, "Anything but Racism: How Sociologists Limit the Significance of Racism," *Race & Society* 4, no. 2 (2001).

73. Crystal Marie Fleming, *How to Be Less Stupid about Race: On Racism, White Supremacy and the Racial Divide* (Boston: Beacon Press, 2018), 31.

74. This passage appeared on pages 1–2 of the retracted version.

75. This passage appeared on page 5 of the retracted version.

76. Lawrence M. Mead, "Poverty and Culture [retracted]," *Society*, July 21, 2020, 1.

77. Retraction Watch, "Hundreds Petition to Retract Paper They Call 'Unscholarly, Overtly Racist' and Full of 'Racially Violent Narratives,'" *Retraction Watch*, July 27, 2020, https://retractionwatch.com/2020/07/27/hundreds-petition-to-retract -paper-they-call-unscholarly-overtly-racist-and-full-of-racially-violent-narratives/.

78. Mario Luis Small and Katherine Newman, "Urban Poverty after the Truly Disadvantaged: The Rediscovery of the Family, the Neighborhood, and Culture," *Annual Review of Sociology* 27 (2001): 39–40. This followed an edited volume also beckoning for renewed conversation between scholars on the topic: Small, Harding, and Lamont, "Introduction: Reconsidering Culture and Poverty."

79. Sociological Inquiry, "Call for Papers: Special Issue on 'The Cultural and the Racial: Stitching Together the Sociologies of Race/Racism/Ethnicity and Culture,' Guest Editors David L. Brunsma and David G. Embrick," 2020, last accessed January 28, 2021, https://onlinelibrary.wiley.com/pb-assets/Special%20Issue%20 -%20Racism%20and%20Culture-1598268806577.pdf.

80. E.g., David C. Rowe and D. Wayne Osgood, "Heredity and Sociological Theories of Delinquency: A Reconsideration," *American Sociological Review* 49, no. 4 (1984).

81. Byrd and colleagues estimate that in 2000–2015 roughly 165 top journal articles substantively linked advances in genetic research to sociological insights.

AJS published roughly 13 percent of these and *Demography* published 29 percent. W. Carson Byrd and Latrica E. Best, "Between (Racial) Groups and a Hard Place: An Exploration of Social Science Approaches to Race and Genetics, 2000–2014," *Biodemography and Social Biology* 62, no. 3 (2016): 292. Moreover, *Annual Review* articles centering on the topic have recently appeared, as have special issues of popular journals (e.g., *AJS* in 2008).

82. Jeremy Freese and Sara Shostak, "Genetics and Social Inquiry," *Annual Review of Sociology* 35, no. 1 (2009): 119.

83. Freese and Shostak, "Genetics and Social Inquiry," 111.

84. Landecker and Panofsky, "From Social Structure to Gene Regulation, and Back," 336.

85. Scholarship on biologists, epidemiologists, and other researchers who use genetic data similarly regularly notes discomfort about the possible abuses of new DNA information—e.g., Martyn Pickersgill, "Negotiating Novelty: Constructing the Novel Within Scientific Accounts of Epigenetics," *Sociology* 55, no. 3 (2021); Abril Saldaña-Tejeda and Peter Wade, "Eugenics, Epigenetics, and Obesity Predisposition among Mexican Mestizos," *Medical Anthropology* 38, no. 8 (2019).

86. Bridget J. Goosby, Jacob E. Cheadle, and Colter Mitchell, "Stress-Related Biosocial Mechanisms of Discrimination and African American Health Inequities," *Annual Review of Sociology* 44, no. 1 (2018): 325–26.

87. Megan Warin, Emma Kowal, and Maurizio Meloni, "Indigenous Knowledge in a Postgenomic Landscape: The Politics of Epigenetic Hope and Reparation in Australia," *Science, Technology, & Human Values* 45, no. 1 (2020): 90. Similarly, Grossi refers to a "strategic racialization"—Elodie Grossi, "New Avenues in Epigenetic Research about Race: Online Activism around Reparations for Slavery in the United States," *Social Science Information* 59, no. 1 (2020): 109.

88. Jayne O. Ifekwunigwe et al., "A Qualitative Analysis of How Anthropologists Interpret the Race Construct," *American Anthropologist* 119, no. 3 (2017): 425.

89. Jenny Reardon and Kim TallBear, "'Your DNA Is Our History': Genomics, Anthropology, and the Construction of Whiteness as Property," *Current Anthropology* 53, no. S5 (2012): S234.

90. Jiannbin Lee Shiao et al., "The Genomic Challenge to the Social Construction of Race," *Sociological Theory* 30, no. 2 (2012); Guang Guo et al., "Genetic Bio-Ancestry and Social Construction of Racial Classification in Social Surveys in the Contemporary United States," *Demography* 51, no. 1 (2014).

91. Ann Morning, "And You Thought We Had Moved Beyond All That: Biological Race Returns to the Social Sciences," *Ethnic and Racial Studies* 37, no. 10 (2014): 1679.

92. Duana Fullwiley, "The 'Contemporary Synthesis': When Politically Inclusive Genomic Science Relies on Biological Notions of Race," *Isis* 105, no. 4 (2014): 812.

93. Roberts and Rollins, "Why Sociology Matters to Race and Biosocial Science," 208.

94. Tesfaye B. Mersha and Tilahun Abebe, "Self-Reported Race/Ethnicity in the Age of Genomic Research: Its Potential Impact on Understanding Health Disparities," *Human Genomics* 9, no. 1 (2015).

95. Byrd and Best, "Between (Racial) Groups and a Hard Place," 292.

96. Laura M. Koehly et al., "Social and Behavioral Science at the Forefront of Genomics: Discovery, Translation, and Health Equity," *Social Science & Medicine* 271 (2019).

97. Troy Duster, "A Post-Genomic Surprise. The Molecular Reinscription of Race in Science, Law and Medicine," *The British Journal of Sociology* 66, no. 1 (2015): 4.

98. W. Carson Byrd and Matthew W. Hughey, "Biological Determinism and Racial Essentialism: The Ideological Double Helix of Racial Inequality," *The ANNALS of the American Academy of Political and Social Science* 661, no. 1 (2015): 12.

99. Duster, "A Post-Genomic Surprise," 13.

100. Byrd and Hughey, "Biological Determinism and Racial Essentialism," 13.

101. Morning, "And You Thought We Had Moved Beyond All That," 1680.

102. Saldaña-Tejeda and Wade, "Eugenics, Epigenetics, and Obesity Predisposition among Mexican Mestizos," 675.

103. Dorothy Roberts, *Fatal Invention: How Science, Politics, and Big Business Re-Create Race in the Twenty-First Century* (New York: New Press, 2011), 309, emphasis added. For another example see Fullwiley, "The 'Contemporary Synthesis,'" 813–14.

104. "This appears akin to the idea that the study of social movements is a revolutionary project in disguise. One needs only to read the literature to be disabused of the notions"—Peter Bearman, "Introduction: Exploring Genetics and Social Structure," *American Journal of Sociology* 114, no. S1 (2008): vi.

105. Bearman, "Introduction: Exploring Genetics and Social Structure," viii.

106. Bearman, viii.

107. Nature, "Life Stresses," Editorial, *Nature* 490, no. 7419 (October 10, 2012): 143.

108. Nature, "Life Stresses," 143.

109. Caroline L. Relton and George Davey Smith, "Is Epidemiology Ready for Epigenetics?" *International Journal of Epidemiology* 41, no. 1 (2012): 8.

110. E.g., Brian Resnick, "What Psychology's Crisis Means for the Future of Science," *Vox*, March 25, 2016, https://www.vox.com/2016/3/14/11219446/psychology-replication-crisis.

111. Zack Beauchamp, "The Controversy around Hoax Studies in Critical Theory, Explained," *Vox*, October 15, 2018, https://www.vox.com/2018/10/15/17951492/grievance-studies-sokal-squared-hoax.

112. Jillian Kay Melchior, "Fake News Comes to Academia," *Wall Street Journal*, October 5, 2018, https://www.wsj.com/articles/fake-news-comes-to-academia-1538520950.

113. As Boltanski and Thévenot showed, actors occasionally attempt to construct "illegitimate orders of worth," which failed to meet measures of logical debate when publicly examined—with eugenics being a key example. Luc Boltanski and Laurent Thévenot, *On Justification: Economies of Worth* (Princeton, NJ: Princeton University Press, 2006), 80–82.

114. Herd et al., for example, examine genetic data on intelligence through the lens of gender equality and demonstrate that genetic markers cannot be trans-

lated into life outcome predictions without social supports. Pamela Herd et al., "Genes, Gender Inequality, and Educational Attainment," *American Sociological Review* 84, no. 6 (2019).

115. Roberts, *Fatal Invention*, 311.

116. See Tukufu Zuberi and Eduardo Bonilla-Silva, *White Logic, White Methods: Racism and Methodology* (Lanham, MD: Rowman & Littlefield, 2008).

117. Ann Morning, *The Nature of Race: How Scientists Think and Teach about Human Difference* (Berkeley: University of California Press, 2011), 228–35.

CHAPTER THREE

1. Corey Dolgon, "Reply to Wright, Embrick, and Henke and Lembcke: Dim Mirrors, Dark Glasses but This Is Not Our Fate," *Humanity & Society* 40, no. 1 (2016): 107.

2. E.g., Lawrence D. Bobo and Michael C. Dawson, "A Change Has Come: Race, Politics, and the Path to the Obama Presidency," *Du Bois Review* 6, no. 1 (2009): 4–5.

3. Most political experts had failed to predict the Brexit outcome. Carter Dougherty, "Brexit Vote 2016: Big Bettors in EU Referendum Have Leg Up on Pollsters in Predicting June 23 Outcome," *International Business Times*, June 16, 2016, https://www.ibtimes.com/brexit-vote-2016-big-bettors-eu-referendum-have -leg-pollsters-predicting-june-23-2382877.

4. Anthony J. Gaughan, "President Trump? Not Likely," *The Conversation*, May 3, 2016, https://theconversation.com/president-trump-not-likely-58758.

5. Eduardo Bonilla-Silva, "The 2008 Elections and the Future of Anti-Racism in 21st Century Amerika or How We Got Drunk with Obama's Hope Liquor and Failed to See Reality," *Humanity & Society* 34, no. 3 (2010).

6. Andrew L. Whitehead and Samuel L. Perry, *Taking America Back for God: Christian Nationalism in the United States* (New York: Oxford University Press, 2020).

7. Ulrich Beck, *The Metamorphosis of the World* (Cambridge, UK, and Malden, MA: Polity, 2016), xi.

8. See Chiapello and Boltanski's conceptualization of the *Projective Cité*, in Luc Boltanski and Ève Chiapello, *The New Spirit of Capitalism* (London and New York: Verso, 2005), 108–21.

9. Peter McMahan and Daniel A. McFarland, "Creative Destruction: The Structural Consequences of Scientific Curation," *American Sociological Review* 86, no. 2 (2021).

10. David Inglis, "Cosmopolitans and Cosmopolitanism: Between and Beyond Sociology and Political Philosophy," *Journal of Sociology* 50, no. 2 (2014).

11. Günter H. Lenz, "Radical Cosmopolitanism: W. E. B. Du Bois, Germany, and African American Pragmatist Visions for Twenty-First-Century Europe," *Journal of Transnational American Studies* 4, no. 2 (2012): 88–91.

12. Vince Marotta, Stan van Hoft, and Wim Vandekerckhove, "The Cosmopolitan Stranger," in *Questioning Cosmopolitanism*, ed. Stan van Hooft and Wim Vandekerckhove (Dordrecht and New York: Springer, 2010).

13. Anthony D. Smith, *Nations and Nationalism in a Global Era* (Cambridge, UK, and Malden, MA: Polity Press and Blackwell, 1995).

14. Liah Greenfeld, "Is Nationalism Legitimate? A Sociological Perspective on a Philosophical Question," *Canadian Journal of Philosophy* 26 (1997): 93.

15. Martha Nussbaum, "Patriotism and Cosmopolitanism," *Boston Review* 19, no. 5 (1994 [1982]): 5.

16. Nussbaum, "Patriotism and Cosmopolitanism," 3.

17. Nussbaum, 5, emphasis added.

18. Martha C. Nussbaum, *For Love of Country: Debating the Limits of Patriotism*, ed. Joshua Cohen (Boston: Beacon Press, 1996).

19. Ulrich Beck and Johannes Willms, *Conversations with Ulrich Beck*, trans. Michael Pollack (Oxford: Polity Press, 2004 [2000]), 116.

20. Beck and Willms, *Conversations with Ulrich Beck*, 117.

21. European Parliament, "Forsmark: How Sweden Alerted the World about the Danger of the Chernobyl Disaster," *European Parliament News*, May 15, 2014, http://www.europarl.europa.eu/news/en/headlines/society/20140514STO47018/forsmark-how-sweden-alerted-the-world-about-the-danger-of-the-chernobyl-disaster.

22. Zygmunt Bauman, *Liquid Modernity* (Cambridge, UK, and Malden, MA: Polity Press and Blackwell, 2000).

23. E.g., Alain Touraine, "Sociology without Societies," *Current Sociology* 51, no. 2 (2003); John Urry, *Mobilities* (Cambridge, UK, and Malden, MA: Polity, 2007).

24. Beck and Willms, *Conversations with Ulrich Beck*, 116.

25. E.g., John Boli and George M. Thomas, "World Culture in the World Polity: A Century of International Non-Governmental Organization," *American Sociological Review* 62, no. 2 (1997); George M. Thomas, "World Polity, World Culture, World Society," *International Political Sociology* 3, no. 1 (2009).

26. Eva Illouz, *Saving the Modern Soul: Therapy, Emotions, and the Culture of Self-Help* (Berkeley: University of California Press, 2008), 20.

27. Peter Redfield, *Life in Crisis: The Ethical Journey of Doctors without Borders* (Berkeley: University of California Press, 2013); Shai M. Dromi, *Above the Fray: The Red Cross and the Making of the Humanitarian Relief Sector* (Chicago: University of Chicago Press, 2020), 116–31.

28. Shai M. Dromi, "Soldiers of the Cross: Calvinism, Humanitarianism, and the Genesis of Social Fields," *Sociological Theory* 34, no. 3 (2016).

29. David Held, *Cosmopolitanism: Ideals and Realities* (Cambridge and Malden, MA: Polity Press, 2010); Mary Kaldor, *Global Civil Society: An Answer to War* (Cambridge, UK: Polity Press, 2003).

30. See for example *British Journal of Sociology* 57, no. 1 (2006): 61, no. 3 (2010), and the first section of *British Journal of Sociology* 68, no. 2 (2017).

31. Ludger Pries, "Configurations of Geographic and Societal Spaces: A Sociological Proposal between 'Methodological Nationalism' and the 'Spaces of Flows,'" *Global Networks* 5, no. 2 (2005).

32. Illouz, *Saving the Modern Soul*, 20.

33. Daniele Archibugi, *The Global Commonwealth of Citizens: Toward Cosmopolitan Democracy* (Princeton, NJ: Princeton University Press, 2008).

34. Kaldor, *Global Civil Society*.

35. Ulrich K. Preuss, "Citizenship in the European Union: A Paradigm for Transnational Democracy," in *Re-Imagining Political Community: Studies in Cos-*

mopolitan Democracy, ed. Daniele Archibugi, David Held, and Martin Köhler (Stanford, CA: Stanford University Press, 1998).

36. Daniele Archibugi and David Held, *Cosmopolitan Democracy: An Agenda for a New World Order* (Cambridge, UK, and Cambridge, MA: Polity Press and Basil Blackwell, 1995).

37. Boltanski and Chiapello describe it as the projective cité (or repertoire) in Boltanski and Chiapello, *The New Spirit of Capitalism*, 103–28. Or the "connectionist" cité.

38. The projective cité, as Boltanski and Chiapello show, emerged as a response to 1960s critiques of capitalism as being too rigid. It grew prevalent over the late twentieth century as a justification for transnational capitalistic projects that deflects such criticisms. See Mohamed Nachi, "Beyond Pragmatic Sociology: A Theoretical Compromise between 'Critical Sociology' and the 'Pragmatic Sociology of Critique,'" in *The Spirit of Luc Boltanski: Essays on the "Pragmatic Sociology of Critique*," ed. Simon Susen and Bryan S. Turner (London: Anthem Press, 2014), 297–302.

39. Bronislaw Szerszynski and John Urry, "Visuality, Mobility and the Cosmopolitan: Inhabiting the World from Afar," *The British Journal of Sociology* 57, no. 1 (2006).

40. Daniele Archibugi, "Cosmopolitical Democracy," *New Left Review* 4, no. 4 (2000): 140.

41. Nussbaum, "Patriotism and Cosmopolitanism," 5.

42. Gerard Delanty, *The Cosmopolitan Imagination: The Renewal of Critical Social Theory* (Cambridge and New York: Cambridge University Press, 2009), 43.

43. John Urry, "Mobile Sociology," *The British Journal of Sociology* 51, no. 1 (2000): 201.

44. Robert Fine, "Taking the 'Ism' Out of Cosmopolitanism: An Essay in Reconstruction," *European Journal of Social Theory* 6, no. 4 (2003): 465.

45. Rogers Brubaker, *Nationalism Reframed: Nationhood and the National Question in the New Europe* (Cambridge and New York: Cambridge University Press, 1996), 2. Migration scholars continue to show that migrants grapple with nation-derived categories, and call attention to the roles nationality plays in migrants' lived experience: e.g., Janine Dahinden, Carolin Fischer, and Joanna Menet, "Knowledge Production, Reflexivity, and the Use of Categories in Migration Studies: Tackling Challenges in the Field," *Ethnic and Racial Studies* 44, no. 4 (2021).

46. Craig Calhoun, "The Class Consciousness of Frequent Travelers: Toward a Critique of Actually Existing Cosmopolitanism," *The South Atlantic Quarterly* 101, no. 4 (2002): 872.

47. Craig J. Calhoun, *Nations Matter: Culture, History, and the Cosmopolitan Dream* (London and New York: Routledge, 2007); see also Shai M. Dromi, "For Good and Country: Nationalism and the Diffusion of Humanitarianism in the Late Nineteenth Century," *Sociological Review Monographs* 64, no. 2 (2016); Shai M. Dromi and Liron Shani, "Love of Land: Nature Protection, Nationalism, and the Struggle over the Establishment of New Communities in Israel," *Rural Sociology* 85, no. 1 (2020).

48. Ulf Hannerz, "Cosmopolitans and Locals in World Culture," *Theory, Culture & Society* 7, no. 2-3 (1990).

49. William Haller and Victor Roudometof, "The Cosmopolitan-Local Continuum in Cross-National Perspective," *Journal of Sociology* (Melbourne, Vic.) 46, no. 3 (2010).

50. Jeevan Vasagar and Rajeev Syal, "LSE Head Quits over Gaddafi Scandal," *The Guardian*, March 3, 2011, https://www.theguardian.com/education/2011/mar/03/lse-director-resigns-gaddafi-scandal.

51. Daniel Finkelstein, "The LSE Scandal Is Intellectual, Not Financial," *The Times*, September 3, 2011, https://www.thetimes.co.uk/article/the-lse-scandal-is-intellectual-not-financial-62mrjkxq8w7.

52. Peter van der Veer, "Colonial Cosmopolitanism," in *Conceiving Cosmopolitanism: Theory, Context and Practice*, ed. Steven Vertovec and Robin Cohen (New York: Oxford University Press, 2003), 178–79.

53. Scholars like Go and Mignolo also pointed to the problematic and potentially colonialist projects cosmopolitanism has inspired, even when those projects were intended to liberate world populations. Julian Go, "Fanon's Postcolonial Cosmopolitanism," *European Journal of Social Theory* 16, no. 2 (2013): 211–14; Walter Mignolo, *The Many Faces of Cosmo-Polis: Border Thinking and Critical Cosmopolitanism* (Durham, NC: Duke University Press, 2002), 721–22.

54. Vivienne Jabri, "Solidarity and Spheres of Culture: The Cosmopolitan and the Postcolonial," *Review of International Studies* 33, no. 4 (2007): 721.

55. Greenfeld, "Is Nationalism Legitimate?" 108.

56. Liah Greenfeld, *Nationalism: Five Roads to Modernity* (Cambridge, MA: Harvard University Press, 1992), 23.

57. Luc Boltanski and Laurent Thévenot, *On Justification: Economies of Worth* (Princeton, NJ: Princeton University Press, 2006), 90.

58. Boltanski and Thévenot similarly refer to the domestic cité as relying on ties of kinship and loyalty—*On Justification*, 90–98.

59. Albert Bandura, "Moral Disengagement in the Perpetration of Inhumanities," *Personality and Social Psychology Review* 3, no. 3 (1999): 206.

60. Calhoun, *Nations Matter*, 48.

61. Craig J. Calhoun, *The Roots of Radicalism: Tradition, the Public Sphere, and Early Nineteenth-Century Social Movements* (Chicago: University of Chicago Press, 2012), 309–11.

62. Dromi, *Above the Fray*.

63. See similar claims about national environmental activism in Dromi and Shani, "Love of Land."

64. Philip S. Gorski and William McMillan, "Barack Obama and American Exceptionalisms," *The Review of Faith & International Affairs* 10, no. 2 (2012): 45–46.

65. Charles Taylor, "Why Democracy Needs Patriotism," *Boston Review* 19, no. 5 (1994): 26.

66. Martha C. Nussbaum, "Toward a Globally Sensitive Patriotism," *Daedalus* 137, no. 3 (2008): 82.

67. Martha C. Nussbaum, *Liberty of Conscience: In Defense of America's Tradition of Religious Equality* (New York: Basic Books, 2008), 83.

68. Martha C. Nussbaum, "Climate Change: Why Theories of Justice Matter," *Chicago Journal of International Law* 13, no. 2 (2013): 473–74.

69. Daniel Hirschman and Isaac Ariail Reed, "Formation Stories and Causality in Sociology," *Sociological Theory* 32, no. 4 (2014): 260.

70. E.g., Nussbaum, "Climate Change," 487–88.

71. Martha C. Nussbaum, *The Cosmopolitan Tradition: A Noble but Flawed Ideal* (Cambridge, MA: Harvard University Press, 2019), 14.

72. See Boltanski and Thévenot's explanation of the Industrial Cité in Boltanski and Thévenot, *On Justification*, 118–23.

73. Max Weber, "Science as a Vocation," in *From Max Weber: Essays in Sociology*, ed. Hans Gerth and C. Wright Mills (Milton Park, Abingdon, UK, and New York: Routledge, 2009 [1919]).

74. Brubaker, *Nationalism Reframed*, 10.

75. Michael Billig, *Banal Nationalism* (London and Thousand Oaks, CA: Sage, 1995), 8.

76. Brubaker, *Nationalism Reframed*, 4.

77. Brubaker, 10.

78. Brubaker, 147.

79. Bart Bonikowski and Paul DiMaggio, "Varieties of American Popular Nationalism," *American Sociological Review* 81, no. 5 (2016): 952.

80. Bonikowski and DiMaggio, "Varieties of American Popular Nationalism," 950. See also Bart Bonikowski, "Nationalism in Settled Times," *Annual Review of Sociology* 42, no. 1 (2016).

81. Andreas Wimmer and Brian Min, "From Empire to Nation-State: Explaining Wars in the Modern World, 1816–2001," *American Sociological Review* 71, no. 6 (2006): 869.

82. George Steinmetz, "The Colonial State as a Social Field: Ethnographic Capital and Native Policy in the German Overseas Empire Before 1914," *American Sociological Review* 73, no. 4 (2008).

83. Julian Go, "Global Fields and Imperial Forms: Field Theory and the British and American Empires," *Sociological Theory* 26, no. 3 (2008).

84. Andrew D. Abbott, *Chaos of Disciplines* (Chicago: University of Chicago Press, 2001), 19.

85. See also John Friedmann and Goetz Wolff, "World City Formation: An Agenda for Research and Action," *International Journal of Urban and Regional Research* 6, no. 3 (1982).

86. Saskia Sassen, "Globalization or Denationalization?" *Review of International Political Economy: RIPE* 10, no. 1 (2003): 13, emphasis added.

87. Sassen, "Globalization or Denationalization?" 5.

88. Roland Robertson, "Glocalization: Time-Space and Homogeneity-Heterogeneity," in *Global Modernities*, ed. Mike Featherstone, Scott Lash, and Roland Robertson (London and Thousand Oaks, CA: Sage Publications, 1995), 40.

89. Andreas Wimmer and Nina Glick Schiller, "Methodological Nationalism, the Social Sciences, and the Study of Migration: An Essay in Historical Epistemology," *The International Migration Review* 37, no. 3 (2003): 600.

90. Harry Enten, "Trump Is Just a Normal Polling Error Behind Clinton,"

FiveThirtyEight, November 4, 2016, https://fivethirtyeight.com/features/trump-is
-just-a-normal-polling-error-behind-clinton/.

91. Jeremy W. Peters and Matt Flegenheimer, "Early Voting Tilts toward Democrats in Swing States," *New York Times*, October 31, 2016, https://www.nytimes.com/
2016/10/31/us/politics/early-voting-trump-clinton.html.

92. *New York Times*, "6 Books to Help Understand Trump's Win," *New York
Times*, November 10, 2016, https://www.nytimes.com/2016/11/10/books/6-books
-to-help-understand-trumps-win.html?searchResultPosition=34.

93. "Philip Gorski," Charlie Rose, updated April 11, 2017, last accessed July 14,
2020, https://charlierose.com/videos/30365.

94. Arlie Russell Hochschild, *Strangers in Their Own Land: Anger and Mourning
on the American Right* (New York: The New Press, 2016).

95. "Strangers in Their Own Land," The New Press, 2016, accessed January 29,
2020, https://thenewpress.com/books/strangers-their-own-land.

96. Gabriel Thompson, "'Strangers in Their Own Land' review: Arlie Russell
Hochschild Listens to the Voices of the American Right," *Newsday*, September
16, 2016, https://www.newsday.com/entertainment/books/strangers-in-their-own
-land-review-arlie-russell-hochschild-listens-to-the-voices-of-the-american-right
-1.12322676.

97. Arlene Stein, "Rage Against the State," *Contemporary Sociology* 46 (2017): 508.

98. Pierre Bourdieu, Jean-Claude Chamboredon, and Jean-Claude Passeron,
The Craft of Sociology: Epistemological Preliminaries, trans. Richard Nice, ed. Beate
Krais (Berlin and New York: Walter de Gruyter, 1991), 33–35.

99. Hochschild, *Strangers in Their Own Land*, 135–38.

100. Harel Shapira, "Who Cares What They Think? Going About the Right the
Wrong Way," *Contemporary Sociology* 46, no. 5 (2017). While we certainly recognize
the potential shortcomings of Hochschild's approach, our point is merely that
Hochschild framed her effort in terms that addressed questions about nation-
alism and civic inclusion, and many others understood this as her aim—e.g.,
Francesca Polletta, "Strangers in Their Own Land: Anger and Mourning on the
American Right by Arlie Russell Hochschild," *American Journal of Sociology* 123,
no. 2 (2017).

101. Rory McVeigh, "Deep Story or Self-Serving Narrative? Understanding the
Paradox of Conservative Politics," *Contemporary Sociology* 46, no. 5 (2017).

CHAPTER FOUR

1. Thomas S. Kuhn, *The Structure of Scientific Revolutions*, 4th ed. (Chicago:
University of Chicago Press, 2012 [1962]), 86–91.

2. Kuhn, *The Structure of Scientific Revolutions*, 53. For an example from neu-
roscience, see Susan Leigh Star and Elihu M. Gerson, "The Management and
Dynamics of Anomalies in Scientific Work," *Sociological Quarterly* 28, no. 2 (1987):
160–63.

3. Luc Boltanski and Ève Chiapello, *The New Spirit of Capitalism* (London and
New York: Verso, 2005), 23.

4. Brian Uzzi et al., "Atypical Combinations and Scientific Impact," *Science*

342, no. 6157 (2013): 471; Jacob G. Foster, Andrey Rzhetsky, and James A. Evans, "Tradition and Innovation in Scientists' Research Strategies," *American Sociological Review* 80, no. 5 (2015): 881–82.

5. Research in scientific communication has argued that review articles, for example, are couched in broader efforts to make sense of an exponentially growing scholarly literature by creating new narratives about where existing knowledge stands. Peter McMahan and Daniel A. McFarland, "Creative Destruction: The Structural Consequences of Scientific Curation," *American Sociological Review* 86, no. 2 (2021): 370–71.

6. Monica Prasad, *Problem-Solving Sociology: A Guide for Students* (New York: Oxford University Press, 2021), 136–37.

7. E.g., Alison Phipps, "Re-Inscribing Gender Binaries: Deconstructing the Dominant Discourse around Women's Equality in Science, Engineering, and Technology," *The Sociological Review* 55, no. 4 (2007): 768–87.

8. Molly McClain, *Ellen Browning Scripps: New Money and American Philanthropy* (Lincoln: University of Nebraska Press, 2017), 1.

9. Arthur A. Campbell and William D. Mosher, "A History of the Measurement of Unintended Pregnancies and Births," *Maternal and Child Health Journal* 4, no. 3 (2000): 164.

10. Campbell and Mosher, "A History of the Measurement of Unintended Pregnancies and Births," 164.

11. Campbell and Mosher, 164.

12. Warren S. Thompson, "Population Trend Foreshadows a New Era: Vast Social and Economic Consequences Are Likely to Follow from the Decline and Eventual Stoppage of the Nation's Growth," *New York Times*, March 18, 1934.

13. Notably, the questions migrated first from a small sample in Indianapolis, then expanded to the US via the inclusion of questions on the National Fertility Survey in 1965, and finally worldwide with the formation of the World Fertility Study in the mid-1970s. See Campbell and Mosher, "A History of the Measurement of Unintended Pregnancies and Births."

14. E.g., Warren S. Thompson, "Population," *American Journal of Sociology* 34, no. 1 (1928).

15. E.g., J. F. Phillips et al., "The Demographic Impact of the Family Planning–Health Services Project in Matlab, Bangladesh," *Studies in Family Planning* 13, no. 5 (1982): 134.

16. P. K. Whelpton and Clyde V. Kiser, "Social and Psychological Factors Affecting Fertility: IV. Developing the Schedules, and Choosing the Type of Couples and the Area to Be Studied," *The Milbank Memorial Fund Quarterly* 23, no. 4 (1945): 391–92.

17. Whelpton and Kiser, "Social and Psychological Factors Affecting Fertility," 388.

18. Whelpton and Kiser, 399–400.

19. The ethos spread beyond the Indianapolis Study. Efficiency of statistical data collection guided studies across the country. Another Scripps venture in the city of Detroit parsed the differences between family expectations (i.e., how many children do you *expect* to have) and family ideals (i.e., how many children

do you *desire* to have) to suggest how multiple measures of fertility ideals could shape analysis. Ronald Freedman, David Goldberg, and Harry Sharp, "'Ideals' about Family Size in the Detroit Metropolitan Area: 1954," *The Milbank Memorial Fund Quarterly* 33, no. 2 (1955).

20. Whelpton and Kiser, "Social and Psychological Factors Affecting Fertility," 398.

21. Edgar F. Borgatta and Charles F. Westoff, "Social and Psychological Factors Affecting Fertility: XXV. The Prediction of Total Fertility," *The Milbank Memorial Fund Quarterly* 32, no. 4 (1954): 385.

22. Charles F. Westoff and Clyde V. Kiser, "Social and Psychological Factors Affecting Fertility: XXI. An Empirical Re-Examination and Intercorrelation of Selected Hypothesis Factors," *The Milbank Memorial Fund Quarterly* 31, no. 4 (1953): 431.

23. Borgatta and Westoff, "Social and Psychological Factors Affecting Fertility," 396.

24. Norman B. Ryder, "A Critique of the National Fertility Study," *Demography* 10, no. 4 (1973): 495.

25. Ryder, "A Critique of the National Fertility Study," 495.

26. E.g., United States Bureau of Census, "Fertility Expectations of American Women: June 1974," *Current Population Reports* Series P-20: Population Characteristics, no. 277 (1975).

27. Charles F. Westoff and Norman B. Ryder, "The Predictive Validity of Reproductive Intentions," *Demography* 14, no. 4 (1977): 449.

28. Lolagene C. Coombs, "The Measurement of Family Size Preferences and Subsequent Fertility," *Demography* 11, no. 4 (1974): 587.

29. S. Philip Morgan, "Floor Discussion," paper presented at the US Census Bureau Conference: The Direction of Fertility in the United States, Washington, DC (2001), 184.

30. Paul Demeny, "Social Science and Population Policy," *Population and Development Review* 14, no. 3 (1988).

31. Quoted in Demeny, "Social Science and Population Policy," 457.

32. Demeny, 457.

33. Steven W. Sinding, John A. Ross, and Allan G. Rosenfield, "Seeking Common Ground: Unmet Need and Demographic Goals," *International Family Planning Perspectives* 20, no. 1 (1994): 25.

34. Because these measures were deemed worthy despite their empirical failings, even efforts to refine their quality were often couched in broader narratives about how scientific advancement could and should contribute to the betterment of global demographic control, and thus society, more generally. See, e.g., Charles F. Westoff, "The Potential Demand for Family Planning: A New Measure of Unmet Need and Estimates for Five Latin American Countries," *International Family Planning Perspectives* 14, no. 2 (1988).

35. Charles F. Westoff, "The Unmet Need for Birth Control in Five Asian Countries," *Family Planning Perspectives* 10, no. 3 (1978): 179.

36. Westoff, "The Unmet Need for Birth Control in Five Asian Countries," 179.

37. Westoff, 179.

38. Ruth Dixon-Mueller and Adrienne Germain, "Stalking the Elusive 'Unmet Need' for Family Planning," *Studies in Family Planning* 23, no. 5 (1992); John Bongaarts, "The KAP-Gap and the Unmet Need for Contraception," *Population and Development Review* 17, no. 2 (1991).

39. Ronald Freedman, "The Contribution of Social Science Research to Population Policy and Family Planning Program Effectiveness," *Studies in Family Planning* 18, no. 2 (1987): 59.

40. Freedman, "The Contribution of Social Science Research to Population Policy," 61.

41. Many demographers at the time repeated this quote as common sense. Lant H. Pritchett, "Desired Fertility and the Impact of Population Policies," *Population and Development Review* 20, no. 1 (1994): 39.

42. Paul M. Kennedy, *Preparing for the Twenty-First Century* (New York: Random House, 1993), 338.

43. John Cleland, "A Critique of KAP Studies and Some Suggestions for Their Improvement," *Studies in Family Planning* 4, no. 2 (1973): 45.

44. Cleland, "A Critique of KAP Studies," 45.

45. Cleland, 43.

46. Cleland, 47.

47. Freedman, "The Contribution of Social Science Research to Population Policy," 76–78.

48. Pritchett, "Desired Fertility and the Impact of Population Policies," 15.

49. Caroline H. Bledsoe et al., "Constructing Natural Fertility: The Use of Western Contraceptive Technologies in Rural Gambia," *Population and Development Review* 20, no. 1 (1994); James P. M. Ntozi and John B. Kabera, "Family Planning in Rural Uganda: Knowledge and Use of Modern and Traditional Methods in Ankole," *Studies in Family Planning* 22, no. 2 (1991); Demeny, "Social Science and Population Policy," 470.

50. Phillips et al., "The Demographic Impact of the Family Planning–Health Services Project," 134.

51. Simon Szreter, "The Idea of Demographic Transition and the Study of Fertility Change: A Critical Intellectual History," *Population and Development Review* 19, no. 4 (1993): 691–92.

52. Hodgson emphasizes the connections between early eugenics movements and the Sangerites and Population Control movements. See Dennis Hodgson, "The Ideological Origins of the Population Association of America," *Population and Development Review* 17, no. 1 (1991).

53. Peter J. Donaldson, *Nature Against Us: The United States and the World Population Crisis, 1965–1980* (Chapel Hill: University of North Carolina Press, 1990), 132.

54. See also Susan Greenhalgh, "The Social Construction of Population Science: An Intellectual, Institutional, and Political History of Twentieth-Century Demography," *Comparative Studies in Society and History* 38, no. 1 (1996): 52–55.

55. Bledsoe et al., "Constructing Natural Fertility," 86. See also John Caldwell et al., "The Role of Traditional Fertility Regulation in Sri Lanka," *Studies in Family Planning* 18, no. 1 (1987).

56. Bledsoe et al., "Constructing Natural Fertility," 83.

57. William G. Axinn, Thomas E. Fricke, and Arland Thornton, "The Micro-demographic Community-Study Approach: Improving Survey Data by Integrating the Ethnographic Method," *Sociological Methods & Research* 20, no. 2 (1991): 191.

58. Westoff and Ryder, "The Predictive Validity of Reproductive Intentions," 449.

59. R. D. Lee, "Aiming at a Moving Target: Period Fertility and Changing Reproductive Goals," *Population Studies* 34, no. 2 (1980): 206.

60. Lee, "Aiming at a Moving Target," 206.

61. E.g., Michel Foucault, *The History of Sexuality. Vol. 1: An Introduction* (New York: Pantheon Books), 115–31.

62. Etienne van de Walle, "Fertility Transition, Conscious Choice, and Numeracy," *Demography* 29, no. 4 (1992): 501.

63. Jennifer Johnson-Hanks, "When the Future Decides: Uncertainty and Intentional Action in Contemporary Cameroon," *Current Anthropology* 46, no. 3 (2005): 367.

64. Johnson-Hanks, "When the Future Decides," 372.

65. Bledsoe et al., "Constructing Natural Fertility," 107.

66. Johnson-Hanks, "When the Future Decides," 377.

67. Johnson-Hanks, 383.

68. Johnson-Hanks, 383.

69. Christine A. Bachrach and S. Philip Morgan, "A Cognitive-Social Model of Fertility Intentions," *Population and Development Review* 39, no. 3 (2013).

70. Jennifer Johnson-Hanks et al., "The Theory of Conjunctural Action," in *Understanding Family Change and Variation: Toward a Theory of Conjunctural action* (Dordrecht: Springer, 2011), 16.

71. Sarah R. Hayford, "The Evolution of Fertility Expectations over the Life Course," *Demography* 46, no. 4 (2009): 779.

72. Véronique Petit and Yves Charbit, "The French School of Demography: Contextualizing Demographic Analysis," *Population and Development Review* 38, no. S1 (2013): 328.

73. Margaret Frye and Lauren Bachan, "The Demography of Words: The Global Decline in Non-Numeric Fertility Preferences, 1993–2011," *Population Studies* 71, no. 2 (2017): 204.

74. Natalie Nitsche and Sarah R. Hayford, "Preferences, Partners, and Parenthood: Linking Early Fertility Desires, Marriage Timing, and Achieved Fertility," *Demography* 57, no. 6 (2020): 25.

75. Jenny Trinitapoli and Sara Yeatman, "The Flexibility of Fertility Preferences in a Context of Uncertainty," *Population and Development Review* 44, no. 1 (2018): 111.

76. Jennifer Johnson-Hanks, "Populations Are Composed One Event at a Time," in *Population in the Human Sciences: Concepts, Models, Evidence*, edited by Philip Kreager, Bruce Winney, Stanley Ulijaszek, and Cristian Capelli (Oxford: Oxford University Press, 2015), 247.

77. Johnson-Hanks, "Populations Are Composed One Event at a Time," 240.

78. Jenny Trinitapoli, "Demography Beyond the Foot," in *Covid-19 and the Global Demographic Research Agenda*, ed. Landis MacKellar and Rachel Friedman (New York: Population Council, 2021), 70. Interestingly, scholars also built on

Johnson-Hanks's work as justification to use fertility intention for fertility predictions: e.g., Rachel M. Shattuck, "Does It Matter What She Wants? The Role of Individual Preferences Against Unmarried Motherhood in Young Women's Likelihood of a Nonmarital First Birth," *Demography* 54, no. 4 (2017): 1471. However, in such forecasts, the use of intentions had been recast—not as direct predictors, but as useful data to compare to a generation's realized fertility, or as part of a larger "data-driven" approach to demographic forecasting. Alison Gemmill, "From Some to None? Fertility Expectation Dynamics of Permanently Childless Women," *Demography* 56, no. 1 (2019): 130; see also Caroline Sten Hartnett and Alison Gemmill, "Recent Trends in U.S. Childbearing Intentions," *Demography* 57, no. 6 (2020): 2044.

79. For similar comments pertaining to social mobility research, see John H. Goldthorpe, "Progress in Sociology: The Case of Social Mobility Research," in *Analyzing Inequality: Life Chances and Social Mobility in Comparative Perspective*, ed. Stefan Svallfors (Stanford, CA: Stanford University Press, 2005), 56.

80. Jacqueline H. Wolf, "Low Breastfeeding Rates and Public Health in the United States," *American Journal of Public Health* 93, no. 12 (2003): 2004.

81. C. Everett Koop, "Preface," in *Report of the Surgeon General's Workshop on Breastfeeding & Human Lactation* (Rochester, NY, and Rockville, MD: United States Department of Health and Human Services, 1984), iii.

82. Department of Health and Human Services, "HHS Blueprint for Action on Breastfeeding," in *Breastfeeding: Laws and Societal Impact*, ed. Sarah W. Ying (Hauppauge, NY: Nova Science Publishers, 2005), 26.

83. C. Everett Koop, "Preface," in *Followup Report: The Surgeon General's Workshop on Breastfeeding and Human Lactation* (Rochester, NY, and Rockville, MD: United States Department of Health and Human Services, 1985), ii.

84. Documented in Orit Avishai, "Managing the Lactating Body: The Breastfeeding Project in the Age of Anxiety," in *Infant Feeding Practices: A Cross-Cultural Perspective*, ed. Pranee Liamputtong (New York: Springer New York, 2010); Joan Wolf, *Is Breast Best? Taking On the Breastfeeding Experts and the New High Stakes of Motherhood* (New York: New York University Press, 2010).

85. Julie E. Artis, "Breastfeed at Your Own Risk," *Contexts* 8, no. 4 (2009); Sharon Hays, *The Cultural Contradictions of Motherhood*, revised ed. (New Haven, CT, and London: Yale University Press, 1998).

86. Rima D. Apple, *Mothers and Medicine: A Social History of Infant Feeding, 1890–1950* (Madison: University of Wisconsin Press, 1987); Jules Law, "The Politics of Breastfeeding: Assessing Risk, Dividing Labor," *Signs: Journal of Women in Culture and Society* 25, no. 2 (2000).

87. Phyllis L. F. Rippeyoung, "Can Breastfeeding Solve Inequality? The Relative Moderating Impact of Breastfeeding on Poverty Gaps in Canadian Child Cognitive Skills," *Canadian Journal of Sociology* 38, no. 1 (2013).

88. Steven J. Haider, Alison Jacknowitz, and Robert F. Schoeni, "Welfare Work Requirements and Child Well-Being: Evidence from the Effects on Breast-Feeding," *Demography* 40, no. 3 (2003): 495.

89. Haider, Jacknowitz, and Schoeni, "Welfare Work Requirements and Child Well-Being," 495.

90. Sara B. Fein and Brian Roe, "The Effect of Work Status on Initiation and Duration of Breast-Feeding," *American Journal of Public Health* 88, no. 7 (1998); Brian Roe et al., "Is There Competition between Breast-Feeding and Maternal Employment?" *Demography* 36, no. 2 (1999).

91. Wolf, *Is Breast Best?* 67.

92. Leah Frerichs et al., "Framing Breastfeeding and Formula-Feeding Messages in Popular U.S. Magazines," *Women & Health* 44, no. 1 (2006).

93. Sara B. Fein, Bidisha Mandal, and Brian E. Roe, "Success of Strategies for Combining Employment and Breastfeeding," *Pediatrics* 122, Supplement (2008); Chinelo Ogbuanu et al., "The Effect of Maternity Leave Length and Time of Return to Work on Breastfeeding," *Pediatrics* 127, no. 6 (2011); Alan S. Ryan, Wenjun Zhou, and Mary Beth Arensberg, "The Effect of Employment Status on Breastfeeding in the United States," *Women's Health Issues* 16, no. 5 (2006).

94. Pinka Chatterji and Kevin Frick, "Does Returning to Work after Childbirth Affect Breastfeeding Practices?" *Review of Economics of the Household* 3, no. 3 (2003).

95. Fein, Mandal, and Roe, "Success of Strategies for Combining Employment and Breastfeeding"; Bidisha Mandal, Brian E. Roe, and Sara B. Fein, "Work and Breastfeeding Decisions Are Jointly Determined for Higher Socioeconomic Status US Mothers," *Review of Economics of the Household* 12, no. 2 (2014).

96. Ryan, Zhou, and Arensberg, "The Effect of Employment Status on Breastfeeding," 250.

97. Alissa Quart, "The Milk Wars," Opinion, *New York Times*, July 14, 2012, https://www.nytimes.com/2012/07/15/opinion/sunday/the-breast-feeding-wars.html.

98. Jacqueline H. Wolf, "What Feminists Can Do for Breastfeeding and What Breastfeeding Can Do for Feminists," *Signs: Journal of Women in Culture and Society* 31, no. 2 (2006): 398.

99. Diane Wiessinger, Diana West, and Teresa Pitman, *The Womanly Art of Breastfeeding*, 8th ed. (New York: Random House, 2010 [1958]).

100. Wolf, "What Feminists Can Do for Breastfeeding," 398.

101. Wolf, 415.

102. Wolf, 417.

103. Law, "The Politics of Breastfeeding."

104. Maria Jansson, "Feeding Children and Protecting Women: The Emergence of Breastfeeding as an International Concern," *Women's Studies International Forum* 32, no. 3 (2009): 241.

105. Jeanne Holcomb, "Resisting Guilt: Mothers' Breastfeeding Intentions and Formula Use," *Sociological Focus* 50, no. 4 (2017): 364.

106. Elizabeth Murphy, "'Breast Is Best': Infant Feeding Decisions and Maternal Deviance," *Sociology of Health & Illness* 21, no. 2 (1999): 205.

107. Ellie Lee, "Health, Morality, and Infant Feeding: British Mothers' Experiences of Formula Milk Use in the Early Weeks," *Sociology of Health & Illness* 29, no. 7 (2007): 1086.

108. Shannon K. Carter and Amanda Koontz Anthony, "Good, Bad, and Extraordinary Mothers: Infant Feeding and Mothering in African American Mothers'

Breastfeeding Narratives," *Sociology of Race and Ethnicity* 1, no. 4 (2015); Nicole Owens et al., "Neutralizing the Maternal Breast: Accounts of Public Breastfeeding by African American Mothers," *Journal of Family Issues* 39, no. 2 (2018).

109. Rebecca Kukla, "Ethics and Ideology in Breastfeeding Advocacy Campaigns," *Hypatia* 21, no. 1 (2006): 177.

110. Vida Maralani and Samuel Stabler, "Intensive Parenting: Fertility and Breastfeeding Duration in the United States," *Demography* 55, no. 5 (2018): 1708.

111. Phyllis L. F. Rippeyoung and Mary C. Noonan, "Is Breastfeeding Truly Cost Free? Income Consequences of Breastfeeding for Women," *American Sociological Review* 77, no. 2 (2012): 245.

112. Ellie Lee, "Breast-Feeding Advocacy, Risk Society and Health Moralism: A Decade's Scholarship," *Sociology Compass* 5, no. 12 (2011).

113. Robyn Lee, "Feeding the Hungry Other: Levinas, Breastfeeding, and the Politics of Hunger," *Hypatia* 31, no. 2 (2016): 269.

114. Cynthia G. Colen and David M. Ramey, "Is Breast Truly Best? Estimating the Effects of Breastfeeding on Long-Term Child Health and Wellbeing in the United States Using Sibling Comparisons," *Social Science & Medicine* 109 (2014): 64.

115. Holcomb, "Resisting Guilt," 372.

116. Wolf, "What Feminists Can Do for Breastfeeding," 417.

117. Wolf, 416.

118. Thomas S. Kuhn, *The Structure of Scientific Revolutions*, ed. Ian Hacking, 4th ed. (Chicago: University of Chicago Press, 2012 [1962]), 122.

119. Karen Benjamin Guzzo et al., "Unpacking the 'Black Box' of Race–Ethnic Variation in Fertility," *Race and Social Problems* 7, no. 2 (2014); Shirley A. Hill and Joey Sprague, "Parenting in Black and White Families: The Interaction of Gender with Race and Class," *Gender & Society* 13, no. 4 (1999).

CONCLUSION

1. George E. Marcus and Michael M. J. Fischer, *Anthropology as Cultural Critique: An Experimental Moment in the Human Sciences* (Chicago: University of Chicago Press, 1986).

2. Robert B. Edgerton, *Sick Societies: Challenging the Myth of Primitive Harmony* (New York and Toronto: Free Press and Maxwell Macmillan, 1992), 208.

3. Contrast Edgerton with postmodern critiques of comparative anthropology, e.g., Richard A. Shweder, *Thinking through Cultures: Expeditions in Cultural Psychology* (Cambridge, MA: Harvard University Press, 1991).

4. E.g., Noëmi Manders-Huits, "What Values in Design? The Challenge of Incorporating Moral Values into Design," *Science and Engineering Ethics* 17, no. 2 (2011).

5. Isaiah Berlin, *The Crooked Timber of Humanity: Chapters in the History of Ideas*, ed. Henry Hardy, 1st American ed. (New York: Knopf; distributed by Random House, 1991).

6. Neil Gross, *Richard Rorty: The Making of an American Philosopher* (Chicago: University of Chicago Press, 2009), 342n5.

7. Jürgen Habermas, *Moral Consciousness and Communicative Action* (Cambridge, MA: MIT Press, 1990), 134.

8. Luc Boltanski, *Love and Justice as Competences: Three Essays on the Sociology of Action*, ed. Catherine Porter (Cambridge and Malden, MA: Polity, 2012); see Boltanski's additional remarks on this topic in Luc Boltanski and Craig Browne, "'Whatever Works': Political Philosophy and Sociology—Luc Boltanski in Conversation with Craig Browne," in *The Spirit of Luc Boltanski: Essays on the "Pragmatic Sociology of Critique*," ed. Simon Susen and Bryan S. Turner (London: Anthem Press, 2014), 550–51.

9. Stephen Cole, "Why Sociology Doesn't Make Progress Like the Natural Sciences," *Sociological Forum* 9, no. 2 (1994): 145.

10. Joseph Raz, "Multiculturalism: A Liberal Perspective," *Dissent* 41, no. 1 (1994): 72.

11. Pragmatist philosophers have long offered positions compatible with value pluralism, beginning famously with William James's discussion of "the one and the many." William James, "The Moral Philosopher and the Moral Life," *International Journal of Ethics* 1, no. 3 (1891). See also James R. O'Shea, "Sources of Pluralism in William James," in *Pluralism: The Philosophy and Politics of Diversity*, ed. Maria Baghramian and Attracta Ingram (London: Routledge, 2000). Conversely, some philosophers have countered that pragmatism and value pluralism are logically incompatible. Robert B. Talisse and Scott F. Aikin, "Why Pragmatists Cannot Be Pluralists," *Transactions of the Charles S. Peirce Society* 41, no. 1 (2005): 101.

12. David Stark, *The Sense of Dissonance: Accounts of Worth in Economic Life* (Princeton, NJ: Princeton University Press, 2009), 192.

13. Luc Boltanski et al., "Sociology of Critique or Critical Theory? Luc Boltanski and Axel Honneth in Conversation with Robin Celikates," in *The Spirit of Luc Boltanski: Essays on the "Pragmatic Sociology of Critique*," ed. Simon Susen and Bryan S. Turner (London: Anthem Press, 2014), 576.

14. Laurent Thévenot suggested that Bourdieusian sociology cannot serve the "strong pluralist requirement" of contemporary societies. Laurent Thévenot, "Power and Oppression from the Perspective of the Sociology of Engagements: A Comparison with Bourdieu's and Dewey's Critical Approaches to Practical Activities," *Irish Journal of Sociology* 19, no. 1 (2011): 43.

15. Gideon Lewis-Kraus, "Can Progressives Be Convinced that Genetics Matters?" *The New Yorker*, September 13, 2021, https://www.newyorker.com/magazine/2021/09/13/can-progressives-be-convinced-that-genetics-matters.

16. Christian Smith, *The Sacred Project of American Sociology* (New York: Oxford University Press, 2014).

17. See further discussion in Gabriel Abend, "Two Main Problems in the Sociology of Morality," *Theory and Society* 37, no. 2 (2008): 92.

18. Chantal Mouffe, "Deconstruction, Pragmatism and the Politics of Democracy," in *Deconstruction and Pragmatism*, ed. Simon Critchley and Chantal Mouffe (London and New York: Routledge, 1996), 8–9.

19. Monica Prasad, "Pragmatism as Problem Solving," *Socius* 7 (2021): 5–6.

20. See as an example Elizabeth Popp Berman, *Thinking Like an Economist: How*

Efficiency Replaced Equality in U.S. Public Policy (Princeton, NJ: Princeton University Press, 2022).

21. Jacob Felson, Amy Adamczyk, and Christopher Thomas, "How and Why Have Attitudes about Cannabis Legalization Changed So Much?" *Social Science Research* 78 (2019). For an overview of the moral justifications used amongst cannabis investors in this transformed environment see Navin Kumar, Cheneal Puljević, and Robert Heimer, "Understanding Motivations for Large US Cannabis Firms' Participation in the Cannabis Space: Qualitative Study Exploring Views of Key Decision-Makers," *Drug and Alcohol Review* 39, no. 4 (2020).

22. Martin A. Lee, *Smoke Signals: A Social History of Marijuana—Medical, Recreational, and Scientific* (New York: Scribner, 2012), 158.

23. For a more detailed reconstruction of the methodological implications of *Becoming a Marijuana User*, see Howard Saul Becker, *What About Mozart? What About Murder? Reasoning from Cases* (Chicago: University of Chicago Press, 2014), 61–93.

24. Howard S. Becker, *Becoming a Marihuana User* (Chicago: University of Chicago Press, 2015 [1953]), xi.

25. Other notable academics included Andrew Weil, a Harvard-trained medical doctor and author of *The Natural Mind*; and Timothy Leary, the Harvard psychologist and author of the mantra "Tune in, turn on, and drop out." See Lee, *Smoke Signals*, 72–115.

26. Emily Dufton, *Grass Roots: The Rise and Fall and Rise of Marijuana in America* (New York: Basic Books, 2017), 45–73.

27. Eduardo Bonilla-Silva and Tyrone A. Forman, "'I Am Not a Racist But . . .': Mapping White College Students' Racial Ideology in the USA," *Discourse & Society* 11, no. 1 (2000).

28. Eduardo Bonilla-Silva, Amanda Lewis, and David G. Embrick, "'I Did Not Get That Job Because of a Black Man . . .': The Story Lines and Testimonies of Color-Blind Racism," *Sociological Forum* 19, no. 4 (2004).

29. Eduardo Bonilla-Silva et al., "'It Wasn't Me!': How Will Race and Racism Work in 21st Century America?" in *Political Sociology for the 21st Century*, ed. Betty A. Dobratz, Lisa K. Waldner, and Tim Buzzell (Amsterdam and Boston: JAI, 2003).

30. Bonilla-Silva distinguished his notion of color-blind racism, which refers to "the dominant racial ideology of post–civil rights America," from Cose, who treats the concept as "a fable [he] wishes to disprove," and from Carr, who relies on a class-based notion of ideology to analyze racial ideology. Eduardo Bonilla-Silva, "Racial Attitudes or Racial Ideology? An Alternative Paradigm for Examining Actors' Racial Views," *Journal of Political Ideologies* 8, no. 1 (2003): 81n8.

31. E.g., Leith Mullings, "Interrogating Racism: Toward an Antiracist Anthropology," *Annual Review of Anthropology* 34, no. 1 (2005).

32. Eduardo Bonilla-Silva, *Racism without Racists: Color-Blind Racism and the Persistence of Racial Inequality in the United States* (Blue Ridge Summit, PA: Rowman & Littlefield Publishing Group, 2006 [2003]).

33. Based on Google Scholar, last accessed August 2, 2021.

34. Nicholas Kristof, "Straight Talk for White Men," *New York Times*, Febru-

ary 22, 2015, https://www.nytimes.com/2015/02/22/opinion/sunday/nicholas
-kristof-straight-talk-for-white-men.html.

35. Bonilla-Silva, *Racism without Racists*, 96–119.

36. Paul Ricœur, *Freud and Philosophy: An Essay on Interpretation* (New Haven,
CT: Yale University Press, 1970), 30, and see more generally 28–36 on the hermeneutics of suspicion.

37. Colin Jerolmack and Shamus Khan, "Talk Is Cheap: Ethnography and the
Attitudinal Fallacy," *Sociological Methods & Research* 43, no. 2 (2014).

AFTERWORD

1. Although see Ilana Silber's important disclaimer about presupposing that
suspicion and recognition are the only two options. Ilana F. Silber, "Luc Boltanski
and the Gift: Beyond Love, Beyond Suspicion . . . ?," in *The Spirit of Luc Boltanski: Essays on the "Pragmatic Sociology of Critique*," ed. Simon Susen and Bryan S.
Turner (London: Anthem Press, 2014): 494–95.

2. Iddo Tavory and Stefan Timmermans, *Abductive Analysis: Theorizing Qualitative Research* (Chicago: University of Chicago Press, 2014).

3. Boltanski developed a response to this charge in Luc Boltanski, *On Critique:
A Sociology of Emancipation* (Malden, MA: Polity, 2011), chapter 3.

4. Paul Lichterman and Isaac Ariail Reed, "Theory and Contrastive Explanation
in Ethnography," *Sociological Methods & Research* 44, no. 4 (2015): 590–91.

5. Our list is heavily influenced by the work of Boltanski and his collaborators,
particularly Laurent Thévenot and Ève Chiapello. The reader is encouraged to
revisit these works, both of which describe the various valuing practices in each of
these repertories in significantly more detail than we do here. Luc Boltanski and
Laurent Thévenot, *On Justification: Economies of Worth* (Princeton, NJ: Princeton
University Press, 2006), 159–213; Luc Boltanski and Ève Chiapello, *The New Spirit
of Capitalism* (London and New York: Verso, 2005), 103–64.

6. We drew here on Boltanski's notion of *regimes of action*. See Luc Boltanski,
Love and Justice as Competences: Three Essays on the Sociology of Action, ed. Catherine Porter (Cambridge and Malden, MA: Polity, 2012), 68–78.

7. Since the two formats are close, we underline that to *reject* an idea is to insist
that a debate about whether and how a certain research trajectory is moral is in
itself unacceptable, whereas what we call *delegitimation* in chapter 2 entails a situation where one rejects the use of an existing moral repertoire and then enters a
debate where they demand that another moral repertoire define the situational.

Bibliography

Abbott, Andrew. "Living One's Theories: Moral Consistency in the Life of Émile Durkheim." *Sociological Theory* 37, no. 1 (2019): 1–34.

———. *Processual Sociology*. Chicago: University of Chicago Press, 2016.

———. "Varieties of Normative Inquiry: Moral Alternatives to Politicization in Sociology." *The American Sociologist* 49, no. 2 (2018): 158–80.

Abbott, Andrew D. *Chaos of Disciplines*. Chicago: University of Chicago Press, 2001.

Abbott, James R. "Critical Sociologies and *Ressentiment*: The Examples of C. Wright Mills and Howard Becker." *The American Sociologist* 37, no. 3 (2006): 15–30.

Abend, G. *The Moral Background: An Inquiry into the History of Business Ethics*. Princeton, NJ: Princeton University Press, 2014.

Abend, Gabriel. "Two Main Problems in the Sociology of Morality." *Theory and Society* 37, no. 2 (2008): 87–125.

Abraham, Margaret, and Bandana Purkayastha. "Making a Difference: Linking Research and Action in Practice, Pedagogy, and Policy for Social Justice: Introduction." *Current Sociology* 60, no. 2 (2012): 123–41.

Adams, Julia, Elisabeth S. Clemens, and Ann Shola Orloff. "Introduction: Social Theory, Modernity, and the Three Waves of Historical Sociology." In *Remaking Modernity: Politics, History, and Sociology*, edited by Julia Adams, Elisabeth S. Clemens, and Ann Shola Orloff, 1–72. Durham, NC: Duke University Press, 2005.

Akresh, Ilana Redstone. "Departmental and Disciplinary Divisions in Sociology: Responses from Departmental Executive Officers." *The American Sociologist* 48, no. 3/4 (2017): 541–60.

Alderfer, Clayton P. "The Science and Nonscience of Psychologists' Responses to *The Bell Curve*." *Professional Psychology: Research and Practice* 34, no. 3 (2003): 287–93.

Alexander, Jeffrey C. "Cultural Pragmatics: Social Performance between Ritual and Strategy." *Sociological Theory* 22, no. 4 (2004): 527–73.

———. "A Cultural Sociology of Evil." In *The Meanings of Social Life: A Cultural Sociology*, 109–20. Oxford and New York: Oxford University Press, 2003.

———. *Fin de Siècle Social Theory: Relativism, Reduction, and the Problem of Reason*. London and New York: Verso, 1995.

———. "Modern, Anti, Post, and Neo: How Social Theories Have Tried to Understand the 'New World' of 'Our Time.'" In *The Meanings of Social Life: A Cultural Sociology*, 193–228. New York: Oxford University Press, 2003.

———. *Theoretical Logic in Sociology, Vol. 1: Positivism, Presuppositions, and Current Controversies*. Berkeley and Los Angeles: University of California Press, 1982.

Almeling, Rene. *GUYnecology: The Missing Science of Men's Reproductive Health*. Berkeley: University of California Press, 2020.

Ammerman, Nancy Tatom. *Sacred Stories, Spiritual Tribes: Finding Religion in Everyday Life*. Oxford: Oxford University Press, 2013.

Anderson, Elijah. *Code of the Street: Decency, Violence, and the Moral Life of the Inner City*. New York: W. W. Norton, 1999.

———. *A Place on the Corner*. Chicago: University of Chicago Press, 1978.

Apple, Rima D. *Mothers and Medicine: A Social History of Infant Feeding, 1890–1950*. Madison: University of Wisconsin Press, 1987.

Archibugi, Daniele. "Cosmopolitical Democracy." *New Left Review* 4, no. 4 (2000): 137–50.

———. *The Global Commonwealth of Citizens: Toward Cosmopolitan Democracy*. Princeton, NJ: Princeton University Press, 2008.

Archibugi, Daniele, and David Held. *Cosmopolitan Democracy: An Agenda for a New World Order*. Cambridge, UK, and Cambridge, MA: Polity Press and Basil Blackwell, 1995.

Artis, Julie E. "Breastfeed at Your Own Risk." *Contexts* 8, no. 4 (2009): 28–34.

Asad, Talal. *Formations of the Secular: Christianity, Islam, Modernity*. Stanford, CA: Stanford University Press, 2003.

Asher, Jeff, and Rob Arthur. "Inside the Algorithm that Tries to Predict Gun Violence in Chicago." *New York Times*, June 13, 2017. https://www.nytimes.com/2017/06/13/upshot/what-an-algorithm-reveals-about-life-on-chicagos-high-risk-list.html.

Avishai, Orit. "Managing the Lactating Body: The Breastfeeding Project in the Age of Anxiety." In *Infant Feeding Practices: A Cross-Cultural Perspective*, edited by Pranee Liamputtong, 23–38. New York: Springer New York, 2010.

Axinn, William G., Thomas E. Fricke, and Arland Thornton. "The Microdemographic Community-Study Approach: Improving Survey Data by Integrating the Ethnographic Method." *Sociological Methods & Research* 20, no. 2 (1991): 187–217.

Bachrach, Christine A., and S. Philip Morgan. "A Cognitive-Social Model of Fertility Intentions." *Population and Development Review* 39, no. 3 (2013): 459–85.

Baker, Joseph O'Brian, and Buster Smith. "None Too Simple: Examining Issues of Religious Nonbelief and Nonbelonging in the United States." *Journal for the Scientific Study of Religion* 48, no. 4 (2009): 719–33.

Bandura, Albert. "Moral Disengagement in the Perpetration of Inhumanities." *Personality and Social Psychology Review* 3, no. 3 (1999): 193–209.

Bargheer, Stefan. *Moral Entanglements: Conserving Birds in Britain and Germany*. Chicago: University of Chicago Press, 2018.

Bartlett, Tom. "The Unraveling of Michael LaCour." *Chronicle of Higher Educa-*

tion, June 2, 2015. https://www.chronicle.com/article/the-unraveling-of-michael -lacour/.

Bateman, Oliver. "The Young Academic's Twitter Conundrum." *The Atlantic*, May 10, 2017. https://www.theatlantic.com/education/archive/2017/05/the -young-academics-twitter-conundrum/525924/.

Bateson, Gregory. *Steps to an Ecology of Mind*. Chicago: University of Chicago Press, 2000.

Bauman, Zygmunt. *Liquid Modernity*. Cambridge and Malden, MA: Polity Press and Blackwell, 2000.

Bearman, Peter. "Introduction: Exploring Genetics and Social Structure." *American Journal of Sociology* 114, no. S1 (2008): v–x.

Beauchamp, Zack. "The Controversy around Hoax Studies in Critical Theory, Explained." *Vox*, October 15, 2018. https://www.vox.com/2018/10/15/17951492/ grievance-studies-sokal-squared-hoax.

Beck, Ulrich. *The Metamorphosis of the World*. Cambridge, UK, and Malden, MA: Polity, 2016.

Beck, Ulrich, and Johannes Willms. *Conversations with Ulrich Beck*. Translated by Michael Pollack. Oxford: Polity Press, 2004 [2000].

Becker, Howard S. *Becoming a Marihuana User*. Chicago: University of Chicago Press, 2015 [1953].

———. "Whose Side Are We On?" *Social Problems* 14, no. 3 (1967): 239–47.

Becker, Howard Saul. *What About Mozart? What About Murder? Reasoning from Cases*. Chicago: University of Chicago Press, 2014.

Bellah, Robert N. "The Ethical Aims of Social Inquiry." In *The Robert Bellah Reader*, 381–401. Durham, NC: Duke University Press, 2006 [1983].

———. "New Religious Consciousness and the Crisis in Modernity." In *The New Religious Consciousness*, edited by Charles Y. Glock, Robert Neelly Bellah, and Randall H. Alfred, 333–52. Berkeley: University of California Press, 1976.

Bénatouïl, Thomas. "A Tale of Two Sociologies: The Critical and the Pragmatic Stance in Contemporary French Sociology." *European Journal of Social Theory* 2, no. 3 (1999): 379–96.

Bender, Courtney. "Pluralism and Secularism." In *Religion on the Edge: De-Centering and Re-Centering the Sociology of Religion*, edited by Courtney Bender, Wendy Cadge, Peggy Levitt, and David Smilde, 138–58. New York: Oxford University Press, 2013.

Benjamin, Ruha. "Cultura Obscura: Race, Power, and 'Culture Talk' in the Health Sciences." *American Journal of Law & Medicine* 43, no. 2–3 (2017): 225–38.

Berlin, Isaiah. *The Crooked Timber of Humanity: Chapters in the History of Ideas*. Edited by Henry Hardy. New York: Knopf; distributed by Random House, 1991.

Berman, Elizabeth Popp. *Thinking Like an Economist: How Efficiency Replaced Equality in U.S. Public Policy*. Princeton, NJ: Princeton University Press, 2022.

Billig, Michael. *Banal Nationalism*. London and Thousand Oaks, CA: Sage, 1995.

Black, Donald. "On the Almost Inconceivable Misunderstandings Concerning the Subject of Value-Free Social Science." *The British Journal of Sociology* 64, no. 4 (2013): 763–80.

Bledsoe, Caroline H., Allan G. Hill, Umberto D'Alessandro, and Patricia Langerock. "Constructing Natural Fertility: The Use of Western Contraceptive Technologies in Rural Gambia." *Population and Development Review* 20, no. 1 (1994): 81–113.

Blokker, Paul. "Pragmatic Sociology: Theoretical Evolvement and Empirical Application." *European Journal of Social Theory* 14, no. 3 (2011): 251–61.

Bobo, Lawrence D., and Michael C. Dawson. "A Change Has Come: Race, Politics, and the Path to the Obama Presidency." *Du Bois Review* 6, no. 1 (2009): 1–14.

Bogusz, Tanja. "Why (Not) Pragmatism?" In *The Spirit of Luc Boltanski: Essays on the "Pragmatic Sociology of Critique,"* edited by Simon Susen and Bryan S. Turner, 129–52. London: Anthem Press, 2014.

Boli, John, and George M. Thomas. "World Culture in the World Polity: A Century of International Non-Governmental Organization." *American Sociological Review* 62, no. 2 (1997): 171–90.

Boltanski, Luc. *Distant Suffering: Morality, Media and Politics*. Cambridge and New York: Cambridge University Press, 1999.

———. *Love and Justice as Competences: Three Essays on the Sociology of Action*. Edited by Catherine Porter. Cambridge and Malden, MA: Polity, 2012.

———. *On Critique: A Sociology of Emancipation*. Malden, MA: Polity, 2011.

Boltanski, Luc, and Craig Browne. "'Whatever Works': Political Philosophy and Sociology—Luc Boltanski in Conversation with Craig Browne." In *The Spirit of Luc Boltanski: Essays on the "Pragmatic Sociology of Critique,"* edited by Simon Susen and Bryan S. Turner, 549–60. London: Anthem Press, 2014.

Boltanski, Luc, and Ève Chiapello. *The New Spirit of Capitalism*. London and New York: Verso, 2005.

Boltanski, Luc, Axel Honneth, Robin Celikates, and Simon Susen. "Sociology of Critique or Critical Theory? Luc Boltanski and Axel Honneth in Conversation with Robin Celikates." In *The Spirit of Luc Boltanski: Essays on the "Pragmatic Sociology of Critique,"* edited by Simon Susen and Bryan S. Turner, 561–90. London: Anthem Press, 2014.

Boltanski, Luc, and Laurent Thévenot. *On Justification: Economies of Worth*. Princeton, NJ: Princeton University Press, 2006.

———. "The Reality of Moral Expectations: A Sociology of Situated Judgement." *Philosophical Explorations* 3, no. 3 (2000): 208–31.

———. "The Sociology of Critical Capacity." *European Journal of Social Theory* 2, no. 3 (1999): 359–77.

Bongaarts, John. "The KAP-Gap and the Unmet Need for Contraception." *Population and Development Review* 17, no. 2 (1991): 293–313.

Bonikowski, Bart. "Nationalism in Settled Times." *Annual Review of Sociology* 42, no. 1 (2016): 427–49.

Bonikowski, Bart, and Paul DiMaggio. "Varieties of American Popular Nationalism." *American Sociological Review* 81, no. 5 (2016): 949–80.

Bonilla-Silva, Eduardo. "Racial Attitudes or Racial Ideology? An Alternative Paradigm for Examining Actors' Racial Views." *Journal of Political Ideologies* 8, no. 1 (2003): 63–82.

———. *Racism without Racists: Color-Blind Racism and the Persistence of Racial In-*

equality in the United States. Blue Ridge Summit, PA: Rowman & Littlefield Publishing Group, 2006 [2003].

———. "The 2008 Elections and the Future of Anti-Racism in 21st Century Amerika or How We Got Drunk with Obama's Hope Liquor and Failed to See Reality." *Humanity & Society* 34, no. 3 (2010): 222–32.

Bonilla-Silva, Eduardo, and Gianpaolo Baiocchi. "Anything but Racism: How Sociologists Limit the Significance of Racism." *Race & Society* 4, no. 2 (2001): 117–31.

Bonilla-Silva, Eduardo, and Tyrone A. Forman. "'I Am Not a Racist But . . .': Mapping White College Students' Racial Ideology in the USA." *Discourse & Society* 11, no. 1 (2000): 50–85.

Bonilla-Silva, Eduardo, Tyrone A. Forman, Amanda E. Lewis, and David G. Embrick. "'It Wasn't Me!': How Will Race and Racism Work in 21st Century America?" In *Political Sociology for the 21st Century*, edited by Betty A. Dobratz, Lisa K. Waldner, and Tim Buzzell, 111–34. Amsterdam and Boston: JAI, 2003.

Bonilla-Silva, Eduardo, Amanda Lewis, and David G. Embrick. "'I Did Not Get That Job Because of a Black Man . . .': The Story Lines and Testimonies of Color-Blind Racism." *Sociological Forum* 19, no. 4 (2004): 555–81.

Borgatta, Edgar F., and Charles F. Westoff. "Social and Psychological Factors Affecting Fertility: XXV. The Prediction of Total Fertility." *The Milbank Memorial Fund Quarterly* 32, no. 4 (1954): 383–419.

Bourdieu, Pierre. *Homo Academicus.* Stanford, CA: Stanford University Press, 1988.

———. *Pascalian Meditations.* Translated by Richard Nice. Stanford, CA: Stanford University Press, 2000.

———. *Science of Science and Reflexivity.* Edited by Richard Nice. Chicago: University of Chicago Press, 2004.

———. *Sketch for a Self-Analysis.* Translated by Richard Nice. Cambridge: Polity, 2007.

———. *The Sociologist and the Historian.* Edited by Roger Chartier and David Fernbach. Cambridge, UK, and Malden, MA: Polity Press, 2015.

———. *Sociology Is a Martial Art: Political Writings by Pierre Bourdieu.* Edited by Gisèle Sapiro, Priscilla Parkhurst Ferguson, Richard W. Nice, and Loïc J. D. Wacquant. New York: New Press, 2010.

Bourdieu, Pierre, Jean-Claude Chamboredon, and Jean-Claude Passeron. *The Craft of Sociology: Epistemological Preliminaries.* Translated by Richard Nice. Edited by Beate Krais. Berlin and New York: Walter de Gruyter, 1991.

Bourdieu, Pierre, and Roger Chartier. "The Sociologist's Craft." Translated by David Fernbach. In *The Sociologist and the Historian*, 1–18. Cambridge: Polity, 2015.

Bourdieu, Pierre, and Loïc J. D. Wacquant. "Epilogue: On the Possibility of a Field of World Sociology." In *Social Theory for a Changing Society*, edited by Pierre Bourdieu and James S. Coleman, 373–87. Boulder, CO, and New York: Westview Press and Russell Sage Foundation, 1991.

Breslau, Daniel. "The American Spencerians: Theorizing a New Science." In *Sociology in America: A History*, edited by Craig J. Calhoun. Chicago: University of Chicago Press, 2007.

Briggs, Laura. *Reproducing Empire: Race, Sex, Science, and U.S. Imperialism in Puerto Rico.* Berkeley: University of California Press, 2002. doi:10.1525/j.ctt1pncqs.

Broockman, David, Joshua Kalla, and P. M. Aronow. "Irregularities in LaCour (2014)." *MetaArXiv Preprints*, January 7, 2020 [2015]. https://doi.org/doi:10.31222/osf.io/qy2se.

Brubaker, Rogers. *Nationalism Reframed: Nationhood and the National Question in the New Europe.* Cambridge and New York: Cambridge University Press, 1996.

———. *Trans: Gender and Race in an Age of Unsettled Identities.* Princeton, NJ: Princeton University Press, 2016.

Bruce, Steve. *Secularization: In Defence of an Unfashionable Theory.* Oxford: Oxford University Press, 2011. doi:10.1093/acprof:osobl/9780199654123.001.0001.

Brunsma, David L., and Jennifer Padilla Wyse. "The Possessive Investment in White Sociology." *Sociology of Race and Ethnicity* 5, no. 1 (2018): 1–10.

Burawoy, Michael. "Sociology as a Vocation." *Contemporary Sociology* 45, no. 4 (2016): 379–93.

Butler, Anthea D. *White Evangelical Racism: The Politics of Morality in America.* Chapel Hill: University of North Carolina Press, 2021.

Byrd, W. Carson, and Latrica E. Best. "Between (Racial) Groups and a Hard Place: An Exploration of Social Science Approaches to Race and Genetics, 2000–2014." *Biodemography and Social Biology* 62, no. 3 (2016): 281–99.

Byrd, W. Carson, and Matthew W. Hughey. "Biological Determinism and Racial Essentialism: The Ideological Double Helix of Racial Inequality." *The ANNALS of the American Academy of Political and Social Science* 661, no. 1 (2015): 8–22.

Caldwell, John, K. H. W. Gaminiratne, Pat Caldwell, Soma de Silva, Bruce Caldwell, Nanda Weeraratne, and Padmini Silva. "The Role of Traditional Fertility Regulation in Sri Lanka." *Studies in Family Planning* 18, no. 1 (1987): 1–21.

Calhoun, Craig. "The Class Consciousness of Frequent Travelers: Toward a Critique of Actually Existing Cosmopolitanism." *The South Atlantic Quarterly* 101, no. 4 (2002): 869–97.

Calhoun, Craig J. *Nations Matter: Culture, History, and the Cosmopolitan Dream.* London and New York: Routledge, 2007.

———. *The Roots of Radicalism: Tradition, the Public Sphere, and Early Nineteenth-Century Social Movements.* Chicago: University of Chicago Press, 2012.

Calhoun, Craig Jackson. "The Radicalism of Tradition: Community Strength or Venerable Disguise and Borrowed Language?" *American Journal of Sociology* 88, no. 5 (1983): 886–914.

Camic, Charles, and Neil Gross. "The New Sociology of Ideas." In *Blackwell Companion to Sociology*, edited by J. Blau, 236–50. Oxford: Blackwell Publishing, 2004.

Camic, Charles, Neil Gross, and Michèle Lamont. *Social Knowledge in the Making.* Chicago: University of Chicago Press, 2011.

Campbell, Arthur A., and William D. Mosher. "A History of the Measurement of Unintended Pregnancies and Births." *Maternal and Child Health Journal* 4, no. 3 (2000): 163–69.

Campos, Paul F. "Alice Goffman's Implausible Ethnography." *Chronicle of Higher Education*, August 21, 2015. https://www.chronicle.com/article/alice-goffmans-implausible-ethnography/.

Carey, Benedict. "Gay Advocates Can Shift Same-Sex Marriage Views." *New York*

Times, December 11, 2014. https://www.nytimes.com/2014/12/12/health/gay -marriage-canvassing-study-science.html.

Carreira da Silva, Filipe. "Following the Book: Towards a Pragmatic Sociology of the Book." *Sociology* 50, no. 6 (2016): 1185–1200.

Carter, Shannon K., and Amanda Koontz Anthony. "Good, Bad, and Extraordinary Mothers: Infant Feeding and Mothering in African American Mothers' Breastfeeding Narratives." *Sociology of Race and Ethnicity* 1, no. 4 (2015): 517–31.

Casanova, José. *Public Religions in the Modern World*. Chicago: University of Chicago Press, 1994.

———. "Rethinking Secularization: A Global Comparative Perspective." *The Hedgehog Review* 8, no. 1–2 (2006): 7–22.

Chatterji, Pinka, and Kevin Frick. "Does Returning to Work after Childbirth Affect Breastfeeding Practices?" *Review of Economics of the Household* 3, no. 3 (2003): 315–35.

Chaves, Mark, and Philip S. Gorski. "Religious Pluralism and Religious Participation." *Annual Review of Sociology* 27 (2001): 261–81.

Chen, Carolyn. *Work Pray Code: When Work Becomes Religion in Silicon Valley*. Princeton, NJ: Princeton University Press, 2022.

Cheng, Simon, and Brian Powell. "Measurement, Methods, and Divergent Patterns: Reassessing the Effects of Same-Sex Parents." *Social Science Research* 52 (2015): 615–26.

Clayman, Steven E. "Review Article: The Dialectic of Ethnomethodology." *Semiotica* 107, no. 1-2 (1995): 105–23.

Cleland, John. "A Critique of KAP Studies and Some Suggestions for Their Improvement." *Studies in Family Planning* 4, no. 2 (1973): 42–47.

Cohen, Andrew C., and Shai M. Dromi. "Advertising Morality: Maintaining Moral Worth in a Stigmatized Profession." *Theory & Society* 47, no. 2 (2018): 175–206.

Cole, Stephen. "Why Sociology Doesn't Make Progress Like the Natural Sciences." *Sociological Forum* 9, no. 2 (1994): 133–54.

Coleman, James S. "The Rational Reconstruction of Society: 1992 Presidential Address." *American Sociological Review* 58, no. 1 (1993): 1–15.

Colen, Cynthia G., and David M. Ramey. "Is Breast Truly Best? Estimating the Effects of Breastfeeding on Long-term Child Health and Wellbeing in the United States Using Sibling Comparisons." *Social Science & Medicine* 109 (2014): 55–65.

Collins, Mali, and Jennifer C. Nash. "The Language Through Which Black Feminist Theory Speaks: A Conversation with Jennifer C. Nash." In *Black Feminist Sociology: Perspectives and Praxis*, edited by Zakiya Luna and Whitney Pirtle, 57–70. Milton: Taylor and Francis, 2021.

Collins, Patricia Hill. *Black Feminist Thought: Knowledge, Consciousness, and the Politics of Empowerment*. London and New York: Routledge, 2014.

———. *On Intellectual Activism*. Philadelphia, PA: Temple University Press, 2013.

Collins, Randall. "Why the Social Sciences Won't Become High-Consensus, Rapid-Discovery Science." *Sociological Forum* 9, no. 2 (1994): 155–78.

Connell, Raewyn. *Southern Theory: The Global Dynamics of Knowledge in Social Science*. Cambridge and Malden, MA: Polity, 2007.

Contreras, Randol. "Transparency and Unmasking Issues in Ethnographic Crime

Research: Methodological Considerations." *Sociological Forum* 34, no. 2 (2019): 293–312.

Cook, Gary A. *George Herbert Mead: The Making of a Social Pragmatist.* Urbana: University of Illinois Press, 1993.

Coombs, Lolagene C. "The Measurement of Family Size Preferences and Subsequent Fertility." *Demography* 11, no. 4 (1974): 587–611.

Cordero, Rodrigo. *Crisis and Critique: On the Fragile Foundations of Social Life.* New York: Routledge, 2017.

Curtis, Bruce. "Reworking Moral Regulation: Metaphorical Capital and the Field of Disinterest." *Canadian Journal of Sociology* 22, no. 3 (1997): 303–18.

Dahinden, Janine, Carolin Fischer, and Joanna Menet. "Knowledge Production, Reflexivity, and the Use of Categories in Migration Studies: Tackling Challenges in the Field." *Ethnic and Racial Studies* 44, no. 4 (2021): 535–54.

Dalmage, Heather M. "Bringing the Hope Back In: The Sociological Imagination and Dreams of Transformation (the 2020 SSSP Presidential Address)." *Social Problems* 68, no. 4 (2021): 801–8.

Deflem, Mathieu. "The Structural Transformation of Sociology." *Society* 50, no. 2 (2013): 156–66.

Delanty, Gerard. *The Cosmopolitan Imagination: The Renewal of Critical Social Theory.* Cambridge and New York: Cambridge University Press, 2009.

Demeny, Paul. "Social Science and Population Policy." *Population and Development Review* 14, no. 3 (1988): 451–79.

Denzin, Norman K. "Re-Reading *The Sociological Imagination.*" *The American Sociologist* 20, no. 3 (1989): 278–82.

Department of Health and Human Services. "HHS Blueprint for Action on Breastfeeding." In *Breastfeeding: Laws and Societal Impact*, edited by Sarah W. Ying, 15–55. Hauppauge, NY: Nova Science Publishers, 2005.

Desmond-Harris, Jenée. "The Real Reason Research Blaming Black Poverty on Black Culture Has Fallen Out of Favor." *Vox*, March 26, 2015. https://www.vox.com/2015/3/26/8253495/moynihan-report-liberal-backlash.

Dewey, John. *Democracy and Education.* Edited and with a critical introduction by Patricia H. Hinchey. Gorham, ME: Myers Education Press, 2018.

———. "Democracy and Educational Administration." *Planning & Changing* 22, no. 3–4 (1991): 134.

———. *The Ethics of Democracy.* Ann Arbor, MI: Andrews & Company, 1888.

Dewey, John, and James H. Tufts. "Ethics." In *The Middle Works, 1899–1924, Vol. 5*, edited by Jo Ann Boydston, 1–540. Carbondale: Southern Illinois University Press, 1976.

Dixon-Mueller, Ruth, and Adrienne Germain. "Stalking the Elusive 'Unmet Need' for Family Planning." *Studies in Family Planning* 23, no. 5 (1992): 330–35.

Dolgon, Corey. "Reply to Wright, Embrick, and Henke and Lembcke: Dim Mirrors, Dark Glasses but This Is Not Our Fate." *Humanity & Society* 40, no. 1 (2016): 107–9.

Donaldson, Peter J. *Nature Against Us: The United States and the World Population Crisis, 1965–1980.* Chapel Hill: University of North Carolina Press, 1990.

Dougherty, Carter. "Brexit Vote 2016: Big Bettors in EU Referendum Have Leg up on Pollsters in Predicting June 23 Outcome." *International Business Times*, June 16, 2016. https://www.ibtimes.com/brexit-vote-2016-big-bettors-eu-referendum-have-leg-pollsters-predicting-june-23-2382877.

Dromi, Shai M. *Above the Fray: The Red Cross and the Making of the Humanitarian Relief Sector*. Chicago: University of Chicago Press, 2020.

———. "For Good and Country: Nationalism and the Diffusion of Humanitarianism in the Late Nineteenth Century." *The Sociological Review* 64, no. S2 (2016): 79–97.

———. "Penny for Your Thoughts: Beggars and the Exercise of Morality in Daily Life." *Sociological Forum* 27, no. 4 (2012): 847–71.

———. "Soldiers of the Cross: Calvinism, Humanitarianism, and the Genesis of Social Fields." *Sociological Theory* 34, no. 3 (2016): 196–219.

Dromi, Shai M., and Eva Illouz. "Recovering Morality: Pragmatic Sociology and Literary Studies." *New Literary History* 41, no. 2 (2010): 351–69.

Dromi, Shai M., and Liron Shani. "Love of Land: Nature Protection, Nationalism, and the Struggle over the Establishment of New Communities in Israel." *Rural Sociology* 85, no. 1 (2020): 111–36.

Dromi, Shai M., and Samuel D. Stabler. "Good on Paper: Sociological Critique, Pragmatism, and Secularization Theory." *Theory and Society* 48, no. 2 (2019): 325–50.

Du Bois, W. E. B. "The Atlanta Conferences." In *W. E. B. Du Bois on Sociology and the Black Community*, edited by Dan S. Green and Edwin D. Driver, 53–60. Chicago: University of Chicago Press, 1978.

———. "Sociology Hesitant." *Boundary* 2 27, no. 3 (2000): 37–44.

Dufton, Emily. *Grass Roots: The Rise and Fall and Rise of Marijuana in America*. New York: Basic Books, 2017.

Durkheim, Émile. *The Rules of Sociological Method*. Translated by Sarah A. Solovay and John Henry Mueller. 8th ed. Edited by George Edward Gordon Catlin. New York: Free Press, 1966.

Duster, Troy. "A Post-Genomic Surprise. The Molecular Reinscription of Race in Science, Law and Medicine." *The British Journal of Sociology* 66, no. 1 (2015): 1–27.

Edgell, Penny. "A Cultural Sociology of Religion: New Directions." *Annual Review of Sociology* 38, no. 1 (2012): 247–65.

Edgerton, Robert B. *Sick Societies: Challenging the Myth of Primitive Harmony*. New York and Toronto: Free Press and Maxwell Macmillan, 1992.

Engels, Friedrich. *The Origin of the Family, Private Property, and the State*. Edited by Lewis Henry Morgan and Friedrich Engels. New York: Pathfinder Press, 1972 [1884].

Enten, Harry. "Trump Is Just a Normal Polling Error Behind Clinton." *FiveThirtyEight*, November 4, 2016. https://fivethirtyeight.com/features/trump-is-just-a-normal-polling-error-behind-clinton/.

Erikson, Emily. *Trade and Nation: How Companies and Politics Reshaped Economic Thought*. New York: Columbia University Press, 2021.

European Parliament. "Forsmark: How Sweden Alerted the World about the Danger of the Chernobyl Disaster." *European Parliament News*, May 15, 2014. http://www

.europarl.europa.eu/news/en/headlines/society/20140514STO47018/forsmark
-how-sweden-alerted-the-world-about-the-danger-of-chernobyl-disaster.

Evans, John H. "Consensus and Knowledge Production in an Academic Field." *Poetics* 35, no. 1 (2007): 1–21.

Eyal, Gil. *The Crisis of Expertise*. Cambridge, UK, and Medford, MA: Polity Press, 2019.

Fanon, Frantz. *Black Skin, White Masks*. Edited by Charles Lam Markmann. New York: Grove Press, Inc., 1967.

Fassin, Didier. "On Resentment and *Ressentiment*: The Politics and Ethics of Moral Emotions." *Current Anthropology* 54, no. 3 (2013): 249–67.

Fein, Sara B., Bidisha Mandal, and Brian E. Roe. "Success of Strategies for Combining Employment and Breastfeeding." *Pediatrics* 122, Supplement (2008): S56–S62.

Fein, Sara B., and Brian Roe. "The Effect of Work Status on Initiation and Duration of Breast-Feeding." *American Journal of Public Health* 88, no. 7 (1998): 1042–46.

Felski, Rita. "Remember the Reader." *Chronicle of Higher Education*, December 19, 2008. https://www.chronicle.com/article/remember-the-reader/.

Felson, Jacob, Amy Adamczyk, and Christopher Thomas. "How and Why Have Attitudes about Cannabis Legalization Changed So Much?" *Social Science Research* 78 (2019): 12–27.

Feyerabend, Paul. *Against Method: Outline of an Anarchistic Theory of Knowledge*. London and Atlantic Highlands, NJ: NLB and Humanities Press, 1975.

Fine, Robert. "Taking the 'Ism' out of Cosmopolitanism: An Essay in Reconstruction." *European Journal of Social Theory* 6, no. 4 (2003): 451–70.

Finke, Roger. "Presidential Address: Origins and Consequences of Religious Freedoms: A Global Overview." *Sociology of Religion* 74, no. 3 (2013): 297–313.

Finke, Roger, and Rodney Stark. *The Churching of America, 1776–1990: Winners and Losers in Our Religious Economy*. New Brunswick, NJ: Rutgers University Press, 1992.

Finkelstein, Daniel. "The LSE Scandal Is Intellectual, Not Financial." *The Times*, September 3, 2011. https://www.thetimes.co.uk/article/the-lse-scandal-is -intellectual-not-financial-62mrjkxq8w7.

Fleming, Crystal Marie. *How to Be Less Stupid about Race: On Racism, White Supremacy, and the Racial Divide*. Boston: Beacon Press, 2018.

Fontdevila, Jorge, M. Pilar Opazo, and Harrison C. White. "Order at the Edge of Chaos: Meanings from Netdom Switchings across Functional Systems." *Sociological Theory* 29, no. 3 (2011): 178–98.

Foster, Jacob G., Andrey Rzhetsky, and James A. Evans. "Tradition and Innovation in Scientists' Research Strategies." *American Sociological Review* 80, no. 5 (2015): 875–908.

Foucault, Michel. *The History of Sexuality. Vol. 1: An Introduction*. Edited by Michel Foucault. New York: Pantheon Books, 1978.

Fourcade, Marion. *Economists and Societies: Discipline and Profession in the United States, Britain, and France, 1890s to 1990s*. Princeton, NJ: Princeton University Press, 2009.

Francis, Mark. "Herbert Spencer and the Myth of Laissez-Faire." *Journal of the History of Ideas* 39, no. 2 (1978): 317–28.

Freedman, Ronald. "The Contribution of Social Science Research to Population Policy and Family Planning Program Effectiveness." *Studies in Family Planning* 18, no. 2 (1987): 57–82.

Freedman, Ronald, David Goldberg, and Harry Sharp. "'Ideals' about Family Size in the Detroit Metropolitan Area: 1954." *The Milbank Memorial Fund Quarterly* 33, no. 2 (1955): 187–97.

Freese, Jeremy, and Sara Shostak. "Genetics and Social Inquiry." *Annual Review of Sociology* 35, no. 1 (2009): 107–28.

Frerichs, Leah, Julie L. Andsager, Shelly Campo, Mary Aquilino, and Carolyn Stewart Dyer. "Framing Breastfeeding and Formula-Feeding Messages in Popular U.S. Magazines." *Women & Health* 44, no. 1 (2006): 95–118.

Friedmann, John, and Goetz Wolff. "World City Formation: An Agenda for Research and Action." *International Journal of Urban and Regional Research* 6, no. 3 (1982): 309–44.

Froese, Paul. *The Plot to Kill God: Findings from the Soviet Experiment in Secularization.* Berkeley: University of California Press, 2008.

Frontiers of Sociology, Symposium. "Repertoires of Contention in America and Britain, 1750–1830." In *The Dynamics of Social Movements: Resource Mobilization, Social Control, and Tactics*, edited by Mayer N. Zald and John D. McCarthy, 126–55. Cambridge, MA: Winthrop Publishers, 1979.

Frye, Margaret, and Lauren Bachan. "The Demography of Words: The Global Decline in Non-Numeric Fertility Preferences, 1993–2011." *Population Studies* 71, no. 2 (2017): 187–209.

Fullwiley, Duana. "The 'Contemporary Synthesis': When Politically Inclusive Genomic Science Relies on Biological Notions of Race." *Isis* 105, no. 4 (2014): 803–14.

Galton, Francis. "Eugenics: Its Definition, Scope, and Aims." *American Journal of Sociology* 10, no. 1 (1904): 1–25.

———. "The History of Twins, as a Criterion of the Relative Powers of Nature and Nurture (1, 2)." *International Journal of Epidemiology* 41, no. 4 (2012 [1875]): 905–11.

Garfinkel, Harold. *Studies in Ethnomethodology.* Cambridge, UK: Polity Press, 1984.

Gaughan, Anthony J. "President Trump? Not Likely." *The Conversation*, May 3, 2016. https://theconversation.com/president-trump-not-likely-58758.

Geary, Daniel. *Beyond Civil Rights: The Moynihan Report and Its Legacy.* Philadelphia: University of Pennsylvania Press, 2015.

Gemmill, Alison. "From Some to None? Fertility Expectation Dynamics of Permanently Childless Women." *Demography* 56, no. 1 (2019): 129–49.

Gill, Anthony James. *The Political Origins of Religious Liberty.* Cambridge and New York: Cambridge University Press, 2008.

Gillham, Nicholas W. "Sir Francis Galton and the Birth of Eugenics." *Annual Review of Genetics* 35, no. 1 (2001): 83–101.

Go, Julian. "Fanon's Postcolonial Cosmopolitanism." *European Journal of Social Theory* 16, no. 2 (2013): 208–25.

———. "Global Fields and Imperial Forms: Field Theory and the British and American Empires." *Sociological Theory* 26, no. 3 (2008): 201–29.

———. "Race, Empire, and Epistemic Exclusion; or, The Structures of Sociological Thought." *Sociological Theory* 38, no. 2 (2020): 79–100.

Go, Julian, and Monika Krause. "Fielding Transnationalism: An Introduction." *The Sociological Review* 64, no. 2 (Supplement) (2016): 6–30.

Goldthorpe, John H. "Progress in Sociology: The Case of Social Mobility Research." In *Analyzing Inequality: Life Chances and Social Mobility in Comparative Perspective*, edited by Stefan Svallfors, 56–82. Stanford, CA: Stanford University Press, 2005.

Goosby, Bridget J., Jacob E. Cheadle, and Colter Mitchell. "Stress-Related Biosocial Mechanisms of Discrimination and African American Health Inequities." *Annual Review of Sociology* 44, no. 1 (2018): 319–40.

Gorski, Philip S. "Beyond the Fact/Value Distinction: Ethical Naturalism and the Social Sciences." *Society* 50, no. 6 (2013): 543–53.

———. *The Disciplinary Revolution: Calvinism and the Rise of the State in Early Modern Europe*. Chicago: University of Chicago Press, 2003.

———. "Historicizing the Secularization Debate: Church, State, and Society in Late Medieval and Early Modern Europe, Ca. 1300 to 1700." *American Sociological Review* 65, no. 1 (2000): 138–67.

———. "The Poverty of Deductivism: A Constructive Realist Model of Sociological Explanation." *Sociological Methodology* 34, no. 1 (2004): 1–33.

———. "The Return of the Repressed: Religion and the Political Unconscious of Historical Sociology." In *Remaking Modernity: Politics, History, and Sociology*. Durham, NC: Duke University Press, 2005.

Gorski, Philip S., and Ateş Altınordu. "After Secularization?" *Annual Review of Sociology* 34 (2008): 55–85.

Gorski, Philip S., and William McMillan. "Barack Obama and American Exceptionalisms." *The Review of Faith & International Affairs* 10, no. 2 (2012): 41–50.

Gorski, Philip S., and Gülay Türkmen-Dervişoğlu. "Religion, Nationalism, and Violence: An Integrated Approach." *Annual Review of Sociology* 39, no. 1 (2013): 193–210.

Gouldner, Alvin W. "Anti-Minotaur: The Myth of a Value-Free Sociology." *Social Problems* 9, no. 3 (1962): 199–213.

———. *The Coming Crisis of Western Sociology*. New York: Basic Books, 1970.

———. "The Sociologist as Partisan: Sociology and the Welfare State." *The American Sociologist* 3, no. 2 (1968): 103–16.

Greenfeld, Liah. "Is Nationalism Legitimate? A Sociological Perspective on a Philosophical Question." *Canadian Journal of Philosophy* 26 (1997): 93–108.

———. *Nationalism: Five Roads to Modernity*. Cambridge, MA: Harvard University Press, 1992.

Greenhalgh, Susan. "The Social Construction of Population Science: An Intellectual, Institutional, and Political History of Twentieth-Century Demography." *Comparative Studies in Society and History* 38, no. 1 (1996): 26–66.

Grim, Brian J., and Roger Finke. *The Price of Freedom Denied: Religious Persecu-*

tion and Conflict in the Twenty-First Century. New York: Cambridge University Press, 2011.

Gross, Neil. "Pragmatism and the Study of Large-Scale Social Phenomena." *Theory and Society* 47, no. 1 (2018): 87–111.

———. *Richard Rorty: The Making of an American Philosopher*. Chicago: University of Chicago Press, 2009.

———. *Why Are Professors Liberal and Why Do Conservatives Care?* Cambridge, MA: Harvard University Press, 2013.

Grossi, Elodie. "New Avenues in Epigenetic Research about Race: Online Activism around Reparations for Slavery in the United States." *Social Science Information* 59, no. 1 (2020): 93–116.

Grüning, Barbara, and Marco Santoro. "Is There a Canon in This Class?" *International Review of Sociology* 31, no. 1 (2021): 7–25.

Guo, Guang, Yilan Fu, Hedwig Lee, Tianji Cai, Kathleen Mullan Harris, and Yi Li. "Genetic Bio-Ancestry and Social Construction of Racial Classification in Social Surveys in the Contemporary United States." *Demography* 51, no. 1 (2014): 141–72.

Guzzo, Karen Benjamin, Sue P. Nash, Wendy D. Manning, Monica A. Longmore, and Peggy C. Giordano. "Unpacking the 'Black Box' of Race—Ethnic Variation in Fertility." *Race and Social Problems* 7, no. 2 (2014): 135–49.

Habermas, Jürgen. *Moral Consciousness and Communicative Action*. Cambridge, MA: MIT Press, 1990.

Haider, Steven J., Alison Jacknowitz, and Robert F. Schoeni. "Welfare Work Requirements and Child Well-Being: Evidence from the Effects on Breast-Feeding." *Demography* 40, no. 3 (2003): 479–97.

Hall, Peter A., and Michèle Lamont. *Successful Societies: How Institutions and Culture Affect Health*. Cambridge and New York: Cambridge University Press, 2009.

Haller, William, and Victor Roudometof. "The Cosmopolitan-Local Continuum in Cross-National Perspective." *Journal of Sociology* 46, no. 3 (2010): 277–97.

Hallett, Tim, Orla Stapleton, and Michael Sauder. "Public Ideas: Their Varieties and Careers." *American Sociological Review* 84, no. 3 (2019): 545–76.

Halperin, David M. *Saint Foucault: Towards a Gay Hagiography*. New York: Oxford University Press, 1995.

Hannerz, Ulf. "Cosmopolitans and Locals in World Culture." *Theory, Culture & Society* 7, no. 2–3 (1990): 237–51.

Haraway, Donna. "Situated Knowledges: The Science Question in Feminism and the Privilege of Partial Perspective." *Feminist Studies* 14, no. 3 (1988): 575–99.

Hartnett, Caroline Sten, and Alison Gemmill. "Recent Trends in U.S. Childbearing Intentions." *Demography* 57, no. 6 (2020): 2035–45.

Hayford, Sarah R. "The Evolution of Fertility Expectations over the Life Course." *Demography* 46, no. 4 (2009): 765–83.

Hays, Sharon. *The Cultural Contradictions of Motherhood*. New Haven, CT, and London: Yale University Press, 1998.

Healy, Kieran. "Fuck Nuance." *Sociological Theory* 35, no. 2 (2017): 118–27.

Heinich, Nathalie. *L'Épreuve de la grandeur: Prix littéraires et reconnaissance*. Paris: Découverte, 1999.

Held, David. *Cosmopolitanism: Ideals and Realities*. Cambridge and Malden, MA: Polity Press, 2010.

Herd, Pamela, Jeremy Freese, Kamil Sicinski, Benjamin W. Domingue, Kathleen Mullan Harris, Caiping Wei, and Robert M. Hauser. "Genes, Gender Inequality, and Educational Attainment." *American Sociological Review* 84, no. 6 (2019): 1069–98.

Herrnstein, Richard J., and Charles A. Murray. *The Bell Curve: Intelligence and Class Structure in American Life*. Intelligence and Class Structure in American Life. New York: Free Press, 1994.

Hill, Shirley A., and Joey Sprague. "Parenting in Black and White Families: The Interaction of Gender with Race and Class." *Gender & Society* 13, no. 4 (1999): 480–502.

Hirschman, Daniel. "Stylized Facts in the Social Sciences." *Sociological Science* 3, no. 26 (2016): 604–26.

Hirschman, Daniel, and Isaac Ariail Reed. "Formation Stories and Causality in Sociology." *Sociological Theory* 32, no. 4 (2014): 259–82.

Hitlin, Steven, and Stephen Vaisey. "The New Sociology of Morality." *Annual Review of Sociology* 39, no. 1 (2013): 51–68.

Hochschild, Arlie Russell. *Strangers in Their Own Land: Anger and Mourning on the American Right*. New York: The New Press, 2016.

Hodgson, Dennis. "The Ideological Origins of the Population Association of America." *Population and Development Review* 17, no. 1 (1991): 1–34.

Holcomb, Jeanne. "Resisting Guilt: Mothers' Breastfeeding Intentions and Formula Use." *Sociological Focus* 50, no. 4 (2017): 361–74.

Horowitz, Irving Louis. *C. Wright Mills: An American Utopian*. New York and London: Free Press and Collier Macmillan, 1983.

Horowitz, Mark, Anthony Haynor, and Kenneth Kickham. "Sociology's Sacred Victims and the Politics of Knowledge: Moral Foundations Theory and Disciplinary Controversies." *The American Sociologist* 49, no. 4 (2018): 459–95.

Iannaccone, Laurence R. "Why Strict Churches Are Strong." *American Journal of Sociology* 99, no. 5 (1994): 1180–1211.

Iannaccone, Laurence R., Roger Finke, and Rodney Stark. "Deregulating Religion: The Economics of Church and State." *Economic Inquiry* 35, no. 2 (1997): 350–64.

Ifekwunigwe, Jayne O., Jennifer K. Wagner, Joon-Ho Yu, Tanya M. Harrell, Michael J. Bamshad, and Charmaine D. Royal. "A Qualitative Analysis of How Anthropologists Interpret the Race Construct." *American Anthropologist* 119, no. 3 (2017): 422–34.

Ignatow, Gabriel. "Culture and Embodied Cognition: Moral Discourses in Internet Support Groups for Overeaters." *Social Forces* 88, no. 2 (2009): 643–69.

Illouz, Eva. *Saving the Modern Soul: Therapy, Emotions, and the Culture of Self-Help*. Berkeley: University of California Press, 2008.

Inglis, David. "Cosmopolitans and Cosmopolitanism: Between and Beyond Sociology and Political Philosophy." *Journal of Sociology* 50, no. 2 (2014): 99–114.

Itzigsohn, José, and Karida L. Brown. *The Sociology of W. E. B. Du Bois: Racialized Modernity and the Global Color Line*. New York: New York University Press, 2020.

Jabri, Vivienne. "Solidarity and Spheres of Culture: The Cosmopolitan and the Postcolonial." *Review of International Studies* 33, no. 4 (2007): 715–28.

James, William. "The Moral Philosopher and the Moral Life." *International Journal of Ethics* 1, no. 3 (1891): 330–54.

Janker, Judith. "Moral Conflicts, Premises and the Social Dimension of Agricultural Sustainability." *Agriculture and Human Values* 37, no. 1 (2020): 97–111.

Jansson, Maria. "Feeding Children and Protecting Women: The Emergence of Breastfeeding as an International Concern." *Women's Studies International Forum* 32, no. 3 (2009): 240–48.

Jeffries, Vincent. "Altruism, Morality, and Social Solidarity as a Field of Study." In *The Palgrave Handbook of Altruism, Morality, and Social Solidarity: Formulating a Field of Study*, edited by Vincent Jeffries. New York: Palgrave Macmillan US, 2014.

Jeffries, Vincent, ed. *The Palgrave Handbook of Altruism, Morality, and Social Solidarity: Formulating a Field of Study*. New York: Palgrave Macmillan US, 2014.

Jerolmack, Colin, and Shamus Khan. "Talk Is Cheap: Ethnography and the Attitudinal Fallacy." *Sociological Methods & Research* 43, no. 2 (2014): 178–209.

Joas, Hans. *The Creativity of Action*. Cambridge: Polity Press, 1996.

Johnson-Hanks, Jennifer. "Populations Are Composed One Event at a Time." In *Population in the Human Sciences: Concepts, Models, Evidence*, edited by Philip Kreager, Bruce Winney, Stanley Ulijaszek, and Cristian Capelli, 238–55. Oxford: Oxford University Press, 2015.

———. "When the Future Decides: Uncertainty and Intentional Action in Contemporary Cameroon." *Current Anthropology* 46, no. 3 (2005): 363–85.

Johnson-Hanks, Jennifer, Christine A. Bachrach, S. Philip Morgan, and Hans-Peter Kohler. "The Theory of Conjunctural Action." In *Understanding Family Change and Variation: Toward a Theory of Conjunctural Action*, 1–22. Dordrecht: Springer, 2011.

Kahan, Dan. "Don't Select on the Dependent Variable in Studying the Science Communication Problem." The Cultural Cognition Project at Yale Law School, January 17, 2013. http://www.culturalcognition.net/blog/2013/11/19/dont-select-on-the-dependent-variable-in-studying-the-scienc.html.

Kaldor, Mary. *Global Civil Society: An Answer to War*. Cambridge, UK: Polity Press, 2003.

Kempner, Joanna, Jon F. Merz, and Charles L. Bosk. "Forbidden Knowledge: Public Controversy and the Production of Nonknowledge." *Sociological Forum* 26, no. 3 (2011): 475–500.

Kennedy, Paul M. *Preparing for the Twenty-First Century*. New York: Random House, 1993.

King, Gary, Robert O. Keohane, and Sidney Verba. *Designing Social Inquiry: Scientific Inference in Qualitative Research*. Princeton, NJ: Princeton University Press, 1994.

Klein, Ezra. "The Sam Harris Debate." *Vox*, January 30, 2018. https://www.vox.com/2018/4/9/17210248/sam-harris-ezra-klein-charles-murray-transcript-podcast.

Klenk, Michael. "Moral Philosophy and the 'Ethical Turn' in Anthropology." *Zeitschrift für Ethik und Moralphilosophie* 2, no. 2 (2019): 331–53.

Koehly, Laura M., Susan Persky, Philip Shaw, Vence L. Bonham, Christopher S. Marcum, Gustavo P. Sudre, Dawn E. Lea, and Sharon K. Davis. "Social and Behavioral Science at the Forefront of Genomics: Discovery, Translation, and Health Equity." *Social Science & Medicine* 271 (2019): 112450.

Koop, C. Everett. "Preface." In *Followup Report: The Surgeon General's Workshop on Breastfeeding and Human Lactation*. Rochester, NY, and Rockville, MD: United States Department of Health and Human Services, 1985.

———. "Preface." In *Report of the Surgeon General's Workshop on Breastfeeding & Human Lactation*, iii. Rochester, NY, and Rockville, MD: United States Department of Health and Human Services, 1984.

Krause, Monika. "'Western Hegemony' in the Social Sciences: Fields and Model Systems." *The Sociological Review* 64, no. 2 (2016): 194–211.

Kristof, Nicholas. "Straight Talk for White Men." *New York Times*, February 22, 2015. https://www.nytimes.com/2015/02/22/opinion/sunday/nicholas-kristof-straight-talk-for-white-men.html.

Kuhn, Thomas S. *The Structure of Scientific Revolutions*. Fourth edition. Edited by Ian Hacking. Chicago: University of Chicago Press, 2012 [1962].

Kukla, Rebecca. "Ethics and Ideology in Breastfeeding Advocacy Campaigns." *Hypatia* 21, no. 1 (2006): 157–80.

Kumar, Navin, Cheneal Puljević, and Robert Heimer. "Understanding Motivations for Large US Cannabis Firms' Participation in the Cannabis Space: Qualitative Study Exploring Views of Key Decision-Makers." *Drug and Alcohol Review* 39, no. 4 (2020): 347–55.

Kuru, Ahmet T. *Secularism and State Policies toward Religion: The United States, France, and Turkey*. Cambridge and New York: Cambridge University Press, 2009.

LaCour, Michael J., and Donald P. Green. "When Contact Changes Minds: An Experiment on Transmission of Support for Gay Equality [retracted]." *Science* 346, no. 6215 (2014): 1366–69. [Retraction: https://www.science.org/doi/10.1126/science.aac6638.]

Lagos, Danya. "Looking at Population Health Beyond 'Male' and 'Female': Implications of Transgender Identity and Gender Nonconformity for Population Health." *Demography* 55, no. 6 (2018): 2097–117.

Lamont, Michèle. *How Professors Think: Inside the Curious World of Academic Judgment*. Cambridge, MA: Harvard University Press, 2009.

———. *Money, Morals, and Manners: The Culture of the French and the American Upper-Middle Class*. Chicago: University of Chicago Press, 1992.

———. "Toward a Comparative Sociology of Valuation and Evaluation." *Annual Review of Sociology* 38, no. 1 (2012): 201–21.

Lamont, Michèle, Hanna Herzog, Nissim Mizrachi, Graziella Moraes Silva, Elisa Reis, and Jessica Welburn. *Getting Respect: Responding to Stigma and Discrimination in the United States, Brazil, and Israel*. Princeton, NJ: Princeton University Press, 2016.

Lamont, Michèle, and Laurent Thévenot. "Introduction: Toward a Renewed Comparative Cultural Sociology." In *Rethinking Comparative Cultural Sociology: Repertoires of Evaluation in France and the United States*, edited by Michèle Lamont and Laurent Thévenot, 1–22. Cambridge, UK, and New York: Cambridge University Press, 2000.

Lamont, Michèle, and Laurent Thévenot, eds. *Rethinking Comparative Cultural Sociology: Repertoires of Evaluation in France and the United States*. Cambridge, UK, and New York: Cambridge University Press, 2000.

Landecker, Hannah, and Aaron Panofsky. "From Social Structure to Gene Regulation, and Back: A Critical Introduction to Environmental Epigenetics for Sociology." *Annual Review of Sociology* 39, no. 1 (2013): 333–57.

Latour, Bruno. *Science in Action: How to Follow Scientists and Engineers through Society*. Cambridge, MA: Harvard University Press, 1987.

Law, Jules. "The Politics of Breastfeeding: Assessing Risk, Dividing Labor." *Signs: Journal of Women in Culture and Society* 25, no. 2 (2000): 407–50.

Lee, Ellie. "Breast-Feeding Advocacy, Risk Society and Health Moralism: A Decade's Scholarship." *Sociology Compass* 5, no. 12 (2011): 1058–69.

———. "Health, Morality, and Infant Feeding: British Mothers' Experiences of Formula Milk Use in the Early Weeks." *Sociology of Health & Illness* 29, no. 7 (2007): 1075–90.

Lee, Martin A. *Smoke Signals: A Social History of Marijuana—Medical, Recreational, and Scientific*. New York: Scribner, 2012.

Lee, Monica, and John Levi Martin. "Coding, Counting and Cultural Cartography." *American Journal of Cultural Sociology* 3, no. 1 (2014): 1–33.

Lee, R. D. "Aiming at a Moving Target: Period Fertility and Changing Reproductive Goals." *Population Studies* 34, no. 2 (1980): 205–26.

Lee, Robyn. "Feeding the Hungry Other: Levinas, Breastfeeding, and the Politics of Hunger." *Hypatia* 31, no. 2 (2016): 259–74.

Lemieux, Cyril. "The Moral Idealism of Ordinary People as a Sociological Challenge: Reflections on the French Reception of Luc Boltanski and Laurent Thévenot's *On Justification*." In *The Spirit of Luc Boltanski: Essays on the "Pragmatic Sociology of Critique,"* edited by Simon Susen and Bryan S. Turner, 153–70. London: Anthem Press, 2014.

Lengermann, Patricia M., and Jill Niebrugge-Brantley. *The Women Founders: Sociology and Social Theory, 1830–1930*. Boston: McGraw-Hill, 1998.

Lenz, Günter H. "Radical Cosmopolitanism: W. E. B. Du Bois, Germany, and African American Pragmatist Visions for Twenty-First-Century Europe." *Journal of Transnational American Studies* 4, no. 2 (2012): 65–96.

Leonard, Thomas C. *Illiberal Reformers: Race, Eugenics, and American Economics in the Progressive Era*. Princeton, NJ: Princeton University Press, 2016.

Lerner, Daniel. *The Passing of Traditional Society: Modernizing the Middle East*. Glencoe, IL: Free Press, 1958.

Levitt, Peggy. "Religion on the Move: Mapping Global Cultural Production and Consumption." In *Religion on the Edge: De-Centering and Re-Centering the Sociology of Religion*, edited by Courtney Bender, Wendy Cadge, Peggy Levitt, and David Smilde, 159–76. New York: Oxford University Press, 2013.

Levy, Marion J. "Some Sources of the Vulnerability of the Structures of Relatively Non-Industrialized Societies to Those of Highly Industrialized Societies." In

The Progress of Underdeveloped Areas, edited by Bert F. Hoselitz, 113–25. Chicago: University of Chicago Press, 1952.

Lewis, Oscar. *Five Families: Mexican Case Studies in the Culture of Poverty*. Edited by Oliver La Farge. New York: Basic Books, 1959.

Lewis-Kraus, Gideon. "Can Progressives Be Convinced that Genetics Matters?" *The New Yorker*, September 13, 2021. https://www.newyorker.com/magazine/2021/09/13/can-progressives-be-convinced-that-genetics-matters.

Lichterman, Paul. "Religion in Public Action: From Actors to Settings." *Sociological Theory* 30, no. 1 (2012): 15–36.

Lichterman, Paul, and Isaac Ariail Reed. "Theory and Contrastive Explanation in Ethnography." *Sociological Methods & Research* 44, no. 4 (2015): 585–635.

Lieberson, Stanley. "Small N's and Big Conclusions: An Examination of the Reasoning in Comparative Studies Based on a Small Number of Cases." *Social Forces* 70, no. 2 (1991): 307–20.

Light, Donald W. "Contributing to Scholarship and Theory through Public Sociology." *Social Forces* 83, no. 4 (2005): 1647–53.

Lim, Chaeyoon, Carol Ann MacGregor, and Robert D. Putnam. "Secular and Liminal: Discovering Heterogeneity among Religious Nones." *Journal for the Scientific Study of Religion* 49, no. 4 (2010): 596–618.

Lizardo, Omar, Robert Mowry, Brandon Sepulvado, Dustin S. Stoltz, Marshall A. Taylor, Justin Van Ness, and Michael Wood. "What Are Dual Process Models? Implications for Cultural Analysis in Sociology." *Sociological Theory* 34, no. 4 (2016): 287–310.

Lorde, Audre. *Sister Outsider: Essays and Speeches*. Trumansburg, NY: The Crossing Press, 1984.

Luker, Kristin. *Salsa Dancing into the Social Sciences: Research in an Age of Info-Glut*. Cambridge, MA: Harvard University Press, 2008.

Lukes, Steven. *Moral Relativism*. New York: Picador, 2008.

Lukianoff, Greg, and Jonathan Haidt. *The Coddling of the American Mind: How Good Intentions and Bad Ideas Are Setting Up a Generation for Failure*. New York: Penguin Press, 2018.

Lumsden, Karen. "'You Are What You Research': Researcher Partisanship and the Sociology of the 'Underdog.'" *Qualitative Research* 13, no. 1 (2013): 3–18.

Mandal, Bidisha, Brian E. Roe, and Sara B. Fein. "Work and Breastfeeding Decisions Are Jointly Determined for Higher Socioeconomic Status US Mothers." *Review of Economics of the Household* 12, no. 2 (2014): 237–57.

Manders-Huits, Noëmi. "What Values in Design? The Challenge of Incorporating Moral Values into Design." *Science and Engineering Ethics* 17, no. 2 (2011): 271–87.

Mannheim, Karl. *Ideology and Utopia*. Translated by Louis Wirth. London: Routledge, 1936.

Manning, Wendy D., Marshal Neal Fettro, and Esther Lamidi. "Child Well-Being in Same-Sex Parent Families: Review of Research Prepared for American Sociological Association Amicus Brief." *Population Research and Policy Review* 33, no. 4 (2014): 485–502.

Maralani, Vida, and Samuel Stabler. "Intensive Parenting: Fertility and

Breastfeeding Duration in the United States." *Demography* 55, no. 5 (2018): 1681–704.

Marcus, George E., and Michael M. J. Fischer. *Anthropology as Cultural Critique: An Experimental Moment in the Human Sciences*. Chicago: University of Chicago Press, 1986.

Markofski, Wes. "The Public Sociology of Religion." *Sociology of Religion* 76, no. 4 (2015): 459–75.

Marotta, Vince, Stan van Hoft, and Wim Vandekerckhove. "The Cosmopolitan Stranger." In *Questioning Cosmopolitanism*, edited by Stan van Hooft and Wim Vandekerckhove, 105–20. Dordrecht and New York: Springer, 2010.

Marres, Noortje, and David Stark. "Put to the Test: For a New Sociology of Testing." *The British Journal of Sociology* 71, no. 3 (2020): 423–43.

Marshall, Joyce L., Mary Godfrey, and Mary J. Renfrew. "Being a 'Good Mother': Managing Breastfeeding and Merging Identities." *Social Science & Medicine* 65, no. 10 (2007): 2147–59.

Martin, John Levi. *The Explanation of Social Action*. New York: Oxford University Press, 2011.

Martineau, Harriet. *How to Observe Morals and Manners*. London: C. Knight and Co., 1838.

Marx, Karl. "Theses on Feuerbach." In *The Marx-Engels Reader*, edited by Robert C. Tucker, 107–9. New York: W. W. Norton, 1972.

Massey, Douglas S., and Robert J. Sampson. "Moynihan Redux: Legacies and Lessons." *The ANNALS of the American Academy of Political and Social Science* 621, no. 1 (2009): 6–27.

Matthews, Ralph. "Committing Canadian Sociology: Developing a Canadian Sociology and a Sociology of Canada." *The Canadian Review of Sociology* 51, no. 2 (2014): 107–27.

McClain, Molly. *Ellen Browning Scripps: New Money and American Philanthropy*. Lincoln: University of Nebraska Press, 2017.

McDonnell, Terence E., Christopher A. Bail, and Iddo Tavory. "A Theory of Resonance." *Sociological Theory* 35, no. 1 (2017): 1–14.

McGee, Harry. "Personal Route to Reach Public Central to Yes Campaign." *The Irish Times*, May 14, 2015. https://www.irishtimes.com/news/politics/personal -route-to-reach-public-central-to-yes-campaign-1.2211282.

McKenzie, Lindsay. "Journal's Board Disavows Apology for 'Transracialism' Article, Making Retraction Unlikely." *Chronicle of Higher Education*, May 18, 2017. https://www.chronicle.com/article/journals-board-disavows-apology-for -transracialism-article-making-retraction-unlikely/.

McMahan, Peter, and Daniel A. McFarland. "Creative Destruction: The Structural Consequences of Scientific Curation." *American Sociological Review* 86, no. 2 (2021): 341–76.

McVeigh, Rory. "Deep Story or Self-Serving Narrative? Understanding the Paradox of Conservative Politics." *Contemporary Sociology* 46, no. 5 (2017): 510–12.

Mead, George Herbert, Daniel R. Huebner, and Hans Joas. *Mind, Self, and Society*. Edited by Charles W. Morris. Chicago: University of Chicago Press, 2015.

Mead, Lawrence M. "Poverty and Culture [retracted]." *Society*, July 21, 2020.

Melchior, Jillian Kay. "Fake News Comes to Academia." *Wall Street Journal*, October 5, 2018. https://www.wsj.com/articles/fake-news-comes-to-academia -1538520950.

Mersha, Tesfaye B., and Tilahun Abebe. "Self-Reported Race/Ethnicity in the Age of Genomic Research: Its Potential Impact on Understanding Health Disparities." *Human Genomics* 9, no. 1 (2015): 1–15.

Mignolo, Walter. *The Many Faces of Cosmo-Polis: Border Thinking and Critical Cosmopolitanism*. Durham, NC: Duke University Press, 2002.

Miles, Andrew. "The (Re)Genesis of Values: Examining the Importance of Values for Action." *American Sociological Review* 80, no. 4 (2015): 680–704.

Mills, C. Wright. "Situated Actions and Vocabularies of Motive." *American Sociological Review* 5, no. 6 (1940): 904–13.

———. *The Sociological Imagination*. New York: Oxford University Press, 1959.

———. *Sociology and Pragmatism: The Higher Learning in America*. New York: Paine-Whitman Publishers, 1964.

Mills, Melinda C., and Felix C. Tropf. "Sociology, Genetics, and the Coming of Age of Sociogenomics." *Annual Review of Sociology* 46, no. 1 (2020): 553–81.

Morgan, S. Philip. "Floor Discussion." Paper presented at the US Census Bureau Conference: The Direction of Fertility in the United States, Washington, DC, 2001.

Morgan, Stephen L., and Jiwon Lee. "Trump Voters and the White Working Class." *Sociological Science* 5 (2018): 234–45.

Morning, Ann. "And You Thought We Had Moved Beyond All That: Biological Race Returns to the Social Sciences." *Ethnic and Racial Studies* 37, no. 10 (2014): 1676–85.

———. *The Nature of Race: How Scientists Think and Teach about Human Difference*. Berkeley: University of California Press, 2011.

Morris, Aldon. "Alternative View of Modernity: The Subaltern Speaks." *American Sociological Review* 87, no. 1 (2022): 1–16.

Morris, Aldon D. "2021 Annual Meeting Theme." *ASA Annual Meeting Bulletin*, February 12, 2020. https://www.asanet.org/annual-meeting-2021/theme-and -program-committee.

———. *The Scholar Denied: W. E. B. Du Bois and the Birth of Modern Sociology*. Oakland: University of California Press, 2015.

———. "The State of Sociology: The Case for Systemic Change." *Social Problems* 64, no. 2 (2017): 206–11.

Mouffe, Chantal. "Deconstruction, Pragmatism and the Politics of Democracy." In *Deconstruction and Pragmatism*, edited by Simon Critchley and Chantal Mouffe, 1–12. London and New York: Routledge, 1996.

Mullings, Leith. "Interrogating Racism: Toward an Antiracist Anthropology." *Annual Review of Anthropology* 34, no. 1 (2005): 667–93.

Murphy, Elizabeth. "'Breast Is Best': Infant Feeding Decisions and Maternal Deviance." *Sociology of Health & Illness* 21, no. 2 (1999): 187–208.

Nachi, Mohamed. "Beyond Pragmatic Sociology: A Theoretical Compromise between 'Critical Sociology' and the 'Pragmatic Sociology of Critique.'" In *The*

Spirit of Luc Boltanski: Essays on the "Pragmatic Sociology of Critique," edited by Simon Susen and Bryan S. Turner, 293–312. London: Anthem Press, 2014.

Nature. "Life Stresses." Editorial. *Nature* 490, no. 7419 (October 10, 2012): 143.

"NCSA Annual Meeting Theme." North Central Sociological Association, 2015. Last accessed April 13, 2015. http://www.ncsanet.org/pdfs/2015%20theme.pdf.

Nelson, Alondra. "Reconciliation Projects: From Kinship to Justice." In *Genetics and the Unsettled Past: The Collision of DNA, Race, and History*, edited by Keith Wailoo, Alondra Nelson, and Catherine Lee, 20–31. New Brunswick, NJ: Rutgers University Press, 2012.

———. *The Social Life of DNA: Race, Reparations, and Reconciliation after the Genome.* Boston: Beacon Press, 2016.

New York Times. "6 Books to Help Understand Trump's Win." *New York Times*, November 10, 2016. https://www.nytimes.com/2016/11/10/books/6-books-to-help-understand-trumps-win.html?searchResultPosition=34.

Nitsche, Natalie, and Sarah R. Hayford. "Preferences, Partners, and Parenthood: Linking Early Fertility Desires, Marriage Timing, and Achieved Fertility." *Demography* 57, no. 6 (2020): 1975–2001.

Norris, Pippa. "Closed Minds? Is a 'Cancel Culture' Stifling Academic Freedom and Intellectual Debate in Political Science?" *SSRN Electronic Journal*, August 2020.

Ntozi, James P. M., and John B. Kabera. "Family Planning in Rural Uganda: Knowledge and Use of Modern and Traditional Methods in Ankole." *Studies in Family Planning* 22, no. 2 (1991): 116–23.

Nussbaum, Martha C. "Climate Change: Why Theories of Justice Matter." *Chicago Journal of International Law* 13, no. 2 (2013): 469–88.

———. *The Cosmopolitan Tradition: A Noble but Flawed Ideal.* Cambridge, MA: Harvard University Press, 2019.

———. *For Love of Country: Debating the Limits of Patriotism.* Edited by Joshua Cohen. Boston: Beacon Press, 1996.

———. *Liberty of Conscience: In Defense of America's Tradition of Religious Equality.* New York: Basic Books, 2008.

———. "Patriotism and Cosmopolitanism." *Boston Review* 19, no. 5 (1994): 3–6.

———. "Toward a Globally Sensitive Patriotism." *Daedalus* 137, no. 3 (2008): 78–93.

Ogbuanu, Chinelo, Saundra Glover, Janice Probst, Jihong Liu, and James Hussey. "The Effect of Maternity Leave Length and Time of Return to Work on Breastfeeding." *Pediatrics* 127, no. 6 (2011): E1414–E1427.

O'Shea, James R. "Sources of Pluralism in William James." In *Pluralism: The Philosophy and Politics of Diversity*, edited by Maria Baghramian and Attracta Ingram, 17–43. London: Routledge, 2000.

Owens, Nicole, Shannon K. Carter, Chelsea J. Nordham, and Jason A. Ford. "Neutralizing the Maternal Breast: Accounts of Public Breastfeeding by African American Mothers." *Journal of Family Issues* 39, no. 2 (2018): 430–50.

Padavic, Irene, and Jonniann Butterfield. "Mothers, Fathers, and 'Mathers.'" *Gender & Society* 25, no. 2 (2011): 176–96.

Parry, Marc. "Conflict over Sociologist's Narrative Puts Spotlight on Ethnography." *Chronicle of Higher Education*, June 12, 2015.

Parsons, Talcott. *The Evolution of Societies*. Edited by Jackson Toby and Talcott Parsons. Englewood Cliffs, NJ: Prentice-Hall, 1977.

———. "Full Citizenship for the Negro American? A Sociological Problem." *Daedalus* 94, no. 4 (1965): 1009–54.

———. *The Social System*. Glencoe, IL: Free Press, 1951.

———. *The Structure of Social Action: A Study in Social Theory with Special Reference to a Group of Recent European Writers*. New York: McGraw-Hill, 1937.

Patterson, Orlando. "A Poverty of the Mind." *New York Times*, March 26, 2006. https://www.nytimes.com/2006/03/26/opinion/a-poverty-of-the-mind.html.

———. "Taking Culture Seriously: A Framework and an Afro-American Illustration." In *Culture Matters: How Values Shape Human Progress*, edited by Samuel P. Huntington and Lawrence E. Harrison, 202–18. New York: Basic Books, 2000.

Pearson, Karl. "Discussion." *American Journal of Sociology* 10, no. 1 (1904): 6–7.

Perry, Samuel. "Excited to Announce My New Book Project Now Under Contract." Twitter post. Updated November 19, 2021, last accessed January 24, 2022. https://twitter.com/socofthesacred/status/1461693449040797706.

Peters, Jeremy W., and Matt Flegenheimer. "Early Voting Tilts toward Democrats in Swing States." *New York Times*, October 31, 2016. https://www.nytimes.com/2016/10/31/us/politics/early-voting-trump-clinton.html.

Petit, Véronique, and Yves Charbit. "The French School of Demography: Contextualizing Demographic Analysis." *Population and Development Review* 38, no. S1 (2013): 322–33.

"Philip Gorski." Charlie Rose. Updated April 11, 2017; last accessed July 14, 2020. https://charlierose.com/videos/30365.

Phillips, J. F., W. S. Stinson, S. Bhatia, M. Rahman, and J. Chakraborty. "The Demographic Impact of the Family Planning–Health Services Project in Matlab, Bangladesh." *Studies in Family Planning* 13, no. 5 (1982): 131–40.

Phipps, Alison. "Re-Inscribing Gender Binaries: Deconstructing the Dominant Discourse around Women's Equality in Science, Engineering, and Technology." *The Sociological Review* 55, no. 4 (2007): 768–87.

Pickersgill, Martyn. "Negotiating Novelty: Constructing the Novel within Scientific Accounts of Epigenetics." *Sociology* 55, no. 3 (2021): 600–618.

Polletta, Francesca. "Strangers in Their Own Land: Anger and Mourning on the American Right by Arlie Russell Hochschild." *American Journal of Sociology* 123, no. 2 (2017): 606–8.

Prasad, Monica. "Pragmatism as Problem Solving." *Socius* 7 (2021): 2378023121993991.

———. *Problem-Solving Sociology: A Guide for Students*. New York: Oxford University Press, 2021.

Preuss, Ulrich K. "Citizenship in the European Union: A Paradigm for Transnational Democracy." In *Re-Imagining Political Community: Studies in Cosmopolitan Democracy*, edited by Daniele Archibugi, David Held, and Martin Köhler, 138–51. Stanford, CA: Stanford University Press, 1998.

Pries, Ludger. "Configurations of Geographic and Societal Spaces: A Sociological Proposal between 'Methodological Nationalism' and the 'Spaces of Flows.'" *Global Networks* 5, no. 2 (2005): 167–90.

Pritchett, Lant H. "Desired Fertility and the Impact of Population Policies." *Population and Development Review* 20, no. 1 (1994): 1–55.

Putnam, Hilary. "Beyond the Fact/Value Dichotomy." In *Science and the Quest for Reality*, edited by Alfred I. Tauber, 363–69. London: Palgrave Macmillan, 1982.

Quart, Alissa. "The Milk Wars." *New York Times*, July 14, 2012. https://www.nytimes.com/2012/07/15/opinion/sunday/the-breast-feeding-wars.html.

Quéré, Louis, and Cédric Terzi. "Did You Say 'Pragmatic'? Luc Boltanski's Sociology from a Pragmatist Perspective." In *The Spirit of Luc Boltanski: Essays on the "Pragmatic Sociology of Critique,"* edited by Simon Susen and Bryan S. Turner, 91–128. London: Anthem Press, 2014.

Quinn, Sarah. "The Transformation of Morals in Markets: Death, Benefits, and the Exchange of Life Insurance Policies." *American Journal of Sociology* 114, no. 3 (2008): 738–80.

Rainwater, Lee, and William L. Yancey. *The Moynihan Report and the Politics of Controversy: A Trans-Action Social Science and Public Policy Report.* Cambridge, MA: MIT Press, 1967.

Raz, Joseph. "Multiculturalism: A Liberal Perspective." *Dissent* 41, no. 1 (1994): 67–79.

Reardon, Jenny, and Kim TallBear. "'Your DNA Is Our History': Genomics, Anthropology, and the Construction of Whiteness as Property." *Current Anthropology* 53, no. S5 (2012): S233–S245.

Redfield, Peter. *Life in Crisis: The Ethical Journey of Doctors without Borders.* Berkeley: University of California Press, 2013.

Reed, Isaac Ariail. "Cultural Sociology as Research Program: Post-Positivism, Meaning, and Causality." In *The Oxford Handbook of Cultural Sociology*, edited by Jeffrey C. Alexander, Ronald N. Jacobs, and Philip Smith, 27–45. Oxford and New York: Oxford University Press, 2012.

Reid, G. A. Archdall. "Discussion." *American Journal of Sociology* 10, no. 1 (1904): 16–19.

Relton, Caroline L., and George Davey Smith. "Is Epidemiology Ready for Epigenetics?" *International Journal of Epidemiology* 41, no. 1 (2012): 5–9.

Resnick, Brian. "What Psychology's Crisis Means for the Future of Science." *Vox*, March 25, 2016. https://www.vox.com/2016/3/14/11219446/psychology-replication-crisis.

Retraction Watch. "Hundreds Petition to Retract Paper They Call 'Unscholarly, Overtly Racist' and Full of 'Racially Violent Narratives.'" *Retraction Watch*, July 27, 2020. https://retractionwatch.com/2020/07/27/hundreds-petition-to-retract-paper-they-call-unscholarly-overtly-racist-and-full-of-racially-violent-narratives/.

Reynolds, Tracey. "Re-Thinking a Black Feminist Standpoint." *Ethnic and Racial Studies* 25, no. 4 (2002): 591–606.

Ricœur, Paul. *Freud and Philosophy: An Essay on Interpretation.* New Haven, CT: Yale University Press, 1970.

Rippeyoung, Phyllis L. F. "Can Breastfeeding Solve Inequality? The Relative Moderating Impact of Breastfeeding on Poverty Gaps in Canadian Child Cognitive Skills." *Canadian Journal of Sociology* 38, no. 1 (2013): 65–86.

Rippeyoung, Phyllis L. F., and Mary C. Noonan. "Is Breastfeeding Truly Cost Free? Income Consequences of Breastfeeding for Women." *American Sociological Review* 77, no. 2 (2012): 244–67.

Roberts, Dorothy. *Fatal Invention: How Science, Politics, and Big Business Re-Create Race in the Twenty-First Century*. New York: New Press, 2011.

Roberts, Dorothy E., and Oliver Rollins. "Why Sociology Matters to Race and Bio-social Science." *Annual Review of Sociology* 46, no. 1 (2020): 195–214.

Robertson, Roland. "Glocalization: Time-Space and Homogeneity-Heterogeneity." In *Global Modernities*, edited by Mike Featherstone, Scott Lash, and Roland Robertson, 25–44. London and Thousand Oaks, CA: Sage Publications, 1995.

Robey, Derek J., Jocelyn Viterna, and Hannah Katz. "Social Evolutionary Thought in Sociological Theory." Unpublished manuscript, last modified October 8, 2020. PDF file.

Rodríguez-Muñiz, Michael. "Intellectual Inheritances: Cultural Diagnostics and the State of Poverty Knowledge." *American Journal of Cultural Sociology* 3, no. 1 (2015): 89–122.

Roe, Brian, Leslie A. Whittington, Sara Beck Fein, and Mario F. Teisl. "Is There Competition between Breast-Feeding and Maternal Employment?" *Demography* 36, no. 2 (1999): 157–71.

Romero, Mary. "Sociology Engaged in Social Justice." *American Sociological Review* 85, no. 1 (2020): 1–30.

Rowe, David C., and D. Wayne Osgood. "Heredity and Sociological Theories of Delinquency: A Reconsideration." *American Sociological Review* 49, no. 4 (1984): 526–40.

Ryan, Alan S., Wenjun Zhou, and Mary Beth Arensberg. "The Effect of Employment Status on Breastfeeding in the United States." *Women's Health Issues* 16, no. 5 (2006): 243–51.

Ryan, William. "Savage Discovery: The Moynihan Report." *The Nation* 201 (1965): 380–84.

Ryder, Norman B. "A Critique of the National Fertility Study." *Demography* 10, no. 4 (1973): 495–506.

Said, Edward W. *Orientalism*. New York: Vintage Books, 1979.

Saldaña-Tejeda, Abril, and Peter Wade. "Eugenics, Epigenetics, and Obesity Predisposition among Mexican Mestizos." *Medical Anthropology* 38, no. 8 (2019): 664–79.

Sassen, Saskia. "Globalization or Denationalization?" *Review of International Political Economy (RIPE)* 10, no. 1 (2003): 1–22.

Saul, Stephanie. "Dozens of Middlebury Students Are Disciplined for Charles Murray Protest." *New York Times*, May 24, 2017. https://www.nytimes.com/2017/05/24/us/middlebury-college-charles-murray-bell-curve.html.

Sayer, Andrew. "Who's Afraid of Critical Social Science?" *Current Sociology* 57, no. 6 (2009): 767–86.

Sayer, R. Andrew. *Why Things Matter to People: Social Science, Values and Ethical Life*. Cambridge and New York: Cambridge University Press, 2011.

Seamster, Louise, and Victor Ray. "Against Teleology in the Study of Race: Toward the Abolition of the Progress Paradigm." *Sociological Theory* 36, no. 4 (2018): 315–42.

Seawright, Jason, and John Gerring. "Case Selection Techniques in Case Study Research: A Menu of Qualitative and Quantitative Options." *Political Research Quarterly* 61, no. 2 (2008): 294–308.

Seto, Christopher H. "Understanding Delinquency among the Spiritual but Not Religious." *Sociology of Religion* 82, no. 2 (2020): 156–78.

Sewell, William Hamilton. *Logics of History: Social Theory and Social Transformation*. Chicago: University of Chicago Press, 2005.

Shapin, Steven. *The Scientific Life: A Moral History of a Late Modern Vocation*. Chicago: University of Chicago Press, 2008.

Shapin, Steven, and Simon Schaffer. *Leviathan and the Air-Pump: Hobbes, Boyle, and the Experimental Life*. Princeton, NJ: Princeton University Press, 2011.

Shapira, Harel. "Who Cares What They Think? Going about the Right the Wrong Way." *Contemporary Sociology* 46, no. 5 (2017): 512–17.

Shapiro, Ben. "A Genius Academic Hoax Exposed that Liberal Arts Colleges Don't Care about Truth." *Newsweek*, October 5, 2018. https://www.newsweek.com/ben-shapiro-genius-academic-hoax-exposed-liberal-arts-colleges-dont-care-1155013.

Shattuck, Rachel M. "Does It Matter What She Wants? The Role of Individual Preferences against Unmarried Motherhood in Young Women's Likelihood of a Nonmarital First Birth." *Demography* 54, no. 4 (2017): 1451–75.

Shaw, Bernard. "Discussion." *American Journal of Sociology* 10, no. 1 (1904): 21–22.

Shiao, Jiannbin Lee, Thomas Bode, Amber Beyer, and Daniel Selvig. "The Genomic Challenge to the Social Construction of Race." *Sociological Theory* 30, no. 2 (2012): 67–88.

Shils, Edward. "The Great Obsession." *The Spectator*, July 5, 1963, 20.

Shweder, Richard A. *Thinking through Cultures: Expeditions in Cultural Psychology*. Cambridge, MA: Harvard University Press, 1991.

Silber, Ilana F. "The Cultural Worth of 'Economies of Worth': French Pragmatic Sociology from a Cultural Sociological Perspective." In *The Sage Handbook of Cultural Sociology*, edited by David Inglis and Anna-Mari Almila, 159–77. London: Sage, 2016.

———. "Luc Boltanski and the Gift: Beyond Love, Beyond Suspicion . . . ?" In *The Spirit of Luc Boltanski: Essays on the "Pragmatic Sociology of Critique,"* edited by Simon Susen and Bryan S. Turner, 485–500. London: Anthem Press, 2014.

———. "Pragmatic Sociology as Cultural Sociology: Beyond Repertoire Theory?" *European Journal of Social Theory* 6, no. 4 (2003): 427–49.

Sinding, Steven W., John A. Ross, and Allan G. Rosenfield. "Seeking Common Ground: Unmet Need and Demographic Goals." *International Family Planning Perspectives* 20, no. 1 (1994): 23–32.

Skocpol, Theda. "Wallerstein's World Capitalist System: A Theoretical and Historical Critique." *American Journal of Sociology* 82, no. 6 (1977): 1075–90.

Small, Mario Luis, David J. Harding, and Michèle Lamont. "Introduction: Reconsidering Culture and Poverty." *The ANNALS of the American Academy of Political and Social Science* 629 (2010): 6–27.

Small, Mario Luis, and Katherine Newman. "Urban Poverty after the Truly Disadvantaged: The Rediscovery of the Family, the Neighborhood, and Culture." *Annual Review of Sociology* 27 (2001): 23–45.

Smilde, David, and Matthew May. "Causality, Normativity, and Diversity in 40 Years of U.S. Sociology of Religion: Contributions to Paradigmatic Reflection." *Sociology of Religion* 76, no. 4 (2015): 369–88.

Smith, Adam. *The Wealth of Nations. Books 1–3*. Lexington, KY: Seven Treasures Publications, 2009 [1776].

Smith, Anthony D. *Nations and Nationalism in a Global Era*. Cambridge, UK, and Malden, MA: Polity Press and Blackwell, 1995.

Smith, Christian. *The Sacred Project of American Sociology*. New York: Oxford University Press, 2014.

———. *The Secular Revolution: Power, Interests, and Conflict in the Secularization of American Public Life*. Berkeley: University of California Press, 2003.

———. *What Is a Person? Rethinking Humanity, Social Life, and the Moral Good from the Person Up*. Chicago: University of Chicago Press, 2011.

Smith, Christian, Brandon Vaidyanathan, Nancy Tatom Ammerman, José Casanova, Hilary Davidson, Elaine Howard Ecklund, John H. Evans, et al. "Roundtable on the Sociology of Religion: Twenty-Three Theses on the Status of Religion in American Sociology—a Mellon Working-Group Reflection." *Journal of the American Academy of Religion* 81, no. 4 (2013): 903–38.

Smith, Dorothy E. *The Everyday World as Problematic: A Feminist Sociology*. Boston: Northeastern University Press, 1987.

Smock, Raymond. *Booker T. Washington: Black Leadership in the Age of Jim Crow*. Chicago: Ivan R. Dee, 2009.

Sociological Inquiry. "Call for Papers: Special Issue on 'The Cultural and the Racial: Stitching Together the Sociologies of Race/Racism/Ethnicity and Culture,' Guest Editors David L. Brunsma and David G. Embrick." 2020, last accessed January 28, 2021. https://onlinelibrary.wiley.com/pb-assets/Special%20Issue%20-%20Racism%20and%20Culture-1598268806577.pdf.

Spencer, Herbert. *The Study of Sociology*. New York: Appleton, 1901.

Stamatov, Peter. *The Origins of Global Humanitarianism: Religion, Empires, and Advocacy*. Cambridge: Cambridge University Press, 2013.

Star, Susan Leigh, and Elihu M. Gerson. "The Management and Dynamics of Anomalies in Scientific Work." *The Sociological Quarterly* 28, no. 2 (1987): 147–69.

Stark, David. *The Sense of Dissonance: Accounts of Worth in Economic Life*. Princeton, NJ: Princeton University Press, 2009.

Stark, Rodney. "Secularization, R.I.P." *Sociology of Religion* 60, no. 3 (1999): 249–73.

———. *A Theory of Religion*. Edited by William Sims Bainbridge. New York: P. Lang, 1987.

Stark, Rodney, and William Sims Bainbridge. "Networks of Faith: Interpersonal Bonds and Recruitment to Cults and Sects." *American Journal of Sociology* 85, no. 6 (1980): 1376–95.

———. "Of Churches, Sects, and Cults: Preliminary Concepts for a Theory of

Religious Movements." *Journal for the Scientific Study of Religion* 18, no. 2 (1979): 117–31.

Stark, Rodney, and Roger Finke. *Acts of Faith: Explaining the Human Side of Religion.* Berkeley: University of California Press, 2000.

Stein, Arlene. "Rage against the State." *Contemporary Sociology* 46, no. 5 (2017): 507–10.

Steinmetz, George. "The Colonial State as a Social Field: Ethnographic Capital and Native Policy in the German Overseas Empire before 1914." *American Sociological Review* 73, no. 4 (2008): 589–612.

———. "Odious Comparisons: Incommensurability, the Case Study, and 'Small N's' in Sociology." *Sociological Theory* 22, no. 3 (2004): 371–400.

Stets, Jan E., and Michael J. Carter. "A Theory of the Self for the Sociology of Morality." *American Sociological Review* 77, no. 1 (2012): 120–40.

Stets, Jan E., and A. D. Cast. "Resources and Identity Verification from an Identity Theory Perspective." *Sociological Perspectives* 50, no. 4 (2007): 517–43.

"Strangers in Their Own Land." The New Press, 2016. Last accessed January 29, 2020. https://thenewpress.com/books/strangers-their-own-land.

Sullivan, Winnifred Fallers. *The Impossibility of Religious Freedom.* Princeton, NJ: Princeton University Press, 2005.

Sullivan, Winnifred Fallers, and Lori G. Beaman. *Varieties of Religious Establishment.* London and New York: Routledge, 2016.

Sullivan, Winnifred Fallers, Robert A. Yelle, Mateo Taussig-Rubbo, and Robert A. Yelle, eds. *After Secular Law.* Stanford, CA: Stanford Law Books, 2011.

Susen, Simon. "Towards a Dialogue between Pierre Bourdieu's 'Critical Sociology' and Luc Boltanski's 'Pragmatic Sociology of Critique.'" In *The Spirit of Luc Boltanski: Essays on the "Pragmatic Sociology of Critique,"* edited by Simon Susen and Bryan S. Turner, 313–48. London: Anthem Press, 2014.

Susen, Simon, and Bryan S. Turner, eds. *The Spirit of Luc Boltanski: Essays on the "Pragmatic Sociology of Critique."* London: Anthem Books, 2014.

Swidler, Ann. "Comment on Stephen Vaisey's 'Socrates, Skinner, and Aristotle: Three Ways of Thinking about Culture in Action.'" *Sociological Forum* 23, no. 3 (2008): 614–18.

———. "Culture in Action: Symbols and Strategies." *American Sociological Review* 51, no. 2 (1986): 273–86.

Sykes, Gresham M., and David Matza. "Techniques of Neutralization: A Theory of Delinquency." *American Sociological Review* 22, no. 2 (1957): 664–70.

Szerszynski, Bronislaw, and John Urry. "Visuality, Mobility and the Cosmopolitan: Inhabiting the World from Afar." *The British Journal of Sociology* 57, no. 1 (2006): 113–31.

Szreter, Simon. "The Idea of Demographic Transition and the Study of Fertility Change: A Critical Intellectual History." *Population and Development Review* 19, no. 4 (1993): 659–701.

Talisse, Robert B., and Scott F. Aikin. "Why Pragmatists Cannot Be Pluralists." *Transactions of the Charles S. Peirce Society* 41, no. 1 (2005): 101–18.

Tavory, Iddo. "The Question of Moral Action: A Formalist Position." *Sociological Theory* 29, no. 4 (2011): 272–93.

Tavory, Iddo, and Nina Eliasoph. "Coordinating Futures: Toward a Theory of Anticipation." *American Journal of Sociology* 118, no. 4 (2013): 908–42.

Tavory, Iddo, and Stefan Timmermans. *Abductive Analysis: Theorizing Qualitative Research*. Chicago: University of Chicago Press, 2014.

Taylor, Charles. "Why Democracy Needs Patriotism." *Boston Review* 19, no. 5 (1994): 26.

———. "Why We Need a Radical Redefinition of Secularism." In *The Power of Religion in the Public Sphere*, edited by Eduardo Mandieta and Jonathan VanAntwerpen, 34–59. New York: Columbia University Press, 2011.

Thévenot, Laurent. *L'Action au pluriel: Sociologie des régimes d'engagement*. Paris: Découverte, 2006.

———. "Organisation and Power: Critical Plurality of Engagement Regimes." *Sociologia del Lavoro* 104 (2006): 86–106.

———. "Power and Oppression from the Perspective of the Sociology of Engagements: A Comparison with Bourdieu's and Dewey's Critical Approaches to Practical Activities." *Irish Journal of Sociology* 19, no. 1 (2011): 35–67.

Thévenot, Laurent, Michael Moody, and Claudette Lafaye. "Forms of Valuing Nature: Arguments and Modes of Justification in French and American Environmental Disputes." In *Rethinking Comparative Cultural Sociology: Repertoires of Evaluation in France and the United States*, edited by Laurent Thévenot and Michèle Lamont, 229–72. Cambridge Cultural Social Studies. Cambridge: Cambridge University Press, 2000.

Thomas, George M. "World Polity, World Culture, World Society." *International Political Sociology* 3, no. 1 (2009): 115–19.

Thomas, William I. "The Mind of Woman and the Lower Races." *American Journal of Sociology* 12, no. 4 (1907): 435–69.

Thompson, Gabriel. "'Strangers in Their Own Land' Review: Arlie Russell Hochschild Listens to the Voices of the American Right." *Newsday*, September 16, 2016. https://www.newsday.com/entertainment/books/strangers-in-their-own -land-review-arlie-russell-hochschild-listens-to-the-voices-of-the-american -right-1.12322676.

Thompson, Warren S. "Population." *American Journal of Sociology* 34, no. 1 (1928): 3–15.

———. "Population Trend Foreshadows a New Era: Vast Social and Economic Consequences Are Likely to Follow from the Decline and Eventual Stoppage of the Nation's Growth." *New York Times*, March 18, 1934, 1.

Thorpe, Charles. *Oppenheimer: The Tragic Intellect*. Chicago: University of Chicago Press, 2006.

Timmermans, Stefan, and Iddo Tavory. "Racist Encounters: A Pragmatist Semiotic Analysis of Interaction." *Sociological Theory* 38, no. 4 (2020): 295–317.

Torres, Sonia. "La Conciencia de la Mestiza / Towards a New Consciousness: Uma Conversação Inter-Americana Com Gloria Anzaldúa." *Estudos Feministas* 13, no. 3 (2005): 720–37.

Touraine, Alain. "Sociology without Societies." *Current Sociology* 51, no. 2 (2003): 123–31.

Trinitapoli, Jenny. "Demography Beyond the Foot." In *Covid-19 and the Global Demographic Research Agenda*, edited by Landis MacKellar and Rachel Friedman, 68–72. New York: Population Council, 2021.

Trinitapoli, Jenny, and Sara Yeatman. "The Flexibility of Fertility Preferences in a Context of Uncertainty." *Population and Development Review* 44, no. 1 (2018): 87–116.

Turiel, Elliot. *The Culture of Morality: Social Development, Context, and Conflict.* Cambridge and New York: Cambridge University Press, 2002.

Turner, Stephen P. *Explaining the Normative.* Cambridge, UK, and Malden, MA: Polity, 2010.

United States Bureau of Census. "Fertility Expectations of American Women: June 1974." *Current Population Reports* Series P-20: Population Characteristics, no. 277 (1975).

United States Department of Labor. *The Negro Family: The Case for National Action.* Moynihan Report. Edited by Daniel P. Moynihan. Washington, DC: US Government Printing Office, 1965.

Urry, John. "Mobile Sociology." *The British Journal of Sociology* 51, no. 1 (2000): 185–203.

———. *Mobilities.* Cambridge, UK, and Malden, MA: Polity, 2007.

Uzzi, Brian, Satyam Mukherjee, Michael Stringer, and Ben Jones. "Atypical Combinations and Scientific Impact." *Science* 342, no. 6157 (2013): 468–72.

Valverde, Mariana. "Moral Capital." *Canadian Journal of Law and Society* 9, no. 1 (1994): 213–32.

van der Veer, Peter. "Colonial Cosmopolitanism." In *Conceiving Cosmopolitanism: Theory, Context and Practice*, edited by Steven Vertovec and Robin Cohen, 165–79. New York: Oxford University Press, 2003.

van de Walle, Etienne. "Fertility Transition, Conscious Choice, and Numeracy." *Demography* 29, no. 4 (1992): 487–502.

Vargas, Eduardo Viana, Bruno Latour, Bruno Karsenti, Frédérique Aït-Touati, and Louise Salmon. "The Debate between Tarde and Durkheim." *Environment and Planning D: Society and Space* 26, no. 5 (2008): 761–77.

Vasagar, Jeevan, and Rajeev Syal. "LSE Head Quits over Gaddafi Scandal." *The Guardian*, March 3, 2011. https://www.theguardian.com/education/2011/mar/03/lse-director-resigns-gaddafi-scandal.

Wagner, Peter. "A Renewal of Social Theory That Remains Necessary: The Sociology of Critical Capacity Twenty Years After." In *The Spirit of Luc Boltanski: Essays on the "Pragmatic Sociology of Critique,"* edited by Simon Susen and Bryan S. Turner, 235–44. London: Anthem Press, 2014.

Wall Street Journal. "Scientific Fraud and Politics: Look Who Is Lecturing Republicans about Scientific Truth." *Wall Street Journal*, June 5, 2015. https://www.wsj.com/articles/scientific-fraud-and-politics-1433544688.

Walzer, Michael. *Spheres of Justice: A Defense of Pluralism and Equality.* New York: Basic Books, 1983.

Warin, Megan, Emma Kowal, and Maurizio Meloni. "Indigenous Knowledge in a Postgenomic Landscape: The Politics of Epigenetic Hope and Reparation in Australia." *Science, Technology, & Human Values* 45, no. 1 (2020): 87–111.

Warner, Michael, Jonathan VanAntwerpen, and Craig J. Calhoun. *Varieties of Secularism in a Secular Age*. Cambridge, MA: Harvard University Press, 2010.

Warner, R. Stephen. *A Church of Our Own: Disestablishment and Diversity in American Religion*. New Brunswick, NJ: Rutgers University Press, 2005.

Watts, Duncan J. "Common Sense and Sociological Explanations." *American Journal of Sociology* 120, no. 2 (2014): 313–51.

Weber, Max. *Economy and Society: An Outline of Interpretative Sociology*. Edited by Guenther Roth and Claus Wittich. Vol. 1. Berkeley, Los Angeles, and London: University of California Press, 1978.

———. "Science as a Vocation." In *From Max Weber: Essays in Sociology*, edited by Hans Gerth and C. Wright Mills, 129–56. Milton Park, Abingdon, Oxon, and New York: Routledge, 2009 [1919].

Wells-Barnett, Ida B. "Our Women." In *The Light of Truth: Writings of an Anti-Lynching Crusader*, edited by Mia Bay and Henry Louis Gates, 20–21. New York: Penguin Books, 2014 [1887].

———. *The Red Record: Tabulated Statistics and Alleged Causes of Lynchings in the United States, 1892-1893-1894*. Chicago: Donohue & Henneberry, 1895.

Westoff, Charles F. "The Potential Demand for Family Planning: A New Measure of Unmet Need and Estimates for Five Latin American Countries." *International Family Planning Perspectives* 14, no. 2 (1988): 45–53.

———. "The Unmet Need for Birth Control in Five Asian Countries." *Family Planning Perspectives* 10, no. 3 (1978): 173–81.

Westoff, Charles F., and Clyde V. Kiser. "Social and Psychological Factors Affecting Fertility: XXI. An Empirical Re-Examination and Intercorrelation of Selected Hypothesis Factors." *The Milbank Memorial Fund Quarterly* 31, no. 4 (1953): 421–35.

Westoff, Charles F., and Norman B. Ryder. "The Predictive Validity of Reproductive Intentions." *Demography* 14, no. 4 (1977): 431–53.

Whelpton, P. K., and Clyde V. Kiser. "Social and Psychological Factors Affecting Fertility: IV. Developing the Schedules, and Choosing the Type of Couples and the Area to Be Studied." *The Milbank Memorial Fund Quarterly* 23, no. 4 (1945): 386–409.

Whitehead, Andrew L., and Samuel L. Perry. *Taking America Back for God: Christian Nationalism in the United States*. New York: Oxford University Press, 2020.

Wiessinger, Diane, Diana West, and Teresa Pitman. *The Womanly Art of Breastfeeding*. 8th ed. New York: Random House, 2010 [1958].

Wilson, James Q. "Pat Moynihan Thinks about Families." *The ANNALS of the American Academy of Political and Social Science* 621, no. 1 (2009): 28–33.

Wilson, William J. *The Truly Disadvantaged: The Inner City, the Underclass, and Public Policy*. Chicago: University of Chicago Press, 2012 [1987].

Wilson, William Julius. "The Moynihan Report and Research on the Black Community." *The ANNALS of the American Academy of Political and Social Science* 621, no. 1 (2009): 34–46.

Wimmer, Andreas, and Brian Min. "From Empire to Nation-State: Explaining Wars in the Modern World, 1816–2001." *American Sociological Review* 71, no. 6 (2006): 867–97.

Wimmer, Andreas, and Nina Glick Schiller. "Methodological Nationalism, the Social Sciences, and the Study of Migration: An Essay in Historical Epistemology." *The International Migration Review* 37, no. 3 (2003): 576–610.

Wolf, Jacqueline H. "Low Breastfeeding Rates and Public Health in the United States." *American Journal of Public Health* 93, no. 12 (2003): 2000–2010.

———. "What Feminists Can Do for Breastfeeding and What Breastfeeding Can Do for Feminists." *Signs: Journal of Women in Culture and Society* 31, no. 2 (2006): 397–424.

Wolf, Joan. *Is Breast Best? Taking On the Breastfeeding Experts and the New High Stakes of Motherhood.* New York: New York University Press, 2010.

Wood, Peter. "The Regnerus Affair at UT Austin." *Chronicle of Higher Education,* July 15, 2012. https://www-chronicle-com.ezp-prod1.hul.harvard.edu/blogs/innovations/the-regnerus-affair-at-ut-austin.

Wright, Earl II. *The First American School of Sociology: W. E. B. Du Bois and the Atlanta Sociological Laboratory.* Milton Park, UK: Routledge, 2017.

Wright, Erik Olin. "The Real Utopia Theme at the 2012 ASA Annual Meeting." *Footnotes* 40, no. 5 (2012): 1.

———. *Envisioning Real Utopias.* London and New York: Verso, 2010.

Wuthnow, Robert. "General Concepts and Domain-Specific Concepts: An Argument about the Study of Religion in Sociology." *Sociology of Religion* 75, no. 4 (2014): 594–606.

———. *Why Religion Is Good for American Democracy.* Princeton, NJ: Princeton University Press, 2021.

Yang, Fenggang. "Exceptionalism or Chinamerica: Measuring Religious Change in the Globalizing World Today." *Journal for the Scientific Study of Religion* 55, no. 1 (2016): 7–22.

———. "Oligopoly Dynamics: Consequences of Religious Regulation." *Social Compass* 57, no. 2 (2010): 194–205.

Yglesias, Matthew. "The Great Awokening." *Vox,* April 1, 2019. https://www.vox.com/2019/3/22/18259865/great-awokening-white-liberals-race-polling-trump-2020.

Young, Alford A. *The Minds of Marginalized Black Men: Making Sense of Mobility, Opportunity, and Future Life Chances.* Princeton, NJ: Princeton University Press, 2004.

Zamora, Daniel, and Michael C. Behrent. *Foucault and Neoliberalism.* Edited by Daniel Zamora. Malden, MA: Polity Press, 2015.

Zuberi, Tukufu. *Thicker Than Blood: How Racial Statistics Lie.* Minneapolis: University of Minnesota Press, 2001.

Zuberi, Tukufu, and Eduardo Bonilla-Silva. *White Logic, White Methods: Racism and Methodology.* Lanham, MD: Rowman & Littlefield Publishers, 2008.

Zuckerman, Ezra W. "What If We Had Been in Charge? The Sociologist as Builder of Rational Institutions." In *Markets on Trial: The Economic Sociology of the U.S. Financial Crisis: Part B,* edited by M. Lounsbury and P. M. Hirsch, 359–78. Research in the Sociology of Organizations 30, Part B. Bingley, UK: Emerald Publishing Group, 2010.

Index

Abbott, Andrew, 6–8, 85
academic controversy: boundary questioning, as legitimate form of, 67; building solidarity, 45, 57–58, 65; as crisis, 66; disagreeing with, 52–54, 66; and "hot potato" issues, 66; ignoring of, 45, 55–57; knowledge production, hindering of, 68; and no-go zones, 67–68; rejecting of, 45–46, 50–52; responding to, 45–47; scholarly creativity, as sites for, 66–67; and turf wars, 85; as zero-sum game, 62
Addams, Jane, 2
Afghanistan, 78
African Americans. *See* Black Americans
agape, 163n21
Alexander, Jeffrey, 51
American creed, 48
American Dream, 88–89
American exceptionalism, 81
American pragmatism, 22, 151n66, 152n73
American Psychological Association (APA), 41
American Sociological Association (ASA), viii, 2–3, 46–47; Altruism, Morality, and Social Solidarity Section, xii, 8
analytic ontology, 7
Anchored Repertoire, 24, 52, 80–81, 88,

95, 103, 106, 109, 113, 132–33; nationalism, link to, 82
Anderson, Benedict, 71
Anderson, Elijah, 27, 54
ANNALS of the American Academy of Political and Social Science (journal), 54
Annual Review of Sociology (journal), 60
antiracism, 62
Anzaldúa, Gloria, 26
Archibugi, Daniele, 74–76
Asia, 99
atheism, 30, 34, 37
Atlanta University, 19
atomic bomb, xi

baby boom, 97
baby boomers, 107
Bachan, Lauren, 107
Baker, Joseph O'Brian, 37
Bangladesh, Matlab region, 101–2
Bateson, Gregory, 154n92
Beaman, Lori, 39
Bearman, Peter, 64–65, 168n104
Beck, Ulrich, 15–16, 69–74, 79, 85–86, 88–89
Becker, Gary, 32
Becker, Howard, 2, 125–26
Bellah, Robert, 8, 150n54
Bell Curve, The (Herrnstein and Murray), 41